Driving Standards Agency

The **OFFICIAL DSA**
THEORY TEST
for Motorcyclists

London: TSO

D0302387

39128 80092 497 9

Written and compiled by the Learning Materials section of the Driving Standards Agency (DSA).

Questions and answers are compiled by the Item Development Team of the DSA.

Published with the permission of the Driving Standards Agency on behalf of the Controller of Her Majesty's Stationery Office.

First published 2000
Twelfth edition 2012

ISBN 978 0 11 553234 4

A CIP catalogue record for this book is available from the British Library.

Other titles in the Driving Skills series

The Official DSA Guide to Riding – the essential skills
The Official DSA Theory Test for Motorcyclists (DVD-ROM)
The Official DSA Guide to Learning to Ride
Better Biking – the Official DSA Training Aid (DVD)

The Official DSA Theory Test iPhone App
The Official DSA Theory Test Kit iPhone App
The Official Highway Code iPhone App

The Official DSA Guide to Driving – the essential skills
The Official DSA Theory Test for Car Drivers
The Official DSA Theory Test for Car Drivers (DVD-ROM)
The Official DSA Guide to Learning to Drive
Prepare for your Practical Driving Test (DVD)
DSA Driving Theory Quiz (DVD)
The Official Highway Code Interactive CD-ROM

The Official DSA Guide to Driving Buses and Coaches
The Official DSA Guide to Driving Goods Vehicles
The Official DSA Theory Test for Drivers of Large Vehicles
The Official DSA Theory Test for Drivers of Large Vehicles (CD-ROM)
Driver CPC – the official DSA guide for professional bus and coach drivers
Driver CPC – the official DSA guide for professional goods vehicle drivers

The Official DSA Guide to Tractor and Specialist Vehicle Driving Tests

The Official DSA Guide to Hazard Perception (DVD)

Every effort has been made to ensure that the information contained in this publication is accurate at the time of going to press. The Stationery Office cannot be held responsible for any inaccuracies. Information in this book is for guidance only.

All metric and imperial conversions in this book are approximate.

We're turning over a new leaf.

75% **recycled**
This book is printed
on 75% recycled paper

MIX
Paper from
responsible sources
FSC® C002151
www.fsc.org

Find us online

> Information and services about

- car drivers
- motorcyclists
- driving licences
- driving and riding tests
- towing a caravan or trailer
- medical rules
- driving and riding for a living
- online services.

Visit **direct.gov.uk/motoring**

> If you need to contact us

If you can't find the answer to your question online and you need information about DSA's service standards, complaints procedures, out-of-pocket expenses or for other matters, visit **direct.gov.uk/contactdsa**

Or you can call us on **0300 200 1122**

You can also find contact details for other motoring agencies like DVLA at **direct.gov.uk/motoringcontacts**

> Message from Lesley Young, the Chief Driving Examiner

Learning to ride is an exciting experience. As with getting to grips with any new skill, you may be nervous and it may be challenging at first. But, before long, you'll be ready to take the step towards getting your full motorcycle licence and enjoying the freedom that comes with it.

A sound understanding of riding theory will help you reach that stage and to carry on improving right through your riding life. Understanding and practice come together in a safe and responsible rider, so my advice is to get at least some practical lessons with an approved training body under your belt while you're studying for your theory test. It helps to make the theory meaningful, and that helps it to stick.

And you'll be glad of that on the day of your theory test!

I wish you safe riding for life.

Lesley Young
Chief Driving Examiner

Contents

About the theory test

In this section, you'll learn about

- how to use this book
- getting started
- the theory test
- after the theory test
- using the questions and answers sections
- using this book to learn and revise.

How to use this book

To prove that you have the right knowledge, understanding and attitude to be a safe and responsible rider, you'll need to pass the theory test.

It includes

- a multiple choice test, to assess your knowledge of riding theory
- a hazard perception test, to assess your hazard recognition skills.

This book contains hundreds of questions, which are very similar to the questions you'll be asked in the test and cover the same topics. It's easy to read, and explains why the answers are correct. References to the source material also appear with each question.

Everyone learns in different ways so this book has features to help you understand riding theory whatever kind of learner you are, including

- bite-size chunks of information, which are easier to understand at your own pace
- lots of photographs and images to illustrate what you're learning
- fourteen topic-specific case studies and six mixed-topic ones, just like those you'll get in the test
- things to discuss and practise with your trainer, to put your learning about each topic into practise
- meeting the standards, to help you understand how each topic relates to the National Riding Standard.

This book is designed to help you learn about the theory of riding and to practise for the test. To prepare thoroughly, you should also study the source materials that the questions are taken from, which are

The Official Highway Code
Know Your Traffic Signs
The Official DSA Guide to Riding – the essential skills

There's always more you can learn, so keep your knowledge up to date throughout your riding career.

Getting started

> Applying for your licence

You must have a valid provisional driving licence before you can ride on the road.

Licences are issued by the Driver and Vehicle Licensing Agency (DVLA). You'll need to fill in application form D1, which you can download from **direct.gov.uk/motoringforms** or collect from any post office. In Northern Ireland, the issuing authority is the Driver and Vehicle Agency (DVA; online at **dvani.gov.uk**) and the form is a DL1. For more information, see **nidirect.gov.uk/learner-and-new-drivers.htm**

Send your form to the appropriate office, as shown on the form. You must enclose the required passport-type photographs, as all provisional licences are now photocard licences.

When you receive your provisional licence, check that all details are correct before you ride on the road. If you need to contact DVLA, the telephone number is 0300 790 6801 (DVA is 0845 402 4000).

You'll need to show both the photocard and the paper counterpart of your provisional licence when you take your theory test.

> Residency requirements

You can't take a test or get a full licence unless you're normally resident in the United Kingdom. Normal residence means the place where you live because of personal or occupational (work) ties. However, if you moved to the United Kingdom having recently been permanently resident in another state of the EC/EEA (European Economic Area), you must have been normally resident in the UK for 185 days in the 12 months before your application for a driving test or full driving licence.

> Compulsory basic training

Before you take your practical motorcycle tests, you must hold a valid compulsory basic training (CBT) course certificate of completion (DL196) (except in Northern

Ireland). This doesn't apply to riders upgrading from one category A to another; for example, upgrading from category A1 to category A. CBT courses can be given only by training bodies approved by DSA. These are checked frequently to make sure that there's a high standard of instruction.

The course will include classroom training and practical skills training. You can find out about CBT courses from

- DSA (visit **direct.gov.uk/cbt** or call 0115 936 6547)
- your motorcycle dealer
- your local road safety officer, by contacting your local council.

DSA also produces *The Official DSA Guide to Learning to Ride* (see pages 11 and 22 for further details), which will give you details about the course.

> About the theory test

You'll take the theory test on-screen in two parts. It's designed to test your knowledge of riding theory – in particular, the rules of the road and best riding practice.

The first part is a series of multiple choice questions. Some multiple choice questions will be presented as a case study. More information about this part of the test is given on pages 17–19. The revision questions are given in the main part of the book, beginning on page 30.

Each question has references to the learning materials; for example

RES s8, HC r162–163, KYTS p32

RES s indicates the section within *The Official DSA Guide to Riding – the essential skills.*

HC r/HC p indicates the rule or page in *The Official Highway Code.*

KYTS p indicates the page in *Know Your Traffic Signs.*

The second part of the theory test is the hazard perception part. More information about this is given on pages 19–20.

9

Can I take the practical test first?

No. You must pass your theory test before you can book a practical test.

Does everyone have to take the theory test?

Most people in the UK who are learning to ride will have to take the theory test. However, you won't have to take a motorcycle theory test again if you wish to upgrade your category A licence or if you've already passed a motorcycle theory test and then a practical moped test.

If you have any questions about whether you need to take a theory test, write to DSA theory test enquiries, PO Box 381, Manchester M50 3UW. Tel 0300 200 1122 or email **customercare@pearson.com**

For Northern Ireland, contact the Driver Licensing Division, County Hall, Castlerock Road, Coleraine, BT51 3TB. Tel 0845 402 4000.

Foreign licence holders: if you hold a foreign licence issued outside the EC/EEA, first check with DVLA (Tel 0300 790 6801; for Northern Ireland call 0845 402 4000), to see whether you can exchange your licence. If you can't, you'll need to apply for a provisional licence and take a theory and a practical test.

> Preparing for your theory test

Although you must pass your theory test before you can take your practical tests, it's best to start studying for your theory test as soon as possible – but don't actually take it until you have some practical experience of riding.

To prepare for the multiple choice part of the theory test, DSA strongly recommends that you study the books from which the theory test questions are taken, as well as the questions you'll find in this book.

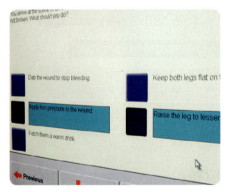

It's important that you study, not just to pass the test, but to become a safer rider.

The Official Highway Code This is essential reading for all road users. It contains the very latest rules of the road, up-to-date legislation and provides advice on road safety and best practice.

Know Your Traffic Signs This contains most of the signs and road markings that you're likely to see.

The Official DSA Guide to Riding – the essential skills This is the official reference book, giving practical advice and best practice for all riders.

The Official DSA Guide to Learning to Ride This gives full details of basic machine handling for compulsory basic training and the full practical test syllabus.

These books will help you to answer the questions correctly and will also help you when studying for your practical tests. The information in them will be relevant throughout your riding life, so make sure you always have an up-to-date copy.

> Other study aids

The Official DSA Theory Test for Motorcyclists (DVD-ROM) This is an alternative way of preparing for the multiple choice part of the theory test. It contains all the revision questions and answers, and also allows you to take mock tests.

All the official training materials listed are available online at **tsoshop.co.uk/dsa** or by mail order from 0870 600 5522.

They're also available from bookshops and selected computer software retailers.

Apps are available from the Apple app store.

eBooks are available from eBook stores.

The Official DSA Guide to Hazard Perception (DVD) We strongly recommend that you use this, preferably with your riding trainer, to prepare for the hazard perception part of the test. The DVD is packed with useful tips, quizzes and expert advice. It also includes interactive hazard perception clips, which you can use to test yourself and see if you're ready to take the real test.

Better Biking – the Official DSA Training Aid (DVD) This DVD gives expert advice on improving your skills. It covers all the key skills including negotiating bends, junctions and roundabouts. An ideal solo ride is demonstrated to show the standard of riding for which you should be aiming.

The Official Highway Code iPhone App All the latest rules of the road and traffic signs at your fingertips.

Why do the questions in the theory test keep changing?

To make sure that all candidates are being tested fairly, questions and video clips are under continuous review. Some questions may be changed as a result of customer feedback. They may also be altered because of changes to legislation, and DSA publications are updated so that the revision questions reflect these changes.

Can I take a mock test?

You can take mock tests for the multiple choice part of the theory test online at **safedrivingforlife.info/practicetheorytest**

The theory test

> Booking your theory test

It's easiest to book online or by phone. You can also book by post.

Booking online or by telephone By using these methods you'll be given the date and time of your test immediately.

Book online at **direct.gov.uk/booktheorytest** (for Northern Ireland, use **dvani.gov.uk**).

To book by telephone, call 0300 200 1122 (0845 600 6700 for Northern Ireland).

If you have hearing or speech difficulties and use a minicom machine, call 0300 200 1166. If you're a Welsh speaker, call 0300 200 1133.

You'll need your

- DVLA or DVA driving licence number
- credit or debit card details (the card holder must book the test). We accept Mastercard, Visa, Delta and Visa Electron.

You'll be given a booking number and you should receive an appointment letter within 10 days.

Where can I take the test?

There are over 150 theory test centres throughout England, Scotland and Wales, and six in Northern Ireland. Most people have a test centre within 20 miles of their home, but this will depend on the density of population in your area. To find your nearest test centre, please visit **direct.gov.uk/motoringnearest**

What should I do if I don't receive an acknowledgement?

If you don't receive an acknowledgement within the time specified, please visit **direct.gov.uk/changetheorytest** or telephone the booking office to check that an appointment has been made. We can't take responsibility for postal delays. If you miss your test appointment, you'll lose your fee.

When are test centres open?

Test centres are usually open on weekdays, some evenings and some Saturdays.

How do I cancel or postpone my test?

You can cancel or postpone your test online by visiting **direct.gov.uk/changetheorytest** or by telephone. You should contact the booking office at least **three clear working days** before your test date, otherwise you'll lose your fee.

Booking by post If you prefer to book by post, you'll need to fill in an application form. These are available from driving test centres, or your riding trainer may have one.

You should receive an appointment letter within 10 days of posting your application form.

If you need the theory test in a language other than English or if you need support for special needs, please turn to page 16.

> Taking your theory test

Arriving at the test centre You must make sure that when you arrive at the test centre you have all the relevant documents with you. If you don't have them, you won't be able to take your test and you'll lose your fee.

You'll need

- your signed photocard licence **and** paper counterpart, or
- your signed driving licence and valid passport (your passport doesn't have to be British).

No other form of identification is acceptable in England, Wales or Scotland.

Other forms of identification may be acceptable in Northern Ireland; please check **dvani.gov.uk** or your appointment letter.

All documents must be original. We can't accept photocopies.

The test centre staff will check your documents and make sure that you take the right category of test.

Remember, if you don't bring your documents your test will be cancelled and you'll lose your fee.

Make sure you arrive in plenty of time so that you aren't rushed. If you arrive after the session has started, you may not be allowed to take the test.

It's an on-screen test and is made up of a multiple choice part and a hazard perception part.

Watch the 'How to pass the theory test' video on DSA's YouTube channel, which explains how to prepare for the theory test, what to expect on the day and what you need to do to pass.

> youtube.com/dsagov

> Languages other than English

In Wales, and at theory test centres on the Welsh borders, you can take your theory test with Welsh text on-screen. A voiceover can also be provided in Welsh.

You can listen through a headset to the test being read out in one of 20 other languages as well as English. These are Albanian, Arabic, Bengali, Cantonese, Dari, Farsi, Gujarati, Hindi, Kashmiri, Kurdish, Mirpuri, Polish, Portuguese, Punjabi, Pushto, Spanish, Tamil, Turkish, Urdu and Welsh.

At some theory test centres you may bring a translator with you so that you can take your test in any other language. The translator must be approved by DSA (DVA in Northern Ireland) and you must make arrangements for this when you book your test. You have to arrange and pay for the services of the translator yourself.

Tests with translators can be taken at the following test centres: Aldershot, Birmingham, Cardiff, Derby, Edinburgh, Glasgow, Ipswich, Leeds, Milton Keynes, Preston, Southgate and all test centres in Northern Ireland.

> Provision for special needs

Every effort is made to ensure that the theory test can be taken by all candidates.

It's important that you state your needs when you book your test so that the necessary arrangements can be made.

Reading difficulties There's an English-language voiceover on a headset to help you if you have reading difficulties or dyslexia.

You can ask for up to twice the normal time to take the multiple choice part of the test.

You'll be asked to provide a letter from a suitable independent person who knows about your reading ability, such as a teacher or employer. Please check with the Special Needs section (call on the normal booking number; see page 13), if you're unsure who to ask.

We can't guarantee to return any original documents, so please send copies only.

Hearing difficulties If you're deaf or have other hearing difficulties, the multiple choice part and the introduction to the hazard perception part of the test can be delivered in British Sign Language (BSL) by an on-screen signer.

A BSL interpreter, signer or lip speaker can be provided if requested at the time of booking. If you have any other requirements, please call the Special Needs section on the normal booking number (see page 13).

Physical disabilities If you have a physical disability that would make it difficult for you to use a touch screen system or a mouse button in the theory test, we may be able to make special arrangements for you to use a different method if you let us know when you book your test.

 # Multiple choice questions

The first part of the theory test consists of 50 multiple choice questions. Some of these will be in the form of a case study. You select your answers for this part of the test by touching the screen or using the mouse.

Before you start, you'll be given the chance to work through a practice session for up to 15 minutes to get used to the system. Staff at the test centre will be available to help you if you have any difficulties.

The questions will cover a variety of topics relating to road safety, the environment and documents. Only one question will appear on the screen at a time.

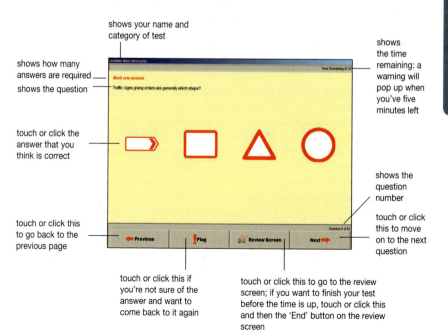

shows your name and category of test

shows the time remaining: a warning will pop up when you've five minutes left

shows how many answers are required

shows the question

touch or click the answer that you think is correct

shows the question number

touch or click this to move on to the next question

touch or click this to go back to the previous page

touch or click this if you're not sure of the answer and want to come back to it again

touch or click this to go to the review screen; if you want to finish your test before the time is up, touch or click this and then the 'End' button on the review screen

Most questions will ask you to mark one correct answer from four possible answers. Some questions may ask for two or more correct answers from a selection, but this will be shown clearly on the screen.

If you try to move on without marking the correct number of answers, you'll be reminded that more answers are needed.

To answer, you need to touch or click the box beside the answer or answers you think are correct. If you change your mind and don't want that answer to be selected, touch or click it again. You can then choose another answer.

Take your time and read the questions carefully. You're given 57 minutes for this part of the test, so relax and don't rush. Some questions will take longer to answer than others, but there are no trick questions. The time remaining is displayed on the screen.

You may be allowed extra time to complete the test if you have special needs and you let us know when you book your test.

You'll be able to move backwards and forwards through the questions and you can also 'flag' questions you'd like to look at again. It's easy to change your answer if you want to.

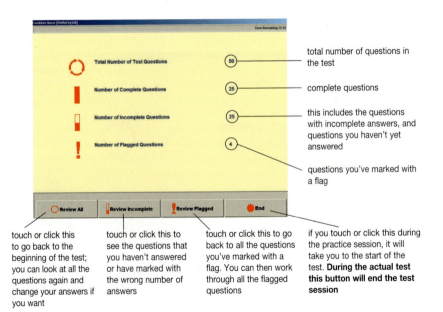

total number of questions in the test

complete questions

this includes the questions with incomplete answers, and questions you haven't yet answered

questions you've marked with a flag

touch or click this to go back to the beginning of the test; you can look at all the questions again and change your answers if you want

touch or click this to see the questions that you haven't answered or have marked with the wrong number of answers

touch or click this to go back to all the questions you've marked with a flag. You can then work through all the flagged questions

if you touch or click this during the practice session, it will take you to the start of the test. **During the actual test this button will end the test session**

Try to answer all the questions. If you're well prepared, you shouldn't find them difficult.

Before you finish this part of the test, if you have time, you can use the 'review' feature to check your answers. If you want to finish your test before the full time, touch or click the 'review' button and then the 'end' button on the review screen. When you touch or click the review button, you'll see the screen on the previous page.

Case studies

Some of the multiple choice questions will be presented as part of a case study. Case studies are designed to test

- knowledge (basic recall of facts)
- comprehension (basic understanding)
- application (practical use of knowledge and understanding).

This is done by creating a set of circumstances that you may encounter in a real-life situation. You'll then be asked some questions relating to the scenario, and you'll have to decide how you would react or behave in each case. For an example of a case study, see page 460.

The case studies at the end of each section in this book set out scenarios and then ask you relevant questions. This is to help you test your knowledge in a format similar to the case studies in the theory test. However, the layout isn't the same as the theory test screens.

Hazard perception

After you've finished the multiple choice part, there's a break of up to three minutes before you start the hazard perception part of the test. You can't leave your seat during this break. This part of the test is a series of film clips, shown from a rider's point of view. You'll be using a mouse for this part of the theory test.

Before you start this part of the test, you'll be shown a short video that explains how the test works and gives you a chance to see a sample film clip. This will help you to understand what you need to do. You can play this video again if you wish.

During the hazard perception part of the test, you'll be shown 14 film clips. Each clip contains one or more developing hazards. You should press the mouse button **as soon as you see** a hazard developing that may need you, the rider, to take some action, such as changing speed or direction.

The earlier you notice a developing hazard and make a response, the higher your score. There are 15 hazards for which you can score points.

Your response won't change what happens in the scene in any way. However, a red flag will appear on the bottom of the screen to show that your response has been noted.

Before each clip starts, there'll be a 10-second pause to allow you to see the new road situation.

The hazard perception part of the test lasts about 20 minutes. For this part of the test no extra time is available, and you can't repeat any of the clips – you don't get a second chance to see a hazard when you're riding on the road.

> Trial questions

We're constantly checking the questions and clips to help us decide whether to use them in future tests. After the hazard perception part of the test, you may be asked to try a few trial questions and clips. You don't have to do these if you don't want to, and if you answer them they won't count towards your final score.

> Customer satisfaction survey

We want to make sure our customers are completely satisfied with the service they receive. At the end of your test you'll be shown some questions designed to give us information about you and how happy you are with the service you received from us.

Your answers will be treated in the strictest confidence. They aren't part of the test and they won't affect your final score or be used for marketing purposes. You'll be asked if you want to complete the survey, but you don't have to.

> The result

You should receive your result at the test centre within 10 minutes of completing the test.

You'll be given a score for each part of the test (the multiple choice part and the hazard perception part). You'll need to pass both parts to pass the theory test. If you fail one of the parts, you'll have to take the whole test again.

Why do I have to retake both parts of the test if I only fail one?

It's really only one test. The theory test has always included questions relating to hazard awareness – the second part simply tests the same skills in a more effective way. The two parts are only presented separately in the theory test because different scoring methods are used.

What's the pass mark?

To pass the multiple choice part of the theory test, you must answer at least 43 out of 50 questions correctly. For learner car drivers and motorcyclists, the pass mark for the hazard perception part is 44 out of 75.

If I don't pass, when can I take the test again?

If you fail your test, you've shown that you're not fully prepared. You'll have to wait at least three clear working days before you can take the theory test again.

Good preparation will save you both time and money.

After the theory test

When you pass your theory test, you'll be given a certificate. Keep this safe as you'll need it when you go for your practical test.

This certificate is valid for two years from the date of your test. This means that you have to take and pass the practical test within this two-year period. If you don't, you'll have to take and pass the theory test again before you can book your practical test.

> Your practical tests

Your next step is to prepare for and take your practical tests. To help you, *The Official DSA Guide to Learning to Ride* has details of the Module 1 off-road and Module 2 on-road practical tests. As well as giving the full test syllabus, it explains the skills that you should show and the faults that you should avoid when taking your tests.

Please refer to the back of this book for information about other publications that will help you prepare for your practical tests.

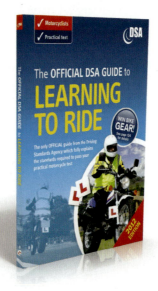

If this is your first full licence and you get six penalty points in the first two years of riding, your licence will be revoked and you'll have to go right back to the beginning and retake your theory test. **Don't risk it, ride safe.**

Using the questions and answers sections

Sections 1 to 14 contain all the revision questions for the multiple choice part of the theory test. These are very similar to the questions you'll be asked in the test and cover the same topics.

The questions are in the left-hand column with a choice of answers below.

For easy reference, the questions are divided into topics. Although this isn't how you'll find them in your test, it's helpful if you want to look at particular subjects.

At the start of each topic, before the questions, there are a few pages of useful information to help you learn more about each topic.

On the right-hand side of the page, there's a brief explanation to help you understand the question. There'll also be some advice on correct riding procedures and some short references to the relevant source materials. These refer to the books listed on page 9.

The correct answers are at the back of the book, in section 16.

Don't just learn the answers; it's important that you know why they're correct. To help you do this, there's a short scenario at the end of each question section with five questions to answer. This will give you an idea of how the case study part of the theory test will assess your understanding of the subject covered. This knowledge will help you with your practical skills and prepare you to become a safe and confident rider.

Taking exams or tests is rarely a pleasant experience, but you can make your test less stressful by being confident that you have the knowledge to answer the questions correctly.

Make studying more enjoyable by involving friends and relations. Take part in a question-and-answer game. Test those 'experienced' riders who've had their licence a while: they might learn something too!

Some of the questions in this book won't be relevant to Northern Ireland theory tests. These questions are marked as follows: **NI EXEMPT**

Best wishes for your theory test. Once you're on the road, remember what you've learnt and be prepared to keep learning.

Using this book to learn and revise

We're all different. We like different foods, listen to different music and learn in different ways.

This book is designed to help you learn the important information that you'll need for the theory test in a variety of different formats, so you can find a way of learning that works best for you.

Features

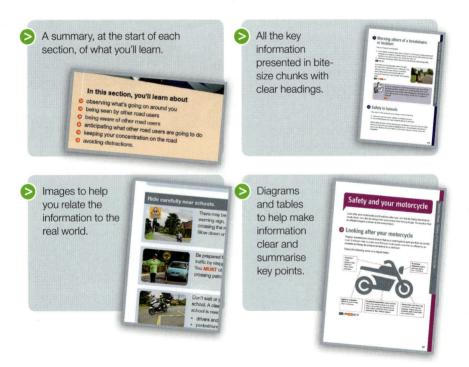

> A summary, at the start of each section, of what you'll learn.

In this section, you'll learn about
- observing what's going on around you
- being seen by other road users
- being aware of other road users
- anticipating what other road users are going to do
- keeping your concentration on the road
- avoiding distractions.

> All the key information presented in bite-size chunks with clear headings.

> Images to help you relate the information to the real world.

> Diagrams and tables to help make information clear and summarise key points.

> Links and QR codes to online videos and interactive activities, to further increase your knowledge and skills. Scan the QR code on your smart phone (you'll need a QR code reader app) to access the online content.

Watch DSA's 'Out of time' video to find out more about the risks of distraction.
youtube.com/dsagov

> Links to other relevant publications, like *The Official Highway Code* and *The Official DSA Guide to Riding – the essential skills*.

• it's safe, legal and necess
• you have enough time to
HC r162–163, 165 RES s8 KYT

> Tips containing useful extra information about riding safely.

TIP At night, if a vehicle overtakes you, dip your headlights as soon as it passes you otherwise your lights could dazzle the other driver.
HC r115

> A summary, at the end of each section, of what you'll need to know and be able to do to meet the National Riding Standard.

Meeting the standards

> Pages for your own notes, with suggested things to think about.

Notes

> Ideas to discuss with your riding trainer and practise when riding.

Things to discuss and prac your trainer
These are just a few examples of what you could dis your trainer. Read more about incidents, accidents a

> Self-assessment – revision questions like the ones you'll get in the test.

11.35 Mark one answer
What shape is a STOP sign at a junction?

11.36 Mark one answer
At a junction you see this sign partly covered by snow. What does it mean?

> Case studies showing how the information might work in practice, and related questions.

Case study practice – 6
Vulnerable road users

The theory test is just one part of the process of learning to ride. You need to learn the facts, but it's important to understand how they relate to real riding.

The combination of knowing rider theory and having good practical riding skills won't only help you pass your test; it will also make you a safer rider for life.

> What kind of learner are YOU?

Ask yourself these questions

- Why are you doing this? What's motivating you?
- When have you learned best in the past? What helped you to remember what you needed to know?
- What are your strengths and weaknesses as a learner?

Think about the way that you learn best. You could try any combination of the following ideas.

I remember what I see or read

- Create flashcards with important facts or statistics
- Make diagrams and charts
- Use mind maps
- Use colour coding
- Watch the DSA short films
- Make your own notes
- Cross-reference information using a variety of books, eg *The Official Highway Code*
- Draw your own diagrams to show key information.

I remember best when I physically do something

- Short study sessions
- Do things – create models or diagrams; make lists
- Use props
- Try the interactive activities
- Watch and copy what your riding trainer does
- Mime or act out different riding moves.

I remember what I hear

- Repeat rules out loud
- Use a voice recorder to make recordings of key information
- Work with others and discuss things
- Watch and listen to the DSA video content.

> Top tips

Remember your motivation

Think about the reason you're learning to ride. Is it for independence? For work? To ride a dream motorcycle? Remind yourself, from time to time, of your motivation for learning. Don't give up!

Relate to your personal experience

Information is more memorable when it's linked to what you already know. Try to picture yourself in the position of the rider. The case studies throughout the book can help you think about how the ideas would work in real life.

Use mnemonics

Mnemonics are little sayings, stories or techniques that help you remember something. A classic example is '**R**ichard **O**f **Y**ork **G**ave **B**attle **I**n **V**ain', which you can use to remember the colours of the rainbow (**r**ed, **o**range, **y**ellow, **g**reen, **b**lue, **i**ndigo, **v**iolet). You can use similar techniques to memorise statistics, facts or information for your riding career.

Question format

However you choose to learn the content, make certain you're familiar with the format of the test and how the questions will be presented. Go through the self-assessment questions in each chapter and see if you can answer them. Mark any you struggle with and try them again at a later date.

Plan your study

Set yourself timelines and targets. Try to set aside dedicated time for study, when you're feeling awake and are unlikely to be interrupted. The environment in which you study is important – try to find an area where you can concentrate.

Getting help

Think about the people you can speak with to ask questions, get advice or share experiences about riding – such as your riding trainer, parents, friends or colleagues at work.

Taking your test

Don't rush into the theory test before you're ready. You need to be confident with the information, and have enough practical experience to give you a deep understanding of the information too.

Alertness

In this section, you'll learn about

- observing what's going on around you
- being seen by other road users
- being aware of other road users
- anticipating what other road users are going to do
- keeping your concentration on the road
- avoiding distractions.

Alertness

Being alert to what's going on around you is vital to riding safely and will help you to avoid dangerous situations.

❯ Observation and awareness

It's important to be aware of what's happening around you while you're riding, including

- other road users
- pedestrians
- signs and road markings
- weather conditions
- the area you're riding through.

Keep scanning the road ahead and to the sides, and assess the changing situations as you ride.

Before you move off, you should

use your mirrors or look around to check how your actions will affect traffic behind you

signal, if necessary

take a final look behind to check your **blind spots**.

`HC` r159–161 `RES` s6

Getting a clear view

If your elbows obstruct your view in the mirrors, fit mirrors with longer stems to get an unobstructed view. Having mirrors fitted to both sides of your motorcycle will give you the best view of the road behind.

Looking over your shoulder before manoeuvring will also warn other drivers that you may be about to change lane, direction or speed. Don't forget your **'lifesaver' check**.

If your view is blocked by parked cars when you're coming out of a junction, move forward slowly and carefully until you have a clear view.

Watch the 'Test your awareness' video on DSA's YouTube channel.

❯ youtube.com/dsagov

Overtaking

Observation is particularly important when you're overtaking another vehicle. Make sure you can see the road ahead clearly, looking out for

- vehicles coming towards you
- whether you're near a junction – vehicles could come out of the junction while you're overtaking

- whether the road gets narrower – there may not be enough space for you to overtake
- bends or dips in the road, which will make it difficult for you to see traffic coming towards you
- road signs that mean you **MUST NOT** overtake.

Before you overtake, check that

- it's safe, legal and necessary
- you have enough time to complete the overtaking manoeuvre.

HC r162–163, 165 **RES** s8 **KYTS** p64

Being seen by others

Other road users can find it difficult to see motorcyclists, so it's important to make sure you can be seen as clearly as possible.

- Wear a light or brightly coloured helmet and fluorescent clothing or strips.
- Use dipped headlamps, even in good daylight, to make yourself easy to see.
- At night, reflective clothing or strips make you visible from a longer distance.
- Where you can't be seen, such as at a hump bridge, you may need to use your horn.

HC r86–87, r115

If you're following a large vehicle, stay well back. This will help the driver to see you in their mirrors. Staying back will also help you see the road ahead much more clearly. This is especially important if you're planning to overtake the vehicle.

HC r164

Remember: if you can't see a large vehicle's mirrors, the driver can't see you.

❯ Anticipation

Anticipation can help you to avoid problems and incidents so that you can ride more safely. For example, a 'give way' sign warns you that a junction is ahead, so you can slow down in good time.

Look at the road signs and markings: these give you information about hazards.

You should

- follow their advice
- slow down if necessary.

 RES s7 KYTS p10, 62

Circles
give orders

Triangles
give warnings

Rectangles
give information

When turning right onto a **dual carriageway**, check that the **central reservation** is wide enough for your vehicle to stop in, especially if you're towing a trailer. Do this in case you have to wait before joining the traffic. If there's not enough space for your vehicle, only emerge when it's clear both to the right and left.

> **Defi**nition
>
> **dual carriageway**
> a road that has a central reservation to separate the carriageways
>
> **central reservation**
> an area of land that separates opposing lanes of traffic

If you're approaching traffic lights that have been green for some time, be prepared to stop because they may change.

Road conditions will affect how easy it is to anticipate what might happen. It's more difficult when

- the weather is very wet or windy
- the light is poor
- the traffic volume is heavy
- the route you're riding is new to you.

In these conditions, you need to be particularly aware of what's happening around you.

RES s8

Anticipating what other road users might do

Watch other road users. Try to anticipate their actions so that you're ready if you need to slow down or change direction.

Be aware of more vulnerable road users. Watch out for

pedestrians approaching a crossing, especially young, older or disabled people who may need more time to cross the road

cyclists – always pass slowly and leave plenty of room, especially if the cyclist is young and may have little experience of dealing with traffic

horses, which may be startled by the noise of your motorcycle – pass them slowly and leave plenty of room.

HC r204–218 **RES** s10

Always be ready to stop

However well prepared you are, you may still have to stop quickly in an emergency. Keep both hands on the handlebars as you brake to keep control of your motorcycle.

RES s6, 10

 # Staying focused

Riding safely takes a lot of concentration – as well as controlling the motorcycle, you need to be aware of what's happening on the road and what could happen next. Stay focused on riding and try not to get distracted.

Always plan your journey so that you

- know which route you need to take
- have regular rest stops.

Avoiding tiredness

You won't be able to concentrate properly if you're tired. It can also be difficult to concentrate if you're riding on a road that isn't very interesting, such as a motorway. Together, boredom and tiredness could make you feel sleepy, especially at night, so

- don't ride continuously for more than two hours
- if you start to feel drowsy, leave at the next exit. Find a safe and legal place to stop and take a break.

 Stop in a safe place and have a cup of coffee or another caffeinated drink. Remember that this is only a short-term solution: it isn't a substitute for proper rest. If possible, take a short nap.

HC r91, 262 **RES** s1, 11

See the Think! road safety website for more information about riding when tired.

➤ **http://think.direct.gov.uk/ fatigue.html**

Keeping warm

It's just as easy to lose concentration if you're cold. Proper motorcycle clothing will keep you warm and will also help to protect you if you're involved in a road traffic incident.

Distraction

It's easy to be distracted by devices such as hands-free phones, intercom systems or music players because your concentration is divided between the road ahead and what you're hearing.

Losing your concentration, or just taking your eyes off the road for a second, could be disastrous. At 60 mph, your motorcycle will travel 27 metres in one second.

HC r149–150 **RES** s1

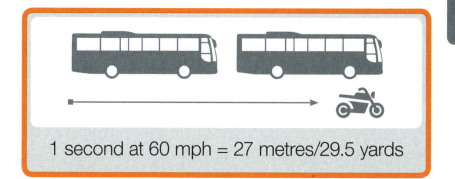

1 second at 60 mph = 27 metres/29.5 yards

Watch DSA's 'Out of time' video to find out more about the risks of distraction.

> **youtube.com/dsagov**

Don't listen to music through an earpiece while you're riding, and make sure you switch off your phone and any hands-free kits. Wait until you're parked in a safe place before you

- retrieve any messages
- make any calls
- send or receive texts
- go online.

If you're riding on a motorway, you should leave the motorway and stop in a safe place before using your phone or adjusting a navigation system.

RES s1, 16, 18

You could also be distracted by something that has happened on the road, such as an incident on the other side of a motorway. Don't slow down or try to see what's happening; continue with your journey and keep your concentration on your riding.

Meeting the standards

The National Riding Standard sets out the skills, knowledge and understanding that DSA believes are required to be a safe and responsible rider. If you know, understand and are able to do the things described in the standard then you'll be not only in a great position to pass your test but well on your way to becoming a safe rider for life.

You can view the National Riding Standard at **dft.gov.uk/dsa/standards**

You must be able to

decide if you're fit to ride. You shouldn't be

- too tired
- too ill
- too emotional
- under the influence of drugs or alcohol

keep concentrating and avoid being distracted

be aware of what's around you (nearby and far away) at all times

ride at such a speed that you can always stop in the clear space ahead of you.

You must know and understand

how these can make you tired

- a poor seating position
- bad posture
- too much noise
- lack of protective clothing

what can distract you. For example

- talking to pillion passengers
- using a sat-nav system

and how to manage these distractions

how helmets and visors may affect your field of vision and how to allow for this

how to read the road ahead and be prepared for the unexpected.

> Notes

You can use this page to make your own notes or diagrams about the key points you need to remember.

Think about

- Which clues can you use to help you anticipate what other road users might do? For example, a filling station at the side of the road could mean traffic slowing down to pull in, or vehicles pulling out.
- Why is it important to keep well back from large vehicles?
- What might you use to plan a long journey, and how would you make sure you took breaks at suitable points?
- Can you find a way to remind yourself to switch off your phone or put it to voicemail before you begin riding?

Your notes

Things to discuss and practise with your trainer

These are just a few examples of what you could discuss and practise with your trainer. Read more about alertness to come up with your own ideas.

Discuss with your trainer

- the 'lifesaver' check. What is it and when should you make it?
- what you need to take into account before overtaking, eg road markings, bends, etc
- what could distract you while riding, eg music via an earpiece, etc.

Practise with your trainer

- seeing and being seen when emerging from junctions, especially when your view is obstructed by parked cars
- turning right onto dual carriageways with different widths of central reservation
- riding at night, to get used to
  - using your dipped and main beam headlights
  - coping with the lights from approaching vehicles
  - wearing the appropriate clothing to be seen.

Mark one answer RES s8, HC r179–181

You are about to turn right. What should you do just before you turn?

☐ Give the correct signal

☐ Take a 'lifesaver' glance over your shoulder

☐ Select the correct gear

☐ Get in position ready for the turn

When you are turning right, plan your approach to the junction. Signal and select the correct gear in good time. Just before you turn, take a 'lifesaver' glance for a final check behind and to the side of you.

1.2 **Mark one answer** RES s8, HC r88

What is the 'lifesaver' when riding a motorcycle?

☐ A certificate every motorcyclist must have

☐ A final, rearward glance before changing direction

☐ A part of the motorcycle tool kit

☐ A mirror fitted to check blind spots

This action makes you aware of what's happening behind and alongside you. The 'lifesaver' glance should be timed so that you still have time to react if it isn't safe to perform the manoeuvre.

1.3 **Mark one answer** RES s9

You see road signs showing a sharp bend ahead. What should you do?

☐ Continue at the same speed

☐ Slow down as you go around the bend

☐ Slow down as you come out of the bend

☐ Slow down before the bend

Always look for any advance warning of hazards, such as road signs and hazard warning lines. Use this information to plan ahead and to help you avoid the need for late, harsh braking. Your motorcycle should be upright and moving in a straight line when you brake. This will help you to keep maximum control when dealing with the hazard.

1.4 **Mark one answer** RES s5

When riding, your shoulders obstruct the view in your mirrors. To overcome this you should

☐ indicate earlier than normal

☐ fit smaller mirrors

☐ extend the mirror arms

☐ brake earlier than normal

It's essential that you have a clear view all around. Adjust your mirrors to give you the best view of the road behind. If your elbows obscure the view try fitting mirrors with longer stems.

1.5
Mark one answer
RES s1, HC r149

On a motorcycle you should only use a mobile telephone when you

☐ have a pillion passenger to help

☐ have parked in a safe place

☐ have a motorcycle with automatic gears

☐ are travelling on a quiet road

It's important that you're in full control at all times. Even using a hands-free kit can distract your attention from the road. Don't take the risk. If you need to use a mobile phone stop at a safe and convenient place.

1.6
Mark one answer
RES s13, HC r115

You are riding at night. You have your headlight on main beam. Another vehicle is overtaking you. When should you dip your headlight?

☐ When the other vehicle signals to overtake

☐ As soon as the other vehicle moves out to overtake

☐ As soon as the other vehicle passes you

☐ After the other vehicle pulls in front of you

At night you should dip your headlight to avoid dazzling oncoming drivers or those ahead of you. If you're being overtaken, dip your headlight as the other vehicle comes past. When you switch to dipped beam your view of the road ahead will be reduced, so look ahead for hazards on your side of the road before you do so.

1.7
Mark one answer
RES s6, HC r159

To move off safely from a parked position you should

☐ signal if other drivers will need to slow down

☐ leave your motorcycle on its stand until the road is clear

☐ give an arm signal as well as using your indicators

☐ look over your shoulder for a final check

Before you move off from the side of the road on a motorcycle you must take a final look around over your shoulder. There may be another road user who is not visible in your mirrors.

1.8
Mark one answer
RES s4

Riding a motorcycle when you are cold could cause you to

☐ be more alert

☐ be more relaxed

☐ react more quickly

☐ lose concentration

It can be difficult to keep warm when riding a motorcycle. Although it isn't cheap, proper motorcycle clothing will help to keep you warm and is essential. It also helps to protect you if you fall off or are involved in a crash.

You are riding at night and are dazzled by the lights of an approaching vehicle. What should you do?

☐ Switch off your headlight

☐ Switch to main beam

☐ Slow down and stop

☐ Flash your headlight

If your view of the road ahead is restricted because you are being dazzled by approaching headlights, slow down and if you need to, pull over and stop.

You should always check the 'blind areas' before

☑ moving off

☐ slowing down

☐ changing gear

☐ giving a signal

These are the areas behind and to either side of you which are not covered by your mirrors. You should always check these areas before moving off or changing direction.

It is vital to check the 'blind area' before

☐ changing gear

☐ giving signals

☐ slowing down

☑ changing lanes

Other vehicles may be hidden in the blind spots that are not covered by your mirrors. Always make sure it is safe before changing lanes by taking a 'lifesaver' check.

Why can it be helpful to have mirrors fitted on each side of your motorcycle?

☐ To judge the gap when filtering in traffic

☐ To give protection when riding in poor weather

☐ To make your motorcycle appear larger to other drivers

☐ To give you the best view of the road behind

When riding on the road you need to know as much about following traffic as you can. A mirror fitted on each side of your motorcycle will help give you the best view of the road behind.

1.13 Mark one answer RES s14

You are about to emerge from a junction. Your pillion passenger tells you it's clear. When should you rely on their judgement?

- ☑ Never, you should always look for yourself
- ☐ When the roads are very busy
- ☐ When the roads are very quiet
- ☐ Only when they are a qualified rider

Your passenger may be inexperienced in judging traffic situations, have a poor view and not have seen a potential hazard. You are responsible for your own safety and your passenger. Always make your own checks to be sure it is safe to pull out.

1.14 Mark one answer RES s8, HC r161

What must you do before stopping normally?

- ☐ Put both feet down
- ☐ Select first gear
- ☑ Use your mirrors
- ☐ Move into neutral

Check your mirrors before slowing down or stopping as there could be vehicles close behind you. If necessary, look behind before stopping.

1.15 Mark two answers RES s8

You want to change lanes in busy, moving traffic. Why could looking over your shoulder help?

- ☐ Mirrors may not cover blind spots
- ☐ To avoid having to give a signal
- ☑ So traffic ahead will make room for you
- ☑ So your balance will not be affected
- ☐ Drivers behind you would be warned

Before changing lanes make sure there's a safe gap to move into. Looking over your shoulder allows you to check the area not covered by your mirrors, where a vehicle could be hidden from view. It also warns following drivers that you want to change lanes.

1.16 Mark one answer RES s8

You have been waiting for some time to make a right turn into a side road. What should you do just before you make the turn?

- ☐ Move close to the kerb
- ☐ Select a higher gear
- ☐ Make a 'lifesaver' check
- ☑ Wave to the oncoming traffic

Remember your 'lifesaver' glance before you start to turn. If you've been waiting for some time and a queue has built up behind you, a vehicle further back may try to overtake. It is especially important to look out for other motorcycles in this situation which may be approaching at speed.

You are turning right onto a dual carriageway. What should you do before emerging?

☐ Stop, and then select a very low gear

☐ Position in the left gutter of the side road

☐ Check that the central reservation is wide enough

☑ Check there is enough room for vehicles behind you

Before emerging right onto a dual carriageway make sure that the central reservation is wide enough to protect your vehicle. If it's not, you should treat it as one road and check that it's clear in both directions before pulling out. Otherwise, you could obstruct part of the carriageway and cause a hazard, both for yourself and other road users.

When riding a different motorcycle you should

☐ ask someone to ride with you for the first time

☐ ride as soon as possible as all controls and switches are the same

☐ leave your gloves behind so switches can be operated more easily

☐ be sure you know where all controls and switches are

Before you ride any motorcycle make sure you're familiar with the layout of all the controls and switches. While control layouts are generally similar, there may be differences in their feel and method of operation.

You are turning right at a large roundabout. Before you cross a lane to reach your exit you should

☑ take a 'lifesaver' glance over your right shoulder

☐ put on your right indicator

☐ take a 'lifesaver' glance over your left shoulder

☐ cancel the left indicator

On busy roundabouts traffic may be moving very quickly and changing lanes suddenly. You need to be aware of what's happening all around you. Before crossing lanes to the left make sure you take a 'lifesaver' glance to the left. This gives you time to react if it's not safe to make the manoeuvre.

1.20
Mark one answer RES s9, HC r184

You are positioned to turn right on a multi-lane roundabout. What should you do before moving to a lane on your left?

☐ Take a 'lifesaver' glance over your right shoulder

☐ Cancel the left signal

☐ Signal to the right

☐ Take a 'lifesaver' glance over your left shoulder

Beware of traffic changing lanes quickly and at the last moment on these roundabouts. Be aware of all signs and road markings so that you can position correctly in good time. Your life could depend on you knowing where other vehicles are.

1.21
Mark one answer RES s9, HC r184

You are turning right on a multi-lane roundabout. When should you take a 'lifesaver' glance over your left shoulder?

☐ After moving into the left lane

☐ After leaving the roundabout

☐ Before signalling to the right

☐ Before moving into the left lane

The 'lifesaver' is essential to motorcyclists and is exactly what it says. It could save your life. Its purpose is to check the blind spot that is not covered by your mirrors. Understand and learn how and when you should use it.

1.22
Mark one answer RES s11, HC r282

You are on a motorway. You see an incident on the other side of the road. Your lane is clear. You should

☐ assist the emergency services

☐ stop, and cross the road to help

☐ concentrate on what is happening ahead

☐ place a warning triangle in the road

Always concentrate on the road ahead. Try not to be distracted by an incident on the other side of the road. Many motorway collisions occur due to traffic slowing down. This is because drivers are looking at something on the other side of the road.

1.23
Mark one answer RES s8, HC r159–161

Before you make a U-turn in the road, you should

☐ give an arm signal as well as using your indicators

☐ signal so that other drivers can slow down for you

☐ look over your shoulder for a final check

☐ select a higher gear than normal

If you want to make a U-turn, slow down and ensure that the road is clear in both directions. Make sure that the road is wide enough to carry out the manoeuvre safely.

As you approach this bridge you should

☐ move into the middle of the road to get a better view

☐ slow down

☐ get over the bridge as quickly as possible

☐ consider using your horn

☐ find another route

☐ beware of pedestrians

This sign gives you a warning. The brow of the hill prevents you seeing oncoming traffic so you must be cautious. The bridge is narrow and there may not be enough room for you to pass an oncoming vehicle at this point. There is no footpath, so pedestrians may be walking in the road. Consider the hidden hazards and be ready to react if necessary.

In which of these situations should you avoid overtaking?

☐ Just after a bend

☐ In a one-way street

☐ On a 30 mph road

☐ Approaching a dip in the road

As you begin to think about overtaking, ask yourself if it's really necessary. If you can't see well ahead stay back and wait for a safer place to pull out.

This road marking warns

☐ drivers to use the hard shoulder

☐ overtaking drivers there is a bend to the left

☐ overtaking drivers to move back to the left

☐ drivers that it is safe to overtake

You should plan your overtaking to take into account any hazards ahead. In this picture the marking indicates that you are approaching a junction. You will not have time to overtake and move back into the left safely.

1.27 · Mark one answer · RES s1, HC r149, 270

Your mobile phone rings while you are travelling. You should

☐ stop immediately
☐ answer it immediately
☐ pull up in a suitable place
☐ pull up at the nearest kerb

The safest option is to switch off your mobile phone before you set off, and use a message service. Even hands-free systems are likely to distract your attention. Don't endanger other road users. If you need to make a call, pull up in a safe place when you can, you may need to go some distance before you can find one. It's illegal to use a hand-held mobile or similar device when driving or riding, except in a genuine emergency.

1.28 · Mark one answer · RES s7, KYTS p68

Why are these yellow lines painted across the road?

☐ To help you choose the correct lane
☐ To help you keep the correct separation distance
☐ To make you aware of your speed
☐ To tell you the distance to the roundabout

These lines are often found on the approach to a roundabout or a dangerous junction. They give you extra warning to adjust your speed. Look well ahead and do this in good time.

1.29 · Mark one answer · RES s7, HC r175–176

You are approaching traffic lights that have been on green for some time. You should

☐ accelerate hard
☐ maintain your speed
☐ be ready to stop
☐ brake hard

The longer traffic lights have been on green, the greater the chance of them changing. Always allow for this on approach and be prepared to stop.

Which of the following should you do before stopping?

- ☐ Sound the horn
- ☐ Use the mirrors
- ☐ Select a higher gear
- ☐ Flash your headlights

Before pulling up check the mirrors to see what is happening behind you. Also assess what is ahead and make sure you give the correct signal if it helps other road users.

When following a large vehicle you should keep well back because this

- ☐ allows you to corner more quickly
- ☐ helps the large vehicle to stop more easily
- ☐ allows the driver to see you in the mirrors
- ☐ helps you to keep out of the wind

If you're following a large vehicle but are so close to it that you can't see the exterior mirrors, the driver can't see you.

Keeping well back will also allow you to see the road ahead by looking past either side of the large vehicle.

When you see a hazard ahead you should use the mirrors. Why is this?

- ☐ Because you will need to accelerate out of danger
- ☐ To assess how your actions will affect following traffic
- ☐ Because you will need to brake sharply to a stop
- ☐ To check what is happening on the road ahead

You should be constantly scanning the road for clues about what is going to happen next. Check your mirrors regularly, particularly as soon as you spot a hazard. What is happening behind may affect your response to hazards ahead.

You are waiting to turn right at the end of a road. Your view is obstructed by parked vehicles. What should you do?

☐ Stop and then move forward slowly and carefully for a proper view

☐ Move quickly to where you can see so you only block traffic from one direction

☐ Wait for a pedestrian to let you know when it is safe for you to emerge

☐ Turn your vehicle around immediately and find another junction to use

At junctions your view is often restricted by buildings, trees or parked cars. You need to be able to see in order to judge a safe gap. Edge forward slowly and keep looking all the time. Don't cause other road users to change speed or direction as you emerge.

Case study practice – 1
Alertness

The morning is clear and fine but very cold.

Joan is riding her motorcycle and is using dipped headlights.

Further on, there's an unmarked junction. Joan looks over her right shoulder before turning right.

Ahead, there's a dip in the road.

Later, she reaches a school crossing patrol area. The officer is signalling traffic to stop while children are crossing.

1.1 Why would Joan be using dipped headlights?
Mark **one** answer

- ☐ To help her see the road ahead
- ☐ To help her be seen by others
- ☐ To help her see other road users
- ☐ To help others see the road ahead

HC r86 **RES** s4

1.2 How should Joan behave at this junction?
Mark **one** answer

- ☐ Check quickly and cross as fast as possible
- ☐ Move slowly while flashing her headlights
- ☐ Check carefully and proceed with great care
- ☐ Wait for someone else to wave her onwards

HC r176 **RES** s9

1.3 What's the name of the final look that Joan gives before turning right?

Mark one answer

- ☐ Lifecycle
- ☐ Lifepreserver
- ☐ Lifeblood
- ☐ Lifesaver

RES s8

1.4 How could the dip affect Joan?

Mark one answer

- ☐ Obstruct her view of the road
- ☐ Increase her fuel consumption
- ☐ Improve her brake function
- ☐ Cause more wear on her tyres

RES s8

1.5 How MUST Joan react to the school crossing patrol warden's signal?

Mark one answer

- ☐ Stop her vehicle and wait patiently
- ☐ Rev up and inch her vehicle forward
- ☐ Stop and wave the children across
- ☐ Move forward slowly with headlights on

HC r105, p105 **RES** s8

> Section two
Attitude

In this section, you'll learn about

- showing consideration and courtesy to other road users
- how to follow other road users safely
- giving priority to emergency vehicles, buses and pedestrians.

Attitude

Safe riding is all about developing the correct attitude and approach to road safety, together with a sound knowledge of riding techniques.

However modern, fast or expensive your motorcycle, it's you, the rider, who determines how safe it is.

> Good manners on the road

Be considerate to other road users. Other types of vehicle, cyclists and horse riders have just as much right to use the road as you. If you ride in a competitive way, you'll make the road less safe for everyone using it.

RES s1

It's also important to be patient with other road users. Unfortunately, not everyone obeys the rules. Try to be calm and tolerant, however difficult it seems. For instance, if someone pulls out in front of you at a junction, slow down and don't get annoyed with them.

HC r147 **RES** s1

Helping other road users

You can help other road users know what you're planning to do by signalling correctly and moving to the correct position at junctions. For instance, if you want to turn right, get into the right-hand lane well before the junction. A badly positioned vehicle could obstruct traffic behind it.

HC r143 **RES** s8, 9

If you're riding slowly, consider the other road users behind you. If there's a queue, pull over as soon as you can do so safely and let the traffic pass. Think how you would feel if you were one of the road users following behind you. They may not be as patient as you are.

HC r169 **RES** s10

If a large vehicle is trying to overtake you but is taking a long time, slow down and let it pass. It will need more time to pass you than a car would.

HC r168 **RES** s8

If you're travelling at the speed limit and a driver comes up behind flashing their headlights or trying to overtake, keep a steady course and allow them to overtake. Don't try to stop them – they could become more frustrated.

HC r168 **RES** s8, 11

Using your horn and lights

Only sound your horn if there's danger and you need to let others know you're there. Don't sound it through impatience.

HC r112 **RES** s5, 6, 10

At night, don't dazzle other road users. Dip your lights when you're

following another vehicle

meeting another vehicle coming towards you.

HC r114 **RES** s13

TIP You should only flash your headlights to show other road users you're there. It's not a signal to show priority, impatience or to greet others.

`HC` r110–111 `RES` s6, 10

Animals on the road

Horses can be frightened easily and a rider could lose control of their horse. When passing horses

- keep your speed right down
- give them plenty of room.

`HC` r214–215 `RES` s10

See the Think! road safety website for more information about horses on the road.

> **http://think.direct.gov.uk/ horses.html**

Take care if there are animals, such as sheep, on the road. If the road is blocked by animals, or if you're asked to, stop and switch off your engine until the road is clear.

`HC` r214

> Following safely

Riding too closely behind another vehicle – known as tailgating – is

- intimidating and distracting for the road user in front
- very dangerous, as it could cause an incident if the vehicle stops suddenly.

`RES` s10

Travelling too closely to another vehicle also means that you can see less of the road ahead, so keep well back, especially from large vehicles. You'll be able to see further down the road and spot any hazards ahead more easily.

`RES` s8, 10

Keep a safe distance from the vehicle in front.

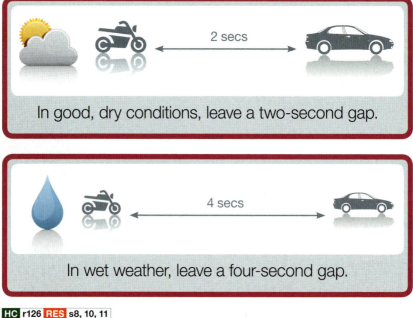

In good, dry conditions, leave a two-second gap.

In wet weather, leave a four-second gap.

HC r126 RES s8, 10, 11

 TIP Use a fixed point, like a road sign, to help you measure the gap between you and the vehicle in front.

See section 4, Safety margins, for more information about the amount of space to leave between you and the vehicle in front.

Keeping well back also allows

- the road user in front to see you in their mirrors
- traffic emerging from junctions ahead to see you more easily.

RES s8, 10

When you're following large vehicles, you may see them move to the centre of the road before turning left – this is because they need more room to manoeuvre. Keep well back and don't try to pass on the left as the rear of the vehicle will cut in.

If the road user behind is following too closely, gradually increase the gap between you and the vehicle in front. This will give you a greater safety margin. If another road user cuts in front of you, drop back until you've restored your safety margin.

HC r168

> Giving priority to others

Who has priority on the road at any time can vary. Sometimes traffic going in one direction is given priority, and this is shown by a road sign. Having priority doesn't mean you can demand right of way. Be careful: the driver coming towards you may not have seen or understood the road sign.

Priority over oncoming vehicles

Emergency vehicles

Always give priority to emergency vehicles. It's important for them to move quickly through traffic because someone's life might depend on it. Pull over to let them through as soon as you can do so safely.

HC r219 **RES** s8

As well as fire, police and ambulance services, other emergency services also use a blue flashing light, including those shown here.

HM coastguard

Bomb disposal

Mountain rescue

Blood transfusion

Doctors' vehicles may use green flashing lights when answering an emergency call.

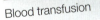

Watch the 'Blue light aware' video to find out more about how to help emergency vehicles get through traffic.

> **motoringassist.com/bluelightaware**

Priority for buses

Give priority to buses pulling out from bus stops, as long as you can do so safely. In some areas, bus lanes allow buses to proceed quickly through traffic. Be aware of road signs and markings so that you don't use bus lanes while they're in operation, unless permitted to do so.

HC r223 **RES** s7, 8, 10

Unmarked crossroads

At unmarked crossroads, no-one has priority. Slow down, look both ways and only emerge into the junction when you can do so safely.

Pedestrian crossings

Be particularly careful around pedestrian crossings so that you're ready to stop if necessary.

Type of crossing	What you need to be aware of
Zebra crossing 	Watch out for pedestrians at or approaching a zebra crossing. • Be ready to slow down and stop. • Be patient if they cross slowly. • Don't encourage them to cross by waving or flashing your headlights – there may be another vehicle coming. **HC** r195 **RES** s8
Pelican crossing	If you're approaching a pelican crossing and the amber light is flashing • give way to pedestrians on the crossing • don't move off until the crossing is clear. **HC** r196–198 **RES** s8

Type of crossing	What you need to be aware of
Puffin crossing 	Puffin crossings are electronically controlled. Sensors ensure that the red light shows until the pedestrian has safely crossed the road. These crossings don't have a flashing amber light; they have a steady amber light, like normal traffic lights. **HC** r199 **RES** s8
Toucan crossing 	Toucan crossings, which work in a similar way to puffin crossings, allow cyclists to cross at the same time as pedestrians. **HC** r199 **RES** s8

Meeting the standards

You must be able to

help other road users to understand what you intend to do by signalling correctly

support the signals that you make with the position of your machine. For example, if you're turning right, position the motorcycle in good time and use the right-turn lane if there is one

control your reaction to other road users. Try not to get annoyed or frustrated

give other road users enough time and space.

You must know and understand

what can happen if you wrongly use the headlights or the horn as a signal

what lane discipline is and why it's important

that it's an offence to ride
- without due care and attention
- without reasonable consideration for other road users.

> Notes

You can use this page to make your own notes or diagrams about the key points you need to remember.

Think about

- To which vehicles do you need to give priority?
- What would you do if someone was tailgating you?
- In what conditions should you keep a four-second distance between you and the vehicle in front?
- What problems might you cause if you're impatient and inconsiderate while riding?

Your notes

_____

_____

_____

_____

_____

_____

_____

_____

_____

_____

_____

Things to discuss and practise with your trainer

These are just a few examples of what you could discuss and practise with your trainer. Read more about attitude to come up with your own ideas.

Discuss with your trainer

- the different crossings you may come across (puffin, toucan, etc) and who can use them
- which emergency vehicles you may see on the road (police, doctors, etc) and how to react to them
- how to behave when other road users don't obey the rules.

Practise with your trainer

- riding in an area with bus lanes, to
  - practise how to react when they're in operation
  - understand when motorcycles may or may not use them
- riding in heavy traffic, to get used to other vehicles that may be following you too closely
- riding in the countryside, or where you're likely to encounter horse riders.

Young, inexperienced and newly qualified motorcyclists can often be involved in crashes. This is due to

☐ being too cautious at junctions

☐ riding in the middle of their lane

☐ showing off and being competitive

☐ wearing full weather protection

Over-confidence, lack of experience and poor judgement can lead to disaster. No matter what anyone says, don't do anything that could endanger lives. It's not worth the risk.

You are riding towards a zebra crossing. Pedestrians are waiting to cross. You should

☐ give way to the elderly and infirm only

☐ slow down and prepare to stop

☐ use your headlight to indicate they can cross

☐ wave at them to cross the road

Look for people waiting to cross and be ready to slow down or stop. Some pedestrians may be hesitant. Children can be unpredictable and may hesitate or run out unexpectedly.

You are riding a motorcycle and following a large vehicle at 40 mph. You should position yourself

☐ close behind to make it easier to overtake the vehicle

☐ to the left of the road to make it easier to be seen

☐ close behind the vehicle to keep out of the wind

☐ well back so that you can see past the vehicle

You need to be able to see well down the road and be ready for any hazards. Staying too close to the vehicle will reduce your view of the road ahead and the driver of the vehicle in front may not be able to see you either. Without a safe separation gap you do not have the time and space necessary to react to any hazards.

2.4 Mark one answer RES s10, HC r214

You are riding on a country road. Two horses with riders are in the distance. You should

☐ continue at your normal speed

☐ change down the gears quickly

☐ slow down and be ready to stop

☐ flash your headlight to warn them

Animals are easily frightened by moving motor vehicles. If you're approaching horses keep your speed down and watch to see if the rider has any difficulty keeping control. Always be ready to stop if necessary.

2.5 Mark one answer RES s8, HC r199

You are approaching a red light at a puffin crossing. Pedestrians are on the crossing. The red light will stay on until

☐ you start to edge forward on to the crossing

☐ the pedestrians have reached a safe position

☐ the pedestrians are clear of the front of your motorcycle

☐ a driver from the opposite direction reaches the crossing

The electronic device will automatically detect when the pedestrians have reached a safe position. Don't proceed until the green light shows it is safe to do so.

2.6 Mark one answer RES s10, HC r169

You are riding a slow-moving scooter on a narrow winding road. You should

☐ keep well out to stop vehicles overtaking dangerously

☐ wave vehicles behind you to pass, if you think they can overtake quickly

☐ pull in safely when you can, to let vehicles behind you overtake

☐ give a left signal when it is safe for vehicles to overtake you

Try not to hold up a queue of traffic. This might lead to other road users becoming impatient and attempting dangerous manoeuvres.

If you're riding a slow-moving scooter or small motorcycle on a narrow road and a queue of traffic has built up behind you, look out for a safe place to pull in.

When riding a motorcycle your normal road position should allow

☐ other vehicles to overtake on your left

☐ the driver ahead to see you in their mirrors

☐ you to prevent vehicles behind from overtaking

☐ you to be seen by traffic that is emerging from junctions ahead

☐ you to ride within half a metre (1 foot 8 ins) of the kerb

Aim to ride in the middle of your lane. Avoid riding in the gutter or in the centre of the road, where you might obstruct overtaking traffic or put yourself in danger from oncoming traffic. Riding in this position could also encourage other traffic to overtake you on the left.

At a pelican crossing the flashing amber light means you MUST

☐ stop and wait for the green light

☐ stop and wait for the red light

☐ give way to pedestrians waiting to cross

☐ give way to pedestrians already on the crossing

Pelican crossings are signal-controlled crossings operated by pedestrians. Push-button controls change the signals. Pelican crossings have no red-and-amber stage before green. Instead, they have a flashing amber light, which means you MUST give way to pedestrians already on the crossing, but if it is clear, you may continue.

You should never wave people across at pedestrian crossings because

☐ there may be another vehicle coming

☐ they may not be looking

☐ it is safer for you to carry on

☐ they may not be ready to cross

If people are waiting to use a pedestrian crossing, slow down and be prepared to stop. Don't wave them across the road since another driver may not have seen them, may not have seen your signal and may not be able to stop safely.

2.10 | Mark one answer | RES s10, HC r126

'Tailgating' means

☐ using the rear door of a hatchback car
☐ reversing into a parking space
☐ following another vehicle too closely
☐ driving with rear fog lights on

'Tailgating' is used to describe this dangerous practice, often seen in fast-moving traffic and on motorways. Following the vehicle in front too closely is dangerous because it

• restricts your view of the road ahead
• leaves you no safety margin if the vehicle in front slows down or stops suddenly.

2.11 | Mark one answer | RES s10, HC r222

Following this vehicle too closely is unwise because

Staying back will increase your view of the road ahead. This will help you to see any hazards that might occur and allow you more time to react.

☐ your brakes will overheat
☐ your view ahead is increased
☐ your engine will overheat
☐ your view ahead is reduced

2.12 | Mark one answer | RES s8, 10, 11, HC r126

You are following a vehicle on a wet road. You should leave a time gap of at least

☐ one second
☐ two seconds
☐ three seconds
☐ four seconds

Wet roads will reduce your tyres' grip on the road. The safe separation gap of at least two seconds in dry conditions should be doubled in wet weather.

2.13 — Mark one answer — RES s8, HC r168

A long, heavily laden lorry is taking a long time to overtake you. What should you do?

☐ Speed up
☐ Slow down
☐ Hold your speed
☐ Change direction

A long lorry with a heavy load will need more time to pass you than a car, especially on an uphill stretch of road. Slow down and allow the lorry to pass.

2.14 — Mark three answers — RES s8

Which of the following vehicles will use blue flashing beacons?

☐ Motorway maintenance
☐ Bomb disposal
☐ Blood transfusion
☐ Police patrol
☐ Breakdown recovery

When you see emergency vehicles with blue flashing beacons, move out of the way as soon as it is safe to do so.

2.15 — Mark one answer — RES s8, HC r219

When being followed by an ambulance showing a flashing blue beacon you should

☐ pull over as soon as safely possible to let it pass
☐ accelerate hard to get away from it
☐ maintain your speed and course
☐ brake harshly and immediately stop in the road

Pull over in a place where the ambulance can pass safely. Check that there are no bollards or obstructions in the road that will prevent it from doing so.

2.16 — Mark one answer — RES s8, HC r219

What type of emergency vehicle is fitted with a green flashing beacon?

☐ Fire engine
☐ Road gritter
☐ Ambulance
☐ Doctor's car

A green flashing beacon on a vehicle means the driver or passenger is a doctor on an emergency call. Give way to them if it's safe to do so. Be aware that the vehicle may be travelling quickly or may stop in a hurry.

2.17   Mark one answer   RES s7, HC r300, KYTS p31

Diamond-shaped signs give instructions to

☐ tram drivers

☐ bus drivers

☐ lorry drivers

☐ taxi drivers

These signs only apply to trams. They are directed at tram drivers but you should know their meaning so that you're aware of the priorities and are able to anticipate the actions of the driver.

2.18   Mark one answer   RES s7, HC r306

On a road where trams operate, which of these vehicles will be most at risk from the tram rails?

☐ Cars

☐ Cycles

☐ Buses

☐ Lorries

The narrow wheels of a bicycle can become stuck in the tram rails, causing the cyclist to stop suddenly, wobble or even lose balance altogether. The tram lines are also slippery which could cause a cyclist to slide or fall off.

2.19   Mark one answer   RES s5, HC r112

What should you use your horn for?

☐ To alert others to your presence

☐ To allow you right of way

☐ To greet other road users

☐ To signal your annoyance

Your horn must not be used between 11.30 pm and 7 am in a built-up area or when you are stationary, unless a moving vehicle poses a danger. Its function is to alert other road users to your presence.

2.20   Mark one answer   RES s8, HC r143

You are in a one-way street and want to turn right. You should position yourself

☐ in the right-hand lane

☐ in the left-hand lane

☐ in either lane, depending on the traffic

☐ just left of the centre line

If you're travelling in a one-way street and wish to turn right you should take up a position in the right-hand lane. This will enable other road users not wishing to turn to proceed on the left. Indicate your intention and take up your position in good time.

2.21
Mark one answer **RES s8, 9, HC r179**

You wish to turn right ahead. Why should you take up the correct position in good time?

- ☐ To allow other drivers to pull out in front of you
- ☐ To give a better view into the road that you're joining
- ☐ To help other road users know what you intend to do
- ☐ To allow drivers to pass you on the right

If you wish to turn right into a side road take up your position in good time. Move to the centre of the road when it's safe to do so. This will allow vehicles to pass you on the left. Early planning will show other traffic what you intend to do.

2.22
Mark one answer **RES s8, HC r25, KYTS p124**

At which type of crossing are cyclists allowed to ride across with pedestrians?

- ☐ Toucan
- ☐ Puffin
- ☐ Pelican
- ☐ Zebra

A toucan crossing is designed to allow pedestrians and cyclists to cross at the same time. Look out for cyclists approaching the crossing at speed.

2.23
Mark one answer **HC r168**

You are travelling at the legal speed limit. A vehicle comes up quickly behind, flashing its headlights. You should

- ☐ accelerate to make a gap behind you
- ☐ touch the brakes sharply to show your brake lights
- ☐ maintain your speed to prevent the vehicle from overtaking
- ☐ allow the vehicle to overtake

Don't enforce the speed limit by blocking another vehicle's progress. This will only lead to the other driver becoming more frustrated. Allow the other vehicle to pass when you can do so safely.

2.24
Mark one answer **RES s6, HC r110–111**

You should ONLY flash your headlights to other road users

- ☐ to show that you are giving way
- ☐ to show that you are about to turn
- ☐ to tell them that you have right of way
- ☐ to let them know that you are there

You should only flash your headlights to warn others of your presence. Don't use them to greet others, show impatience or give priority to other road users. They could misunderstand your signal.

2.25   Mark one answer   RES s9, HC r146

You are approaching unmarked crossroads. How should you deal with this type of junction?

☐ Accelerate and keep to the middle

☐ Slow down and keep to the right

☐ Accelerate looking to the left

☐ Slow down and look both ways

Be extra-cautious, especially when your view is restricted by hedges, bushes, walls and large vehicles etc. In the summer months these junctions can become more difficult to deal with when growing foliage may obscure your view.

2.26   Mark one answer   RES s8, HC r196

You are approaching a pelican crossing. The amber light is flashing. You must

☐ give way to pedestrians who are crossing

☐ encourage pedestrians to cross

☐ not move until the green light appears

☐ stop even if the crossing is clear

While the pedestrians are crossing don't encourage them to cross by waving or flashing your headlights: other road users may misunderstand your signal. Don't harass them by creeping forward or revving your engine.

2.27   Mark one answer   RES s8, 10, 11, HC r126

The conditions are good and dry. You could use the 'two-second rule'

☐ before restarting the engine after it has stalled

☐ to keep a safe gap from the vehicle in front

☐ before using the 'Mirror-Signal-Manoeuvre' routine

☐ when emerging on wet roads

To measure this, choose a fixed reference point such as a bridge, sign or tree. When the vehicle ahead passes the object, say to yourself 'Only a fool breaks the two-second rule.' If you reach the object before you finish saying this, you're TOO CLOSE.

2.28   Mark one answer   RES s8, HC r199

At a puffin crossing, which colour follows the green signal?

☐ Steady red

☐ Flashing amber

☐ Steady amber

☐ Flashing green

Puffin crossings have infra-red sensors which detect when pedestrians are crossing and hold the red traffic signal until the crossing is clear. The use of a sensor means there is no flashing amber phase as there is with a pelican crossing.

You are in a line of traffic. The driver behind you is following very closely. What action should you take?

☐ Ignore the following driver and continue to travel within the speed limit

☐ Slow down, gradually increasing the gap between you and the vehicle in front

☐ Signal left and wave the following driver past

☐ Move over to a position just left of the centre line of the road

It can be worrying to see that the car behind is following you too closely. Give yourself a greater safety margin by easing back from the vehicle in front.

A bus has stopped at a bus stop ahead of you. Its right-hand indicator is flashing. You should

Give way to buses whenever you can do so safely, especially when they signal to pull away from bus stops. Look out for people leaving the bus and crossing the road.

☐ flash your headlights and slow down

☐ slow down and give way if it is safe to do so

☐ sound your horn and keep going

☐ slow down and then sound your horn

> Case study practice – 2
Attitude

David rides his motorcycle to a motorcycle show.
The single-carriageway road surface is damp from overnight rain.

David comes up behind two horse riders on the single carriageway road. He passes them in an appropriate manner.

Near the showground, the traffic volume increases.

There's a large vehicle in front, so David drops back.

He sees a green flashing light in his mirrors so he makes room for the vehicle to pass.

2.1 What's the national speed limit for motorcycles on this road?
Mark **one** answer

☐ 40 mph
☐ 50 mph
☐ 60 mph
☐ 70 mph

HC r124, p40

2.2 How should David ride on this road surface?
Mark **one** answer

☐ Carefully, while increasing the distance from the vehicle in front
☐ Faster, as this will help warm the tyres and dry the road surface
☐ Very slowly, to help prevent surface water spraying over others
☐ As close as possible to the vehicle in front, for added protection

HC r126 **RES** s8

2.3 What's the recommended safest way to pass horse riders?

Mark one answer

☐ Quickly, while flashing headlights
☐ Slowly, while sounding the horn
☐ Quickly, leaving a large gap
☐ Slowly, leaving plenty of room

HC r214–215 **RES** s10

2.4 Why did David drop back?

Mark one answer

☐ To avoid any buffeting from the wind
☐ To allow space for other road users to pull in
☐ To avoid any mud splashing up from the tyres
☐ To allow the driver to see him in the mirrors

HC r164 **RES** s10

2.5 Which vehicle would show a green flashing light?

Mark one answer

☐ Firefighter driving to the fire station
☐ Doctor attending emergency call
☐ Police officer driving home after duty
☐ Council worker driving snow plough

HC r219

Safety and your motorcycle

In this section, you'll learn about

- carrying out basic maintenance on your motorcycle
- what to do if your motorcycle has a fault
- carrying passengers and loads safely
- being seen by, and making sure you can see, other road users
- making your motorcycle secure
- parking safely
- being aware of the environment
- avoiding congestion.

Safety and your motorcycle

Look after your motorcycle and it will look after you, not only by being less likely to break down, but also by being more economical and lasting longer. Remember that an efficient engine is kinder to the environment.

> Looking after your motorcycle

Regular maintenance should ensure that your motorcycle is safe and fit to be on the road. It will also help to make sure that your motorcycle uses fuel as efficiently as possible and keep its exhaust emissions to a minimum.

Check the following items on a regular basis.

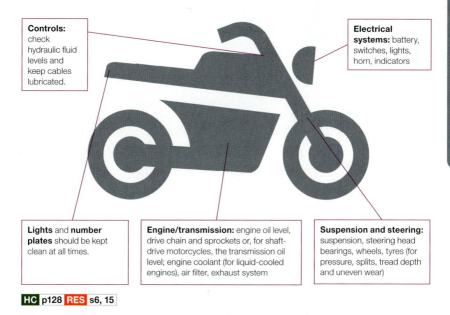

Controls: check hydraulic fluid levels and keep cables lubricated.

Electrical systems: battery, switches, lights, horn, indicators

Lights and **number plates** should be kept clean at all times.

Engine/transmission: engine oil level, drive chain and sprockets or, for shaft-drive motorcycles, the transmission oil level; engine coolant (for liquid-cooled engines), air filter, exhaust system

Suspension and steering: suspension, steering head bearings, wheels, tyres (for pressure, splits, tread depth and uneven wear)

HC p128 RES s6, 15

Helpful tips

The drive chain and sprockets: a loose drive chain and worn sprockets can cause the chain to jump off the rear sprocket and lock the rear wheel. When adjusting the chain tension, check the wheel alignment too as this can increase tyre wear and cause instability when cornering.

Tyre pressures: check them when the tyres are cold. Increase the pressure when you're carrying passengers or loads, or if riding at high speeds. Under-inflation can affect stopping and steering, as well as increase fuel consumption. Check your motorcycle handbook for correct pressures.

Tyre tread: the depth must be more than 1 mm to be legal. When replacing the tyres, replace the tubes as well if necessary. Check the wheel alignment after refitting the rear wheel. Ride carefully on your new tyres until the shiny surface wears off.

HC p129 **RES** s15

Use this handy guide to give your motorcycle a health check.

> **http://think.direct.gov.uk/assets/ pdf/dg_195267.pdf**

Also remember to check

- brake fluid levels regularly: low levels can affect braking efficiency
- oil and coolant levels and tyre pressures before a long journey
- battery fluid levels; if necessary, top up with distilled water to just above the cell plates.

HC p128 **RES** s6, 15

Dealing with faults

A basic understanding of how your motorcycle works will help you recognise when there's a problem with it. It's important that your motorcycle is checked regularly by a qualified mechanic, especially the brakes.

Warning lights on the instrument panel tell you about the performance of the engine and warn you of any faults.

- Check your motorcycle handbook to make sure that you know what all the warning lights mean.
- Don't ignore a warning: it could affect your safety.

HC p128 **RES** s5, 15

Motorcycles fitted with anti-lock braking systems (ABS) will have a warning light on the instrument panel, which should go out at a speed of 5–10 mph. If this doesn't happen, have the ABS checked by a qualified mechanic.

Remember to check oil seals for leakage. Leaks of damping oil from shock absorbers or front forks can

- make your shock absorbers stop working and make your motorcycle difficult to control
- get onto the brakes and increase your stopping distance
- get onto your tyres, causing loss of grip and increased risk of skidding.

 Don't overfill your motorcycle's engine with oil as this could cause damage to engine seals and oil leaks.

Visit a garage as soon as possible if

- the motorcycle vibrates – the wheels may need **wheel balancing**
- the motorcycle becomes difficult to control – the steering head bearings may be worn or need adjustment
- indicators flash too fast – they should flash between one and two times a second
- you notice uneven tyre wear – this can indicate faults with the brakes, suspension or wheel alignment.

RES s6, 15

wheel balancing
making sure that the wheels and tyres are adjusted to minimise any vibrations in the ride

	If this happens while you're riding ...	here's what to do
	The oil pressure light comes on.	Stop as quickly as possible and investigate.
	A tyre bursts.	Slow gently to a stop, holding the handlebars firmly.
	You forget to switch the choke off.	Turn it off as soon as you realise. Leaving it on can cause increased pollution and engine wear, and it wastes fuel.

HC p128 **RES** s6, 15

❯ Carrying passengers and loads

Once you've passed your practical tests, you can carry a passenger if your motorcycle is designed to do so. You're responsible for ensuring that any passenger you carry is

- sitting properly
- facing forward
- on a proper seat with appropriate footrests
- wearing an approved safety helmet, which is correctly fastened.

Make sure that you secure any load or luggage so it doesn't fall off or affect your control of the motorcycle.

HC r83, 85 **RES** s14

> Seeing and being seen

Many road traffic incidents are caused by one road user not seeing another. Motorcyclists are particularly vulnerable in this way, because they take up less space than cars and are more easily hidden by other vehicles.

Visibility

Before you start riding, adjust the mirrors so that you can see as clearly as possible all around. Convex mirrors give a wider view but can make vehicles look further away than they are.

If you're riding in conditions where visibility is seriously reduced, you **MUST** use dipped headlights. It's important for other road users to see you. If there's thick fog, use your fog lights (if fitted) but remember to switch them off again when visibility improves.

Hazard warning lights are fitted so that you can warn road users of a hazard ahead, such as

- when you've broken down
- queuing traffic on a dual carriageway or motorway.

Don't use them as an excuse to park illegally, even for a short time.

HC r116, 226, 274, 277–278 **RES** s5, 11

Clothing

You can make it easier for other road users to see you by wearing a light or brightly coloured helmet, brightly coloured clothing and a high-visibility or reflective jacket or vest. Reflective clothing is especially important at night.

Always wear proper protective clothing and footwear when riding. It can protect you in all types of weather and in the event of an incident. Having a fairing fitted to your motorcycle can protect your hands, legs and feet from bad weather and cold winds.

HC r83–88 **RES** s4

Find out more about protective gear for motorcyclists in this guide.

❯ **http://think.direct.gov.uk/ assets/pdf/dg_195215.pdf**

Use this link to check the safety rating of your helmet.

❯ **http://sharp.direct.gov.uk**

Helmet visors and goggles should be

- kept clean: check manufacturer's guidelines for recommended cleaning materials
- undamaged: replace scratched visors or goggles as soon as possible.

If your visor or goggles become fogged up during a ride, stop as soon as possible to clear them.

HC r83–88 **RES** s4

TIP

Never use a second-hand helmet. Even if the helmet has no obvious damage, it could have damage that can't be seen. This could make it unreliable in a road traffic incident, so it's best not to take the risk.

RES s4

> Security

It's impossible to make a motorcycle completely secure. However, the harder you make it for a potential thief to steal it, the less likely you are to be targeted.

Make it as difficult as you can for a thief to steal your motorcycle.

Use a steering lock.

Use an extra locking device, eg a high-tension steel cable or chain with high-quality padlock, a U-lock or disc lock.

Lock it to an immovable object or another motorcycle.

At night, park in a well-lit area.

HC p131 **RES** s8

To make it more difficult for an opportunist thief, you can

- fit an anti-theft alarm or immobiliser
- have the Vehicle Identification Number (VIN) security-marked onto the motorcycle.

RES s8

You **MUST NOT** leave your vehicle unattended with the engine running.

HC r123

Always switch off the engine and secure your motorcycle before leaving it. Use the steering lock and, if possible, chain the motorcycle to an immovable object for extra security.

Consider joining a Vehicle Watch scheme if there's one in your area. Contact the crime prevention officer at your local police station to find out more.

 Use this link to find out more about thefts from vehicles.

❯ **direct.gov.uk/vehiclecrime**

❯ Parking safely

Where you park your motorcycle can affect the safety of other road users. Avoid parking where your motorcycle would block access or visibility for others, such as

- in front of a property entrance
- at or near a bus stop
- near the brow of a hill where the limited view of the road ahead makes it difficult to see whether it's safe to pass the obstruction
- at a dropped kerb, as this is a place for wheelchair and mobility scooter users to get onto the road or pavement.

HC r243

You **MUST NOT** stop or park on the zigzag lines at a pedestrian crossing. This would block the view of pedestrians and other road users, and endanger people trying to use the crossing.

HC r239–250, 291 **RES** s8

If you have to park on a hill or sloped area, make sure your motorcycle can't roll downhill by

- leaving it in a low gear
- blocking a wheel or wedging it against the kerb.

When leaving your motorcycle on a two-way road at night, park in the direction of the traffic. If the speed limit is more than 30 mph (46 km/h), switch on your parking lights.

❯ Being aware of the environment

Motorcycle engines burn petrol, which is a fossil fuel. Burning fossil fuel causes air pollution and damages the environment, while using up natural resources that can't be replaced.

You can help the environment by riding in an ecosafe way. You'll help to

- improve road safety
- reduce exhaust emissions
- reduce your fuel consumption, which will save you money.

RES s17

Ecosafe riding

Follow these guidelines to make your riding ecosafe.

Reduce your speed. Vehicles travelling at 70 mph (112 km/h) use up to 30% more fuel than those travelling at 50 mph (80 km/h).

Plan well ahead so that you can ride smoothly. Avoiding rapid acceleration and heavy braking can cut your fuel bill by up to 15%.

Follow these guidelines to make your riding ecosafe.

Use selective gear changing: miss out some gears when you're accelerating. This can help by reducing the amount of time you're accelerating, which is the time when your motorcycle uses the most fuel.

Have your motorcycle regularly serviced and tuned properly.

Make sure your tyres are correctly inflated.

RES s17

Avoid

- carrying unnecessary loads
- over-revving the engine in lower gears
- leaving the engine running unnecessarily – if your motorcycle is stationary and likely to remain so for some time, switch off the engine.

HC r123 **RES** s17

Try not to use your motorcycle to make lots of short journeys: consider walking or cycling instead. Using public transport or sharing a vehicle can reduce the volume of traffic and vehicle emissions.

RES s17

Keeping your motorcycle in good condition

Having your motorcycle serviced regularly will give better fuel economy and its exhaust emissions will be reduced. If your motorcycle is over three years old (over four years old in Northern Ireland), it will have to pass an emissions test as part of the MOT test.

If you service your own motorcycle, dispose of old engine oil and batteries responsibly. Take them to a local authority site or a garage. Don't pour oil down the drain.

Make sure your filler cap is securely fastened. If it's loose, it could spill fuel, which wastes both fuel and money. Spilt fuel makes the road slippery for other road users.
HC p130 RES s15

If you notice a strong smell of petrol, check where it's coming from as soon as possible. Use the engine cut-out switch in an emergency.
RES s17

Noise pollution

Don't make excessive noise with your motorcycle. In built-up areas, you **MUST NOT** use your horn between 11.30 pm and 7.00 am, unless another vehicle poses a danger.
HC r112 RES s5

> Avoiding congestion

Sometimes it's impossible to avoid road congestion, but if you can it will make riding less stressful for you.

Always try to

- plan your route before starting out
- avoid riding at times when roads will be busy, if possible
- allow plenty of time for your journey, especially if you have an appointment to keep or a connection to make.

RES s18

Plan your route by

- looking at a map
- using satellite navigation equipment
- checking for roadworks or major events with a motoring organisation
- using a route planner on the internet.

In some towns and cities, you may see red lines on the side of the road, which indicate 'Red Routes'. They help the traffic flow by restricting stopping on these routes.

HC p115 **RES** s7

If you're travelling on a new or unfamiliar route, it's a good idea to print out or write down the route, and also to plan an alternative in case your original route is blocked.

If you can avoid travelling at busy times, you'll

- be less likely to be delayed
- help to ease congestion for those who have to travel at these times.

In some areas, you may have to pay a congestion charge to use congested road space. In London, those exempt from paying include

- disabled people who hold a Blue Badge
- riders of two-wheeled vehicles (and sidecars)
- people living within the area.

RES s18

Find out more about congestion charging in London using this website.

➲ **tfl.gov.uk/roadusers/ congestioncharging**

Meeting the standards

You must be able to

check that all lights and reflectors are

- legal
- clean
- in good working order

make sure that your tyres

- are at the right pressure
- have enough tread depth

get to know the machine if it's the first time you've ridden it

carry out pre-start checks.

You must know and understand

that these must be kept clean at all times

- lights
- indicators
- reflectors
- number plates

how to check that tyres

- are correctly fitted
- are correctly inflated
- have enough tread depth
- are legal to use.

> Notes

You can use this page to make your own notes or diagrams about the key points you need to remember.

Think about

- What maintenance does your motorcycle need each week, month and year?
- What should you do if a warning light appears on your instrument panel while you're riding?
- Which security features does your motorcycle have? How could you improve your machine's security?
- Are there more efficient alternative forms of transport available for your journey?
- How can you find out about local traffic congestion? (For example, local radio stations, websites and mobile phone apps.)

Your notes

Things to discuss and practise with your trainer

These are just a few examples of what you could discuss and practise with your trainer. Read more about safety and your motorcycle to come up with your own ideas.

Discuss with your trainer

- the importance of the state of your tyres, eg on safety, fuel consumption, vehicle handling, etc. Also, discuss how often you should check your tyres
- how you can ride in an ecosafe way, eg use of gears, controlling your speed, etc
- what you think is suitable clothing for riding in different weather conditions.

Practise with your trainer

- riding through built-up areas to get used to different methods of traffic calming
- identifying the warning lights on your instrument panel
- planning your journey. Do this with a new lesson route and see how you can avoid busy times and places.

A loose drive chain on a motorcycle could cause

☐ the front wheel to wobble
☐ the ignition to cut out
☐ the brakes to fail
☐ the rear wheel to lock

Drive chains are subject to wear and require frequent adjustment to maintain the correct tension. Allowing the drive chain to run dry will greatly increase the rate of wear, so it is important to keep it lubricated. If the chain becomes worn or slack it can jump off the sprocket and lock the rear wheel.

What is the most important reason why you should keep your motorcycle regularly maintained?

☐ To accelerate faster than other traffic
☐ So the motorcycle can carry panniers
☐ To keep the machine roadworthy
☐ So the motorcycle can carry a passenger

Whenever you use any motorcycle on the road it must be in a roadworthy condition. Regular maintenance should identify any faults at an early stage and help prevent more serious problems.

How should you ride a motorcycle when NEW tyres have just been fitted?

☐ Carefully, until the shiny surface is worn off
☐ By braking hard especially into bends
☐ Through normal riding with higher air pressures
☐ By riding at faster than normal speeds

New tyres have a shiny finish which needs to wear off before the tyre will give the best grip. Take extra care if the road surface is wet or slippery.

When riding and wearing brightly coloured clothing you will

☐ dazzle other motorists on the road
☐ be seen more easily by other motorists
☐ create a hazard by distracting other drivers
☐ be able to ride on unlit roads at night with sidelights

For your own safety you need other road users to see you easily. Wearing brightly coloured or fluorescent clothing will help you to achieve this during daylight. At night, wearing clothing that includes reflective material is the best way of helping others to see you.

3.5 — Mark one answer — RES s4

You are riding a motorcycle in very hot weather. You should

☐ ride with your visor fully open
☐ continue to wear protective clothing
☐ wear trainers instead of boots
☐ slacken your helmet strap

Always wear your protective clothing, whatever the weather.

In very hot weather it's tempting to ride in light summer clothes. Don't take the risk. If you fall from your motorcycle you'll have no protection from the hard road surface.

3.6 — Mark one answer — RES s4, HC r86

Why should you wear fluorescent clothing when riding in daylight?

☐ It reduces wind resistance
☐ It prevents injury if you come off the machine
☐ It helps other road users to see you
☐ It keeps you cool in hot weather

Motorcycles are smaller and therefore harder to see than most other vehicles on the road. You need to make yourself as visible as possible to other road users. Fluorescent and reflective clothing will help achieve this. You must be visible from all sides.

3.7 — Mark one answer — RES s4, HC r87

Why should riders wear reflective clothing?

☐ To protect them from the cold
☐ To protect them from direct sunlight
☐ To be seen better in daylight
☐ To be seen better at night

Fluorescent clothing will help others to see you during the day. At night, however, you should wear clothing that reflects the light. This allows other road users to see you more easily in their headlights. Ask your local motorcycle dealer about fluorescent and reflective clothing.

3.8 — Mark one answer — RES s4

Which of the following fairings would give you the best weather protection?

☐ Handlebar
☐ Sports
☐ Touring
☐ Windscreen

Fairings give protection to the hands, legs and feet. They also make riding more comfortable by keeping you out of the wind.

Mark one answer

RES s4, HC r84

Your visor becomes badly scratched. You should

☐ polish it with a fine abrasive

☐ replace it

☐ wash it in soapy water

☐ clean it with petrol

Your visor protects your eyes from wind, rain, insects and road dirt. It's therefore important to keep it clean and in good repair. A badly scratched visor can, obscure your view and cause dazzle from lights of oncoming vehicles.

3.10

Mark one answer

RES s15, HC p129

The legal minimum depth of tread for motorcycle tyres is

☐ 1 mm

☐ 1.6 mm

☐ 2.5 mm

☐ 4 mm

The entire original tread should be continuous. Don't ride a motorcycle with worn tyres. Your tyres are your only contact with the road so it's very important that you ensure they are in good condition.

3.11

Mark three answers

RES s4, HC r86

Which of the following makes it easier for motorcyclists to be seen?

☐ Using a dipped headlight

☐ Wearing a fluorescent jacket

☐ Wearing a white helmet

☐ Wearing a grey helmet

☐ Wearing black leathers

☐ Using a tinted visor

Many incidents and collisions involving motorcyclists occur because another road user didn't see them. Do what you can to make yourself more visible to others. Be aware that you are vulnerable and ride defensively.

3.12

Mark one answer

RES s5

Your oil light comes on as you are riding. You should

☐ go to a dealer for an oil change

☐ go to the nearest garage for their advice

☐ ride slowly for a few miles to see if the light goes out

☐ stop as quickly as possible and try to find the cause

If the oil pressure warning light comes on when the engine is running you may have a serious problem. Pull over as soon as you can, stop the engine and investigate the cause.

3.13

Mark two answers

RES s15

Motorcycle tyres MUST

☐ have the same tread pattern

☐ be correctly inflated

☐ be the same size, front and rear

☐ both be the same make

☐ have sufficient tread depth

Your safety and that of others may depend on the condition of your tyres. Before you ride you must check they are correctly inflated and have sufficient tread depth. Make sure these checks become part of a routine.

3.14

Mark one answer

RES s5

You forget to switch the choke off after the engine warms up. This could

☐ flatten the battery

☐ reduce braking distances

☐ use less fuel

☐ cause much more engine wear

Leaving the choke on for too long will cause unnecessary engine wear and waste fuel.

3.15

Mark one answer

RES s15

When riding your motorcycle a tyre bursts. What should you do?

☐ Slow gently to a stop

☐ Brake firmly to a stop

☐ Change to a high gear

☐ Lower the side stand

If a tyre bursts, close the throttle smoothly and slow gently to a stop, holding the handlebars firmly to help you keep a straight course.

3.16

Mark one answer

RES s15, 17

A motorcycle engine that is properly maintained will

☐ use much more fuel

☐ have lower exhaust emissions

☐ increase your insurance premiums

☐ not need to have an MOT

A badly maintained engine can emit more exhaust fumes than one that is correctly serviced. This can be damaging to the environment and also cost you more in fuel.

What should you clean visors and goggles with?

It is very important to keep your visor or goggles clean. Clean them using warm soapy water. Do not use solvents or petrol.

☐ Petrol

☐ White spirit

☐ Antifreeze

☐ Soapy water

You are riding on a quiet road. Your visor fogs up. What should you do?

☐ Continue at a reduced speed

☐ Stop as soon as possible and wipe it

☐ Build up speed to increase air flow

☐ Close the helmet air vents

In cold and wet weather your visor may fog up. If this happens when you are riding choose somewhere safe to stop, and wipe it clean with a damp cloth. Special anti-fog products are available at motorcycle dealers.

You are riding in hot weather. What is the safest type of footwear?

☐ Sandals

☐ Trainers

☐ Shoes

☐ Boots

It is important to wear good boots when you ride a motorcycle. Boots protect your feet and shins from knocks, and give some protection in a crash. They also help keep you warm and dry in cold or wet weather.

Which of the following should not be used to fasten your safety helmet?

☐ Double D ring fastening

☐ Velcro tab

☐ Quick release fastening

☐ Bar and buckle

Some helmet straps have a velcro tab in addition to the main fastening, which is intended to secure the strap so that it does not flap in the wind. It should NOT be used on its own to fasten the helmet.

3.21
Mark two answers — RES s4, HC r87

You want to ride your motorcycle in the dark. What could you wear to be seen more easily?

- ☐ A black leather jacket
- ☐ Reflective clothing
- ☐ A white helmet
- ☐ A red helmet

When riding in the dark you will be easier to see if you wear reflective clothing and a white helmet. A light-coloured helmet contrasts starkly with the surrounding darkness, while reflective clothing reflects the light from other vehicles and makes the rider much more visible.

3.22
Mark one answer — RES s17

Your motorcycle has a catalytic converter. Its purpose is to reduce

- ☐ exhaust noise
- ☐ fuel consumption
- ☐ exhaust emissions
- ☐ engine noise

Catalytic converters reduce the toxic and polluting gases given out by the engine. Never use leaded or lead replacement petrol in a vehicle with a catalytic converter, as even one tankful can permanently damage the system.

3.23
Mark one answer — RES s15

After refitting your rear wheel what should you check?

- ☐ Your steering damper
- ☐ Your side stand
- ☐ Your wheel alignment
- ☐ Your suspension preload

After refitting the rear wheel or adjusting the drive chain you should check your wheel alignment. Incorrect alignment will result in excessive tyre wear and poor road holding.

3.24
Mark one answer — RES s15

You are checking your direction indicators. How often per second must they flash?

- ☐ Between 1 and 2 times
- ☐ Between 3 and 4 times
- ☐ Between 5 and 6 times
- ☐ Between 7 and 8 times

You should check that all your lights work properly before every journey. Make sure that any signals you give can be clearly seen.

If you're not sure whether your signals can be seen you can use arm signals as well to make your intentions clear. Only do this if you're going slowly.

3.25
Mark one answer RES s15

After adjusting the final drive chain what should you check?

- ☐ The rear wheel alignment
- ☐ The suspension adjustment
- ☐ The rear shock absorber
- ☐ The front suspension forks

Always check the rear wheel alignment after adjusting the chain tension. Marks on the chain adjuster may be provided to make this easy. Incorrect alignment can cause instability and increased tyre wear.

3.26
Mark one answer RES s15

Your steering feels wobbly. Which of these is a likely cause?

- ☐ Tyre pressure is too high
- ☐ Incorrectly adjusted brakes
- ☐ Worn steering head bearings
- ☐ A broken clutch cable

Worn bearings in the steering head can make your motorcycle very difficult to control. They should be checked for wear and correct adjustment.

3.27
Mark one answer RES s15

You have a faulty oil seal on a shock absorber. Why is this a serious problem?

- ☐ It will cause excessive chain wear
- ☐ Dripping oil could reduce the grip of your tyre
- ☐ Your motorcycle will be harder to ride uphill
- ☐ Your motorcycle will not accelerate so quickly

Leaking oil could affect the grip of your tyres and also the effectiveness of your brakes. This could result in a loss of control, putting you and other road users in danger.

3.28
Mark one answer RES s15

Oil is leaking from your forks. Why should you NOT ride a motorcycle in this condition?

- ☐ Your brakes could be affected by dripping oil
- ☐ Your steering is likely to seize up
- ☐ The forks will quickly begin to rust
- ☐ The motorcycle will become too noisy

Oil dripping from forks and shock absorbers is dangerous if it gets onto brakes and tyres. Replace faulty oil seals immediately.

3.29 — Mark one answer — RES s15

You have adjusted your drive chain. If this is not done properly, what problem could it cause?

☐ Inaccurate speedometer reading

☐ Loss of braking power

☐ Incorrect rear wheel alignment

☐ Excessive fuel consumption

After carrying out drive chain adjustment, you should always check the rear wheel alignment. Many motorcycles have alignment guides stamped onto the frame to help you do this correctly.

3.30 — Mark one answer — RES s15, HC p129

There is a cut in the sidewall of one of your tyres. What should you do about this?

☐ Replace the tyre before riding the motorcycle

☐ Check regularly to see if it gets any worse

☐ Repair the puncture before riding the motorcycle

☐ Reduce pressure in the tyre before you ride

A cut in the sidewall can be very dangerous. The tyre is in danger of blowing out if you ride the motorcycle in this condition.

3.31 — Mark one answer — RES s15

You need to put air into your tyres. How would you find out the correct pressure to use?

☐ It will be shown on the tyre wall

☐ It will be stamped on the wheel

☐ By checking the vehicle owner's manual

☐ By checking the registration document

Tyre pressures should be checked regularly. Use your vehicle manual to find advice on the correct pressures to use.

3.32 — Mark one answer — RES s15

You can prevent a cable operated clutch from becoming stiff by keeping the cable

☐ tight

☐ dry

☐ slack

☐ oiled

Keeping the cable oiled will help it to move smoothly through its outer casing. This will extend the life of the cable and assist your control of the motorcycle.

When adjusting your chain it is important for the wheels to be aligned accurately. Incorrect wheel alignment can cause

☐ a serious loss of power

☐ reduced braking performance

☐ increased tyre wear

☐ reduced ground clearance

If a motorcycle's wheels are incorrectly aligned tyres may wear unevenly and the motorcycle can become unstable, especially when cornering.

Why should you wear specialist motorcycle clothing when riding?

☐ Because the law requires you to do so

☐ Because it looks better than ordinary clothing

☐ Because it gives best protection from the weather

☐ Because it will reduce your insurance

If you become cold and wet when riding, this can have a serious effect on your concentration and control of your motorcycle.

Proper riding gear can help shield you from the weather, as well as giving protection in the event of a crash.

When leaving your motorcycle parked, you should always

☐ remove the battery lead

☐ pull it onto the kerb

☐ use the steering lock

☐ leave the parking light on

When leaving your motorcycle you should always use the steering lock. You should also consider using additional locking devices such as a U-lock, disc lock or chain. If possible fasten it to an immovable post or another motorcycle.

You are parking your motorcycle. Chaining it to an immovable object will

☐ be against the law

☐ give extra security

☐ be likely to cause damage

☐ leave the motorcycle unstable

Theft of motorcycles is a very common crime. If you can, secure your vehicle to a lamppost or other such object, to help reduce the chances of it being stolen.

3.37 Mark one answer RES s8

You are parking your motorcycle and sidecar on a hill. What is the best way to stop it rolling away?

☐ Leave it in neutral

☐ Put the rear wheel on the pavement

☐ Leave it in a low gear

☐ Park very close to another vehicle

To make sure a sidecar outfit doesn't roll away when parking you should leave it in a low gear, and wedge it against the kerb or place a block behind the wheel.

3.38 Mark one answer RES s5

An engine cut-out switch should be used to

If you are involved in a collision or crash, using the engine cut-out switch will help to reduce any fire hazard. When stopping the engine normally, use the ignition switch.

☐ reduce speed in an emergency

☐ prevent the motorcycle being stolen

☐ stop the engine normally

☐ stop the engine in an emergency

3.39 Mark one answer RES s7, HC r153

You enter a road where there are road humps. What should you do?

☐ Maintain a reduced speed throughout

☐ Accelerate quickly between each one

☐ Always keep to the maximum legal speed

☐ Ride slowly at school times only

The humps are there for a reason; to reduce the speed of the traffic. Don't accelerate harshly between them, as this means you will only have to brake sharply to negotiate the next hump.

Harsh braking and acceleration uses more fuel as well as causing wear and tear to your vehicle.

3.40 Mark one answer RES s15

When should you especially check the engine oil level?

☐ Before a long journey

☐ When the engine is hot

☐ Early in the morning

☐ Every 6000 miles

As well as the oil you will also need to check other items. These include, fuel, water and tyres.

You service your own motorcycle. How should you get rid of the old engine oil?

☐ Take it to a local authority site

☐ Pour it down a drain

☐ Tip it into a hole in the ground

☐ Put it into your dustbin

Never pour the oil down any drain. The oil is highly pollutant and could harm wildlife. Confine it in a container and dispose of it properly at an authorised site.

What safeguard could you take against fire risk to your motorcycle?

☐ Keep water levels above maximum

☐ Check out any strong smell of petrol

☐ Avoid riding with a full tank of petrol

☐ Use unleaded petrol

The fuel in your motorcycle can be a dangerous fire hazard. DON'T use a naked flame if you can smell fuel, or smoke when refuelling.

Which of the following would NOT make you more visible in daylight?

☐ Wearing a black helmet

☐ Wearing a white helmet

☐ Switching on your dipped headlight

☐ Wearing a fluorescent jacket

Wearing bright or fluorescent clothes will help other road users to see you. Wearing a white or brightly coloured helmet can also make you more visible.

It would be illegal to ride with a helmet on when

☐ the helmet is not fastened correctly

☐ the helmet is more than four years old

☐ you have borrowed someone else's helmet

☐ the helmet does not have chin protection

A helmet that is incorrectly fastened or not fastened at all is likely to come off in a crash. It will provide little or no protection. By law, you must wear a helmet when riding on the road and it must be correctly fastened (members of the Sikh religion who wear a turban are exempt).

3.45 — Mark three answers — RES s15

When may you have to increase the tyre pressures on your motorcycle?

- ☐ When carrying a passenger
- ☐ After a long journey
- ☐ When carrying a load
- ☐ When riding at high speeds
- ☐ When riding in hot weather

Read the manufacturer's handbook to see if they recommend increasing tyre pressures under certain conditions.

3.46 — Mark two answers — RES s15, HC p128

Which TWO of these items on a motorcycle MUST be kept clean?

- ☐ Number plate
- ☐ Wheels
- ☐ Engine
- ☐ Fairing
- ☐ Headlight

Maintenance is a vital part of road safety. Lights, indicators, reflectors and number plates MUST be kept clean and clear.

3.47 — Mark one answer — RES s5

You should use the engine cut-out switch on your motorcycle to

- ☐ save wear and tear on the battery
- ☐ stop the engine for a short time
- ☐ stop the engine in an emergency
- ☐ save wear and tear on the ignition

Only use the engine cut-out switch in an emergency. When stopping the engine normally, use the ignition switch. This will remind you to take your keys with you when parking. It could also prevent starting problems if you forget you've left the cut-out switch in the 'off' position. When returning to your motorcycle make sure someone has not done this as a trick.

3.48 — Mark one answer — RES s15

You have adjusted the tension on your drive chain. You should check the

- ☐ rear wheel alignment
- ☐ tyre pressures
- ☐ valve clearances
- ☐ sidelights

Drive chains wear and need frequent adjustment and lubrication. If the drive chain is worn or slack it can jump off the sprocket and lock the rear wheel. When you have adjusted the chain tension, you need to check the rear wheel alignment. Marks by the chain adjusters may be provided to make this easier.

A friend offers you a second-hand safety helmet for you to use. Why may this be a bad idea?

A second-hand helmet may look in good condition but it could have received damage that is not visible externally. A damaged helmet could be unreliable in a crash. Don't take the risk.

☐ It may be damaged

☐ You will be breaking the law

☐ You will affect your insurance cover

☐ It may be a full-face type

You are riding a motorcycle of more than 50 cc. Which FOUR would make a tyre illegal?

☐ Tread less than 1.6 mm deep

☐ Tread less than 1 mm deep

☐ A large bulge in the wall

☐ A recut tread

☐ Exposed ply or cord

☐ A stone wedged in the tread

When checking tyres make sure there are no bulges or cuts in the side walls. Always buy your tyres from a reputable dealer to ensure quality and value for money.

You should maintain cable operated brakes

☐ by regular adjustment when necessary

☐ at normal service times only

☐ yearly, before taking the motorcycle for its MOT

☐ by oiling cables and pivots regularly

Keeping your brakes in good working order is vital for safety. Cables will stretch with use and need checking and adjusting regularly. They will also need lubricating to prevent friction and wear of the cables and pivots.

3.52 — Mark two answers — RES s15

A properly serviced motorcycle will give

- ☐ lower insurance premiums
- ☐ a refund on your road tax
- ☐ better fuel economy
- ☐ cleaner exhaust emissions

When you purchase your motorcycle, check at what intervals you should have it serviced. This can vary depending on model or manufacturer. Use the service manual and keep it up to date.

3.53 — Mark one answer — RES s15

A loosely adjusted drive chain could

- ☐ lock the rear wheel
- ☐ make wheels wobble
- ☐ cause a braking fault
- ☐ affect your headlight beam

A motorcycle chain will stretch as it wears. It needs frequent checking, and adjustment if necessary, to keep the tension correct. In extreme cases a loose chain can jump off the sprocket and become wedged in the rear wheel. This could cause serious loss of control and result in a crash.

3.54 — Mark one answer — RES s12, HC r226

Your motorcycle is NOT fitted with daytime running lights. When MUST you use a dipped headlight during the day?

- ☐ On country roads
- ☐ In poor visibility
- ☐ Along narrow streets
- ☐ When parking

It's important that other road users can see you clearly at all times. It will help other road users to see you if you use a dipped headlight during the day. You MUST use a dipped headlight during the day if visibility is seriously reduced, that is, when you can't see for more than 100 metres (328 feet).

3.55 — Mark one answer — RES s14

Tyre pressures should usually be increased on your motorcycle when

- ☐ riding on a wet road
- ☐ carrying a pillion passenger
- ☐ travelling on an uneven surface
- ☐ riding on twisty roads

Sometimes manufacturers advise you to increase your tyre pressures for high-speed riding and when carrying extra weight. This information can be found in the handbook.

Mark one answer

RES s15

You have too much oil in your engine. What could this cause?

☐ Low oil pressure

☐ Engine overheating

☐ Chain wear

☐ Oil leaks

Too much oil in the engine will create excess pressure and could damage engine seals and cause oil leaks. Any excess oil should be drained off.

3.57

Mark one answer

HC r123

You are leaving your motorcycle unattended on a road. When may you leave the engine running?

☐ When parking for less than five minutes

☐ If the battery is flat

☐ When in a 20 mph zone

☐ Not on any occasion

When you leave your motorcycle parked and unattended on a road, switch off the engine, use the steering lock and remove the ignition key. Also take any tank bags, panniers or loose luggage with you, set the alarm if it has one, and use an additional lock and chain or cable lock.

3.58

Mark one answer

RES s5

You are involved in a crash. To reduce the risk of fire what is the best thing to do?

☐ Keep the engine running

☐ Open the choke

☐ Turn the fuel tap to reserve

☐ Use the engine cut-out switch

The engine cut-out switch is used to stop the engine in an emergency. In the event of a crash this may help to reduce any fire risk.

3.59

Mark two answers

RES s4, 13, HC r87

When riding at night you should

☐ ride with your headlight on

☐ wear reflective clothing

☐ wear a tinted visor

☐ ride in the centre of the road

☐ give arm signals

At night you should wear clothing that includes reflective material to help other road users see you. This could be a vest, tabard or reflective body strap. Use your headlight on dipped or main beam as appropriate without dazzling other road users.

3.60   Mark two answers   RES s15, HC p129

Which TWO are badly affected if the tyres are under-inflated?

☐ Braking

☐ Steering

☐ Changing gear

☐ Parking

Your tyres are your only contact with the road so it is very important to ensure that they are free from defects, have sufficient tread depth and are correctly inflated. Correct tyre pressures help reduce the risk of skidding and provide a safer and more comfortable drive or ride.

3.61   Mark one answer   RES s5, HC r112

You must NOT sound your horn

☐ between 10 pm and 6 am in a built-up area

☐ at any time in a built-up area

☐ between 11.30 pm and 7 am in a built-up area

☐ between 11.30 pm and 6 am on any road

Vehicles can be noisy. Every effort must be made to prevent excessive noise, especially in built-up areas at night. Don't

• rev the engine

• sound the horn

unnecessarily.

It is illegal to sound your horn in a built-up area between 11.30 pm and 7 am, except when another vehicle poses a danger.

3.62   Mark three answers   RES s8

The pictured vehicle is 'environmentally friendly' because it

Trams are powered by electricity and therefore do not emit exhaust fumes. They are also much quieter than petrol or diesel engined vehicles and can carry a large number of passengers.

☐ reduces noise pollution

☐ uses diesel fuel

☐ uses electricity

☐ uses unleaded fuel

☐ reduces parking spaces

☐ reduces town traffic

Supertrams or Light Rapid Transit (LRT) systems are environmentally friendly because

☐ they use diesel power

☐ they use quieter roads

☐ they use electric power

☐ they do not operate during rush hour

This means that they do not emit toxic fumes, which add to city pollution problems. They are also a lot quieter and smoother to ride on.

'Red routes' in major cities have been introduced to

☐ raise the speed limits

☐ help the traffic flow

☐ provide better parking

☐ allow lorries to load more freely

Traffic jams today are often caused by the volume of traffic. However, inconsiderate parking can lead to the closure of an inside lane or traffic having to wait for oncoming vehicles. Driving slowly in traffic increases fuel consumption and causes a build-up of exhaust fumes.

Road humps, chicanes and narrowings are

☐ always at major road works

☐ used to increase traffic speed

☐ at toll-bridge approaches only

☐ traffic calming measures

Traffic calming measures help keep vehicle speeds low in congested areas where there are pedestrians and children. A pedestrian is much more likely to survive a collision with a vehicle travelling at 20 mph than at 40 mph.

It is essential that tyre pressures are checked regularly. When should this be done?

☐ After any lengthy journey

☐ After travelling at high speed

☐ When tyres are hot

☐ When tyres are cold

When you check the tyre pressures do so when the tyres are cold. This will give you a more accurate reading. The heat generated from a long journey will raise the pressure inside the tyre.

3.67   Mark one answer   RES s15, 17

You will use more fuel if your tyres are

- ☐ under-inflated
- ☐ of different makes
- ☐ over-inflated
- ☐ new and hardly used

Check your tyre pressures frequently – normally once a week. If pressures are lower than those recommended by the manufacturer, there will be more 'rolling resistance'. The engine will have to work harder to overcome this, leading to increased fuel consumption.

3.68   Mark two answers   RES s17

How should you dispose of a used battery?

- ☐ Take it to a local authority site
- ☐ Put it in the dustbin
- ☐ Break it up into pieces
- ☐ Leave it on waste land
- ☐ Take it to a garage
- ☐ Burn it on a fire

Batteries contain acid which is hazardous and must be disposed of safely.

3.69   Mark one answer   RES s17, HC r123

What is most likely to cause high fuel consumption?

- ☐ Poor steering control
- ☐ Accelerating around bends
- ☐ Staying in high gears
- ☐ Harsh braking and accelerating

Accelerating and braking gently and smoothly will help to save fuel, reduce wear on your vehicle and is better for the environment.

3.70   Mark one answer   RES s15

The fluid level in your battery is low. What should you top it up with?

- ☐ Battery acid
- ☐ Distilled water
- ☐ Engine oil
- ☐ Engine coolant

Some modern batteries are maintenance-free. Check your vehicle handbook and, if necessary, make sure that the plates in each battery cell are covered.

You are parked on the road at night. Where must you use parking lights?

☐ Where there are continuous white lines in the middle of the road

☐ Where the speed limit exceeds 30 mph

☐ Where you are facing oncoming traffic

☐ Where you are near a bus stop

When parking at night, park in the direction of the traffic. This will enable other road users to see the reflectors on the rear of your vehicle. Use your parking lights if the speed limit is over 30 mph.

Motor vehicles can harm the environment. This has resulted in

☐ air pollution

☐ damage to buildings

☐ less risk to health

☐ improved public transport

☐ less use of electrical vehicles

☐ using up of natural resources

Exhaust emissions are harmful to health. Together with vibration from heavy traffic this can result in damage to buildings. Most petrol and diesel fuels come from a finite and non-renewable source. Anything you can do to reduce your use of these fuels will help the environment.

Excessive or uneven tyre wear can be caused by faults in which THREE of the following?

☐ The gearbox

☐ The braking system

☐ The accelerator

☐ The exhaust system

☐ Wheel alignment

☐ The suspension

Regular servicing will help to detect faults at an early stage and this will avoid the risk of minor faults becoming serious or even dangerous.

You need to top up your battery. What level should you fill to?

☐ The top of the battery

☐ Half-way up the battery

☐ Just below the cell plates

☐ Just above the cell plates

Top up the battery with distilled water and make sure each cell plate is covered.

3.75 — Mark one answer — RES s13

You are parking on a two-way road at night. The speed limit is 40 mph. You should park on the

☐ left with parking lights on

☐ left with no lights on

☐ right with parking lights on

☐ right with dipped headlights on

At night all vehicles must display parking lights when parked on a road with a speed limit greater than 30 mph. They should be close to the kerb, facing in the direction of the traffic flow and not within a distance as specified in The Highway Code.

3.76 — Mark one answer — RES s18

How can you plan your route before starting a long journey?

☐ Check your vehicle's workshop manual

☐ Ask your local garage

☐ Use a route planner on the internet

☐ Consult your travel agents

Various route planners are available on the internet. Most of them give you various options allowing you to choose the most direct, quickest or scenic route. They can also include rest and fuel stops and distances. Print them off and take them with you.

3.77 — Mark one answer — RES s18

Planning your route before setting out can be helpful. How can you do this?

☐ Look in a motoring magazine

☐ Only visit places you know

☐ Try to travel at busy times

☐ Print or write down the route

Print or write down your route before setting out. Some places are not well signed so using place names and road numbers may help you avoid problems en route. Try to get an idea of how far you're going before you leave. You can also use it to re-check the next stage at each rest stop.

3.78 — Mark one answer — RES s18

Why is it a good idea to plan your journey to avoid busy times?

☐ You will have an easier journey

☐ You will have a more stressful journey

☐ Your journey time will be longer

☐ It will cause more traffic congestion

No one likes to spend time in traffic queues. Try to avoid busy times related to school or work travel. As well as moving vehicles you should also consider congestion caused by parked cars, buses and coaches around schools.

Mark one answer

By avoiding busy times when travelling

☐ you are more likely to be held up

☐ your journey time will be longer

☐ you will travel a much shorter distance

☐ you are less likely to be delayed

If possible, avoid the early morning, late afternoon and early evening 'rush hour'. Doing this should allow you to travel in a more relaxed frame of mind, concentrate solely on what you're doing and arrive at your destination feeling less stressed.

Mark one answer

It can help to plan your route before starting a journey. Why should you also plan an alternative route?

☐ Your original route may be blocked

☐ Your maps may have different scales

☐ You may find you have to pay a congestion charge

☐ Because you may get held up by a tractor

It can be frustrating and worrying to find your planned route is blocked by roadworks or diversions. If you have planned an alternative you will feel less stressed and more able to concentrate fully on your driving or riding. If your original route is mostly on motorways it's a good idea to plan an alternative using non-motorway roads. Always carry a map with you just in case you need to refer to it.

Mark one answer

You are making an appointment and will have to travel a long distance. You should

☐ allow plenty of time for your journey

☐ plan to go at busy times

☐ avoid all national speed limit roads

☐ prevent other drivers from overtaking

Always allow plenty of time for your journey in case of unforeseen problems. Anything can happen: punctures, breakdowns, road closures, diversions, etc. You will feel less stressed and less inclined to take risks if you are not 'pushed for time'.

Mark one answer

Rapid acceleration and heavy braking can lead to

☐ reduced pollution

☐ increased fuel consumption

☐ reduced exhaust emissions

☐ increased road safety

Using the controls smoothly can reduce fuel consumption by about 15% as well as reducing wear and tear on your vehicle. Plan ahead and anticipate changes of speed well in advance. This will reduce the need to accelerate rapidly or brake sharply.

Which of these, if allowed to get low, could cause you to crash?

☐ Anti-freeze level

☐ Brake fluid level

☐ Battery water level

☐ Radiator coolant level

You should carry out frequent checks on all fluid levels but particularly brake fluid. As the brake pads or shoes wear down the brake fluid level will drop. If it drops below the minimum mark on the fluid reservoir, air could enter the hydraulic system and lead to a loss of braking efficiency or complete brake failure.

Section three Questions

> Case study practice – 3 Safety and your motorcycle

Julia is riding her motorcycle to work. The weather is dry but chilly.

Julia wears leather riding gear, boots and gauntlets, helmet and a fluorescent reflective jacket. She makes herself as visible as possible.

At the service station, she buys fuel and cleans both handlebar mirrors, which have longer stems.

She also makes her weekly check of tyre pressures and tread depths. The depth is well above the legal limit.

3.1 What should Julia do about protective clothing in warmer weather?

Mark **one** answer

- ☐ Wear some summer clothing
- ☐ Continue using protective gear
- ☐ Use boots and trousers only
- ☐ Discard the gloves and boots

 RES s12

3.2 What colour and type of helmet are recommended for maximum visibility and safety?

Mark **one** answer

☐ Black with a full-face visor
☐ Black without a full-face visor
☐ White with a full-face visor
☐ White without a full-face visor

RES s4

3.3 How can Julia's reflective clothing help her while riding?

Mark **one** answer

☐ With braking and stopping
☐ With speed and gears
☐ With signalling and turning
☐ With visibility and safety

HC r86, 87 **RES** s4

3.4 Why might Julia have this sort of mirror?

Mark **one** answer

☐ Because they look very cool and fashionable
☐ So that her view is completely unobstructed
☐ Because other vehicles then allow more room
☐ They help to balance and control the motorcycle

RES s5

3.5 What's the minimum legal tread depth for motorcycle tyres?

Mark **one** answer

☐ At least 1 mm over three-quarters of the tread breadth and all around
☐ At least 2 mm over the entire surface of tread breadth and all around
☐ At least 2 mm over three-quarters of the tread breadth and all around
☐ At least 1 mm over the entire surface of tread breadth and all around

HC p129 **RES** s15

> Section four
Safety margins

In this section, you'll learn about

- ❯ keeping yourself and others safe by staying within safety margins
- ❯ stopping, thinking and braking distances
- ❯ risks caused by different weather conditions and road surfaces
- ❯ the risk of skidding
- ❯ contraflow systems.

Safety margins

It's essential that you always keep your safety, and that of your passenger and other road users, in mind as you're riding.

You can reduce your chances of being involved in an incident on the road by knowing the safety margins and what can happen if you don't ride within them. Never take risks.

Keep control of your motorcycle by using the correct procedures. For instance, when you're travelling on a long downhill stretch of road, control your speed by selecting a lower gear and using your brakes carefully. Excessive braking on hills can cause your brakes to overheat and become less effective.

HC r160 **RES** s6, 8

Don't 'coast' – this means travelling in neutral or with the clutch disengaged – as this can reduce your control over the machine.

HC r122

> Stopping distance

Leave enough room between your motorcycle and the vehicle in front so that you can pull up safely if it slows down or stops suddenly.

Your overall stopping distance is the distance your motorcycle travels from the moment you realise that you must brake to the moment your motorcycle stops.

HC r126 **RES** s8

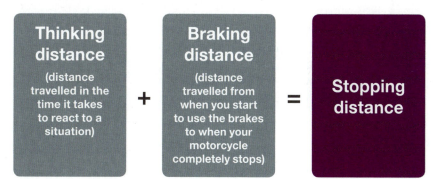

Thinking distance		Braking distance		Stopping distance
(distance travelled in the time it takes to react to a situation)	**+**	(distance travelled from when you start to use the brakes to when your motorcycle completely stops)	**=**	

> Typical stopping distances

Look at the typical stopping, thinking and braking distances given in *The Official Highway Code*. Remember that these are based on vehicles travelling

- with good tyres and brakes
- on a dry road
- in good conditions.

HC r126 **RES** s8

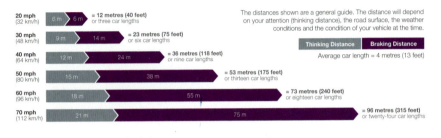

	Thinking Distance	Braking Distance

The distances shown are a general guide. The distance will depend on your attention (thinking distance), the road surface, the weather conditions and the condition of your vehicle at the time.

Average car length = 4 metres (13 feet)

20 mph (32 km/h) — 6 m | 6 m = 12 metres (40 feet) or three car lengths
30 mph (48 km/h) — 9 m | 14 m = 23 metres (75 feet) or six car lengths
40 mph (64 km/h) — 12 m | 24 m = 36 metres (118 feet) or nine car lengths
50 mph (80 km/h) — 15 m | 38 m = 53 metres (175 feet) or thirteen car lengths
60 mph (96 km/h) — 18 m | 55 m = 73 metres (240 feet) or eighteen car lengths
70 mph (112 km/h) — 21 m | 75 m = 96 metres (315 feet) or twenty-four car lengths

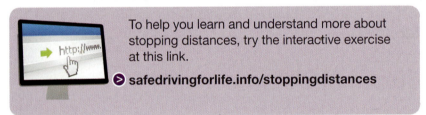

To help you learn and understand more about stopping distances, try the interactive exercise at this link.

> **safedrivingforlife.info/stoppingdistances**

Don't just learn the stopping distance figures: you need to be able to judge the distance when you're riding.

HC r126 **RES** s12

TIP

In good conditions, leave a two-second gap between your motorcycle and the vehicle in front. Use a fixed point, like a road sign, to measure the time gap between your motorcycle and the vehicle in front. You can measure two seconds by saying the sentence, 'Only a fool breaks the two-second rule.'

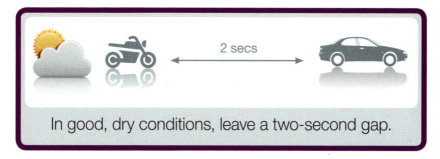

In good, dry conditions, leave a two-second gap.

In other conditions, you need to increase this distance.

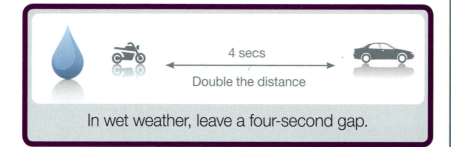

In wet weather, leave a four-second gap.

In icy weather, leave a 20-second gap.

Keeping a safe distance from the vehicle in front will help to lower your risk of having a collision. If someone overtakes you and pulls into the gap in front, drop back to keep a safe distance from them.

HC r126 **RES** s12

Remember, your overall stopping distance may be longer when carrying a passenger.

RES s14

> Weather conditions

Weather conditions have a major effect on your safety margins. If there's bad weather, such as snow, ice or thick fog, think about whether you really need to make your journey. Never underestimate the dangers and always wear suitable clothing.

HC r228–231 **RES** s4

Read more about protective clothing and riding in bad weather at this link.

> **direct.gov.uk/en/Motoring/ LearnerAndNewDrivers/ RidingMotorcyclesAndMopeds/ DG_4022434**

Weather	Actions to take
Heavy rain/wet road  	When there's heavy rainfall, water can collect on the road surface and may cause aquaplaning. This is where the tyres lift off the road surface and skate on a film of water. If this happens, • ease off the throttle smoothly • don't brake or try to change direction until you can feel the tyres gripping again. **HC** r121, 227 **RES** s12 Use a low gear when riding through a ford or flood water, and test your brakes afterwards. If necessary, dry them out by applying the brakes lightly as you go along. **HC** r121 **RES** s12 If it rains after a long dry spell, the road surface can be unusually slippery and requires extra care. **HC** r237

Weather	Actions to take
Hot and/or bright 	Hot weather can also be dangerous. The road surface can become soft and may begin to melt. This could affect your braking and steering. Bright sunlight can dazzle. Other drivers might not be able to see your indicators flashing. Give an arm signal if you think it will be helpful. **HC** r237 **RES** s12
Foggy 	Fog reduces your visibility. Remember to <ul><li>think about whether you could use a different form of transport or delay your journey until conditions improve</li><li>allow more time for your journey</li><li>slow down, because you can't see as far ahead as usual</li><li>increase the gap between your motorcycle and the vehicle in front</li><li>keep your visor or goggles clear</li><li>beware of other road users not using their headlights</li><li>use dipped headlights, even in daylight.</li></ul> If visibility falls below 100 metres (328 feet), use fog lights if you've got them. You **MUST** switch them off when the fog lifts. **HC** r234–236 **RES** s12
Windy 	High winds can blow you off course, especially on an open stretch of road. The wind can affect all road users but those worst-affected include <ul><li>high-sided vehicles</li><li>other motorcyclists</li><li>vehicles towing trailers or caravans</li><li>cyclists.</li></ul> Take care and allow extra room if you pass these road users, as they may be blown off course by a sudden gust of wind. **HC** r232–233 **RES** 12

Weather	Actions to take
Freezing 	Freezing conditions can make roads very slippery, which will make your motorcycle harder to control. Before starting a journey, think about • whether your journey is necessary • whether you could use a different form of transport. If you must travel, clear ice and snow from your lights, mirrors and number plate. **RES** 12 When riding, • try and keep to main roads • keep your speed down • brake gently and in plenty of time. **HC** r234–236 **RES** s12

 Take extra care when there are crosswinds from your left. These can blow you off course and into the path of oncoming vehicles.

At night

When riding at night,

- wear reflective clothing
- use dipped headlights (you can also use these in the day to become more visible to others)
- don't use tinted glasses, lenses or visors.

RES s13

> Skidding

Skidding is when the tyres lose grip on the road, and it's caused by the rider. Road surface and tyre conditions can increase the risk of skidding, but skids are the result of how the rider controls acceleration, braking, speed and steering.

There's a greater risk of skidding in wet or icy conditions. To reduce the risk of skidding in slippery conditions, ride

* at a low speed
* in the highest gear you can use effectively.

Skidding can be caused by

* heavy or uncoordinated braking, which can lock one or both wheels
* too much acceleration, causing rear wheel spin
* steering harshly – making a sudden change of direction
* travelling too fast and leaning over too far when cornering, which may cause tyres to lose grip.

If you accelerate too harshly and start to skid,

* ease off the throttle to regain control
* steer in the direction of the skid; for example, if the back of the motorcycle skids to the right, steer to the right.

If the skid is caused by braking, release the brakes to allow the wheels to turn again, then apply the brakes again as firmly as you can in the riding conditions.

HC r119, 231 **RES** s8, 12

To reduce the risk of skidding, look at the road ahead for clues such as road signs and markings, and hazards like potholes, debris, drain covers, oil patches or loose gravel. You can then plan your riding so that you can

* slow down gradually before you reach a hazard, such as a bend
* avoid sudden steering movements.

HC r119, 231 **RES** s6, 8, 12

Anti-lock braking systems

An anti-lock braking system (ABS) will help to prevent wheel lock caused by excessive braking, such as in an emergency. The sensor will keep the wheel at the point of lock-up for as long as the rider continues to brake hard enough to activate the system, or until the motorcycle stops. Refer to your motorcycle handbook for details of the manufacturer's recommended method of use.

HC r120 **RES** s5

ABS doesn't necessarily reduce your stopping distance, but you can continue to steer while braking because the wheels are prevented from locking. It may not work as well if there's

- surface water, such as when there's been heavy rainfall
- a loose road surface, such as gravel.

❯ Contraflow systems

contraflow system
where one or more lanes have a direction of traffic against that of the rest of the carriageway

When you enter a **contraflow system**, you should

- reduce your speed in good time
- choose a suitable lane in good time: look for signs advising you to use a particular lane if you want to take an exit that will be coming up soon
- keep a safe distance behind the vehicle in front.

HC r290 **RES** s11

Meeting the standards

You must be able to

keep a safe distance from the vehicle in front

use the throttle and brakes correctly to
- regulate your speed
- bring the machine to a stop safely

always use a safe, systematic approach to keep you and other road users safe.
For example **observation, signal, manoeuvre, position, speed, look.**

You must know and understand

the importance of keeping a safe separation distance in all weather and traffic conditions

about skidding
- why a skid may occur
- how to avoid skids
- how to correct them if they do occur

the distance that a machine needs to stop
- from different speeds
- in different road conditions
- in different weather conditions

how traffic and weather conditions may affect other road users and what to do.
For example, their visibility may be reduced.

> Notes

You can use this page to make your own notes or diagrams about the key points you need to remember.

Think about

- What are typical stopping distances and how do wet or icy roads affect them?
- What extra considerations or precautions might you need to take if the weather is
  - snowy or icy
  - wet
  - foggy
  - hot
  - bright and dazzling
  - windy?
- How can you reduce the risk of skidding and what should you do if your motorcycle starts to skid?
- How does the manufacturer recommend using ABS on your motorcycle?
- Picture yourself entering a contraflow system. What actions can you take to reduce risk?

Your notes

Things to discuss and practise with your trainer

These are just a few examples of what you could discuss and practise with your trainer. Read more about safety margins to come up with your own ideas.

Discuss with your trainer

- how you should ride when you see various road markings, eg bus stop markings
- what lights you may use in foggy conditions
- stopping distances on dry, wet and icy roads.

Practise with your trainer

- riding in different weather conditions to practise vehicle handling, eg high winds, heavy rain
- leaving a two-second gap between yourself and the vehicle in front on dry roads.

Your overall stopping distance will be longer when riding

☐ at night

☐ in the fog

☐ with a passenger

☐ up a hill

When carrying a passenger on a motorcycle the overall weight will be much more than when riding alone. This additional weight will make it harder for you to stop quickly in an emergency.

On a wet road what is the safest way to stop?

☐ Change gear without braking

☐ Use the back brake only

☐ Use the front brake only

☐ Use both brakes

Motorcyclists need to take extra care when stopping on wet road surfaces. Plan well ahead so that you're able to brake in good time. You should ensure your motorcycle is upright and brake when travelling in a straight line.

You are riding in heavy rain when your rear wheel skids as you accelerate. To get control again you must

☐ change down to a lower gear

☐ ease off the throttle

☐ brake to reduce speed

☐ put your feet down

If you feel your back wheel beginning to skid as you pull away, ease off the throttle. This will give your rear tyre the chance to grip the road and stop the skid.

It is snowing. Before starting your journey you should

☐ think if you need to ride at all

☐ try to avoid taking a passenger

☐ plan a route avoiding towns

☐ take a hot drink before setting out

Do not ride in snowy or icy conditions unless your journey is essential. If you must go out, try and keep to main roads which are more likely to be treated and clear.

4.5

Mark one answer

RES s4, HC r86

Why should you ride with a dipped headlight on in the daytime?

☐ It helps other road users to see you

☐ It means that you can ride faster

☐ Other vehicles will get out of the way

☐ So that it is already on when it gets dark

Make yourself as visible as possible, from the side as well as from the front and rear. Having your headlight on, even in good daylight, can help make you more conspicuous.

4.6

Mark one answer

RES s12, HC r114, 226, 236

Motorcyclists are only allowed to use high-intensity rear fog lights when

☐ a pillion passenger is being carried

☐ they ride a large touring machine

☐ visibility is 100 metres (328 feet) or less

☐ they are riding on the road for the first time

If your motorcycle is fitted with high-intensity rear fog lights you must only use them when visibility is seriously reduced, that is, when you can see no further than 100 metres (328 feet). This rule also applies to all other motor vehicles using these lights.

4.7

Mark three answers

RES s13, HC r113–114, 226

You MUST use your headlight

☐ when riding in a group

☐ at night when street lighting is poor

☐ when carrying a passenger

☐ on motorways during darkness

☐ at times of poor visibility

☐ when parked on an unlit road

Your headlight helps you to see in the dark and helps other road users to see you. You must also use your headlight at any time when visibility is seriously reduced.

4.8

Mark one answer

RES s13

You are riding in town at night. The roads are wet after rain. The reflections from wet surfaces will

☐ affect your stopping distance

☐ affect your road holding

☐ make it easy to see unlit objects

☐ make it hard to see unlit objects

If you can't see clearly, slow down and stop. Make sure that your visor or goggles are clean. Be extra-cautious in these conditions and allow twice the normal separation distance.

You have just ridden through a flood. When clear of the water you should test your

☐ starter motor

☐ headlight

☐ steering

☐ brakes

If you have ridden through deep water your brakes may be less effective. If they have been affected, ride slowly while gently applying both brakes until normal braking is restored.

When going through flood water you should ride

☐ quickly in a high gear

☐ slowly in a high gear

☐ quickly in a low gear

☐ slowly in a low gear

If you have to go through a flood, ride slowly in a low gear. Keep the engine running fast enough to keep water out of the exhaust. You may need to slip the clutch to do this.

When riding at night you should NOT

☐ switch on full beam headlights

☐ overtake slower vehicles in front

☐ use dipped beam headlights

☐ use tinted glasses, lenses or visors

Do not use tinted glasses, lenses or visors at night because they reduce the amount of available light reaching your eyes. It's also important to keep your visor or goggles clean to give a clear view of the road at all times.

Which of the following should you do when riding in fog?

☐ Keep close to the vehicle in front

☐ Use your dipped headlight

☐ Ride close to the centre of the road

☐ Keep your visor or goggles clear

☐ Keep the vehicle in front in view

You must use your dipped headlight when visibility is seriously reduced. In fog a film of mist can form over the outside of your visor or goggles. This can further reduce your ability to see. Be aware of this hazard and keep your visor or goggles clear.

4.13   Mark one answer   RES s8

You are riding in heavy rain. Why should you try to avoid this marked area?

☐ It is illegal to ride over bus stops

☐ The painted lines may be slippery

☐ Cyclists may be using the bus stop

☐ Only emergency vehicles may drive over bus stops

Painted lines and road markings can be very slippery, especially for motorcyclists. Try to avoid them if you can do so safely.

4.14   Mark one answer   RES s4, HC r87

When riding at night you should

☐ wear reflective clothing

☐ wear a tinted visor

☐ ride in the middle of the road

☐ always give arm signals

You need to make yourself as visible as possible, from the front and rear and also from the side. Don't just rely on your headlight and tail light. Wear clothing that uses reflective material as this stands out in other vehicles' headlights.

4.15   Mark one answer   RES s4

When riding in extremely cold conditions what can you do to keep warm?

☐ Stay close to the vehicles in front

☐ Wear suitable clothing

☐ Lie flat on the tank

☐ Put one hand on the exhaust pipe

Motorcyclists are exposed to the elements and can become very cold when riding in wintry conditions. It's important to keep warm or your concentration could be affected. The only way to stay warm is to wear suitable clothing. If you do find yourself getting cold then stop at a suitable place to warm up.

4.16

You are riding at night. To be seen more easily you should

- ☐ ride with your headlight on dipped beam
- ☐ wear reflective clothing
- ☐ keep the motorcycle clean
- ☐ stay well out to the right
- ☐ wear waterproof clothing

Reflective clothing works by reflecting light from the headlights of the other vehicles. This will make it easier for you to be seen.

Fluorescent clothing, although effective during the day, won't show up as well as reflective clothing at night.

4.17

Your overall stopping distance will be much longer when riding

- ☐ in the rain
- ☐ in fog
- ☐ at night
- ☐ in strong winds

Extra care should be taken in wet weather. Wet roads will affect the time it takes you to stop. Your stopping distance could be at least doubled.

4.18

The road surface is very important to motorcyclists. Which FOUR of these are more likely to reduce the stability of your motorcycle?

- ☐ Potholes
- ☐ Drain covers
- ☐ Concrete
- ☐ Oil patches
- ☐ Tarmac
- ☐ Loose gravel

Apart from the weather conditions, the road surface and any changes in it can affect the stability of your motorcycle. Be on the lookout for poor road surfaces and be aware of any traffic around you, in case you need to take avoiding action.

4.19
Mark one answer
RES s8, HC r167

You are riding past queuing traffic. Why should you be more cautious when approaching this road marking?

When riding past queuing traffic look out for 'keep clear' road markings that will indicate a side road or entrance on the left. Vehicles may emerge between gaps in the traffic.

☐ Lorries will be unloading here

☐ Schoolchildren will be crossing here

☐ Pedestrians will be standing in the road

☐ Traffic could be emerging and may not see you

4.20
Mark one answer
RES s8

What can cause your tyres to skid and lose their grip on the road surface?

☐ Giving hand signals

☐ Riding one handed

☐ Looking over your shoulder

☐ Heavy braking

You can cause your motorcycle to skid by heavy or uncoordinated braking, as well as excessive acceleration, swerving or changing direction too sharply, and leaning over too far.

4.21
Mark one answer
RES s12, HC r227

When riding in heavy rain a film of water can build up between your tyres and the road. This is known as aquaplaning. What should you do to keep control?

☐ Use your rear brakes gently

☐ Steer to the crown of the road

☐ Ease off the throttle smoothly

☐ Change up into a higher gear

If your vehicle starts to aquaplane ease off the throttle smoothly. Do not brake or turn the steering until tyre grip has been restored.

4.22　Mark one answer　RES s12, HC r121

After riding through deep water you notice your scooter brakes do not work properly. What would be the best way to dry them out?

☐ Ride slowly, braking lightly

☐ Ride quickly, braking harshly

☐ Stop and dry them with a cloth

☐ Stop and wait for a few minutes

You can help to dry out brakes by riding slowly and applying light pressure to the brake pedal/lever. DO NOT ride at normal speeds until they are working normally again.

4.23　Mark two answers　RES s12, HC r226, 235

You have to ride in foggy weather. You should

☐ stay close to the centre of the road

☐ switch only your sidelights on

☐ switch on your dipped headlights

☐ be aware of others not using their headlights

☐ always ride in the gutter to see the kerb

Only travel in fog if your journey is absolutely necessary. Fog is often patchy and visibility can suddenly reduce without warning.

4.24　Mark one answer　RES s8, HC r126

Only a fool breaks the two-second rule refers to

☐ the time recommended when using the choke

☐ the separation distance when riding in good conditions

☐ restarting a stalled engine in busy traffic

☐ the time you should keep your foot down at a junction

It is very important that you always leave a safe gap between yourself and any vehicle you're following. In good conditions you need to leave at least one metre for every mile per hour of your speed or a two-second time interval.

4.25　Mark one answer　RES s9

At a mini roundabout it is important that a motorcyclist should avoid

☐ turning right

☐ using signals

☐ taking 'lifesavers'

☐ the painted area

Avoid riding over the painted area as these can become very slippery, especially when wet. Even on dry roads only a small part of the motorcycle's tyre makes contact with the road. Any reduction in grip can therefore affect the stability of your machine.

4.26 — Mark two answers — RES s11

You are riding on a motorway in a crosswind. You should take extra care when

- ☐ approaching service areas
- ☐ overtaking a large vehicle
- ☐ riding in slow-moving traffic
- ☐ approaching an exit
- ☐ riding in exposed places

Take extra care when overtaking large vehicles as they can cause air turbulence and buffeting. Beware of crosswinds when riding on exposed stretches of road, which can suddenly blow you off course. Bear in mind that strong winds can also affect the stability of other road users.

4.27 — Mark one answer — RES s12

Why should you try to avoid riding over this marked area?

Try to anticipate slippery road surfaces. Watch out for oil patches at places where vehicles stop for some time, such as bus stops, lay-bys and busy junctions.

- ☐ It is illegal to ride over bus stops
- ☐ It will alter your machine's centre of gravity
- ☐ Pedestrians may be waiting at the bus stop
- ☐ A bus may have left patches of oil

4.28 — Mark one answer — RES s8, HC r126

Your overall stopping distance comprises thinking and braking distance. You are on a good, dry road surface with good brakes and tyres. What is the typical BRAKING distance at 50 mph?

- ☐ 14 metres (46 feet)
- ☐ 24 metres (79 feet)
- ☐ 38 metres (125 feet)
- ☐ 55 metres (180 feet)

Different factors can affect how long it takes you to stop, such as weather and road conditions, vehicle condition and loading. You also need to add reaction time to this. The overall stopping distance at 50 mph includes 15 metres thinking distance (the reaction time before braking starts) plus your braking distance of 38 metres, giving a typical overall stopping distance of 53 metres (175 feet) in good conditions.

Braking distances on ice can be

☐ twice the normal distance

☐ five times the normal distance

☐ seven times the normal distance

☐ ten times the normal distance

In icy and snowy weather, your stopping distance will increase by up to ten times compared to good, dry conditions.

Take extra care when braking, accelerating and steering, to cut down the risk of skidding.

Freezing conditions will affect the distance it takes you to come to a stop. You should expect stopping distances to increase by up to

☐ two times

☐ three times

☐ five times

☐ ten times

Your tyre grip is greatly reduced on icy roads and you need to allow up to ten times the normal stopping distance.

In windy conditions you need to take extra care when

☐ using the brakes

☐ making a hill start

☐ turning into a narrow road

☐ passing pedal cyclists

You should always give cyclists plenty of room when overtaking. When it's windy, a sudden gust could blow them off course.

When approaching a right-hand bend you should keep well to the left. Why is this?

☐ To improve your view of the road

☐ To overcome the effect of the road's slope

☐ To let faster traffic from behind overtake

☐ To be positioned safely if you skid

Doing this will give you an earlier view around the bend and enable you to see any hazards sooner.

It also reduces the risk of collision with an oncoming vehicle that may have drifted over the centre line while taking the bend.

4.33 — Mark one answer — RES s12, HC r121

You have just gone through deep water. To dry off the brakes you should

☐ accelerate and keep to a high speed for a short time

☐ go slowly while gently applying the brakes

☐ avoid using the brakes at all for a few miles

☐ stop for at least an hour to allow them time to dry

Water on the brakes will act as a lubricant, causing them to work less efficiently. Using the brakes lightly as you go along will dry them out.

4.34 — Mark two answers — RES s12, HC r237

In very hot weather the road surface can become soft. Which TWO of the following will be most affected?

☐ The suspension

☐ The grip of the tyres

☐ The braking

☐ The exhaust

Only a small part of your tyres is in contact with the road. This is why you must consider the surface on which you're travelling, and alter your speed to suit the road conditions.

4.35 — Mark one answer — RES s12, HC r232

Where are you most likely to be affected by a side wind?

☐ On a narrow country lane

☐ On an open stretch of road

☐ On a busy stretch of road

☐ On a long, straight road

In windy conditions, care must be taken on exposed roads. A strong gust of wind can blow you off course. Watch out for other road users who are particularly likely to be affected, such as cyclists, motorcyclists, high-sided lorries and vehicles towing trailers.

4.36 — Mark one answer — HC r126

In good conditions, what is the typical stopping distance at 70 mph?

☐ 53 metres (175 feet)

☐ 60 metres (197 feet)

☐ 73 metres (240 feet)

☐ 96 metres (315 feet)

Note that this is the typical stopping distance. It will take at least this distance to think, brake and stop in good conditions. In poor conditions it will take much longer.

What is the shortest overall stopping distance on a dry road at 60 mph?

☐ 53 metres (175 feet)

☐ 58 metres (190 feet)

☐ 73 metres (240 feet)

☐ 96 metres (315 feet)

This distance is the equivalent of 18 car lengths. Try pacing out 73 metres and then look back. It's probably further than you think.

You are following a vehicle at a safe distance on a wet road. Another driver overtakes you and pulls into the gap you have left. What should you do?

☐ Flash your headlights as a warning

☐ Try to overtake safely as soon as you can

☐ Drop back to regain a safe distance

☐ Stay close to the other vehicle until it moves on

Wet weather will affect the time it takes for you to stop and can affect your control. Your speed should allow you to stop safely and in good time. If another vehicle pulls into the gap you've left, ease back until you've regained your stopping distance.

You are travelling at 50 mph on a good, dry road. What is your typical overall stopping distance?

☐ 36 metres (118 feet)

☐ 53 metres (175 feet)

☐ 75 metres (245 feet)

☐ 96 metres (315 feet)

Even in good conditions it will usually take you further than you think to stop. Don't just learn the figures, make sure you understand how far the distance is.

You are on a good, dry, road surface. Your brakes and tyres are good. What is the typical overall stopping distance at 40 mph?

☐ 23 metres (75 feet)

☐ 36 metres (118 feet)

☐ 53 metres (175 feet)

☐ 96 metres (315 feet)

Stopping distances are affected by a number of variable factors. These include the type, model and condition of your vehicle, road and weather conditions, and your reaction time. Look well ahead for hazards and leave enough space between you and the vehicle in front. This should allow you to pull up safely if you have to, without braking sharply.

4.41
Mark one answer
RES s12, HC r233

You are overtaking a motorcyclist in strong winds. What should you do?

☐ Allow extra room

☐ Give a thank you wave

☐ Move back early

☐ Sound your horn

It is easy for motorcyclists to be blown off course. Always give them plenty of room if you decide to overtake, especially in strong winds. Decide whether you need to overtake at all. Always check to the left as you pass.

4.42
Mark one answer
HC r126

Overall stopping distance is made up of thinking and braking distance. You are on a good, dry road surface with good brakes and tyres. What is the typical BRAKING distance from 50 mph?

☐ 14 metres (46 feet)

☐ 24 metres (80 feet)

☐ 38 metres (125 feet)

☐ 55 metres (180 feet)

Be aware this is just the braking distance. You need to add the thinking distance to this to give the OVERALL STOPPING DISTANCE. At 50 mph the typical thinking distance will be 15 metres (50 feet), plus a braking distance of 38 metres (125 feet), giving an overall stopping distance of 53 metres (175 feet). The distance could be greater than this depending on your attention and response to any hazards. These figures are a general guide.

4.43
Mark one answer
RES s8, HC r126

In heavy motorway traffic the vehicle behind you is following too closely. How can you lower the risk of a collision?

☐ Increase your distance from the vehicle in front

☐ Operate the brakes sharply

☐ Switch on your hazard lights

☐ Move onto the hard shoulder and stop

On busy roads traffic may still travel at high speeds despite being close together. Don't follow too closely to the vehicle in front. If a driver behind seems to be 'pushing' you, gradually increase your distance from the vehicle in front by slowing down gently. This will give you more space in front if you have to brake, and lessen the risk of a collision involving several vehicles.

You are following other vehicles in fog. You have your lights on. What else can you do to reduce the chances of being in a collision?

☐ Keep close to the vehicle in front

☐ Use your main beam instead of dipped headlights

☐ Keep up with the faster vehicles

☐ Reduce your speed and increase the gap in front

When it's foggy use dipped headlights. This will help you see and be seen by other road users. If visibility is seriously reduced consider using front and rear fog lights. Keep a sensible speed and don't follow the vehicle in front too closely. If the road is wet and slippery you'll need to allow twice the normal stopping distance.

To avoid a collision when entering a contraflow system, you should

☐ reduce speed in good time

☐ switch lanes at any time to make progress

☐ choose an appropriate lane in good time

☐ keep the correct separation distance

☐ increase speed to pass through quickly

☐ follow other motorists closely to avoid long queues

In a contraflow system you will be travelling close to oncoming traffic and sometimes in narrow lanes. You should obey the temporary speed limit signs, get into the correct lane at the proper time and keep a safe separation distance from the vehicle ahead. When traffic is at a very low speed, merging in turn is recommended if it's safe and appropriate.

> Case study practice – 4 Safety margins

Kim is collecting her new motorcycle. Steve is taking her as a passenger on his machine.

The weather is fine with a strong crosswind.

There's a cyclist in front of Steve.

The road surface is cracked and in need of repair. There are also areas of loose and crumbled tarmac.

Further on, the traffic is heavier.

On reaching their destination, they turn right into the dealer's forecourt.

4.1 What might Steve need to adjust on his motorcycle before the journey?

Mark **one** answer

☐ Tyre pressures and headlight angle
☐ Front forks and handlebar height
☐ Pillion seating and wheel alignment
☐ Passenger foot rests and brake linings

RES s8

4.2 How could crosswinds affect Steve and Kim?

Mark **one** answer

☐ Speed up their journey
☐ Increase fuel consumption
☐ Blow them off course
☐ Make them feel colder

HC r232 **RES** s12

4.3 How might the cyclist react on the road surface described?

Mark **one** answer

- [ ] Make a U-turn and go back home
- [ ] Get off and walk along the road
- [ ] Swerve to avoid cracks and holes
- [ ] Ride faster over the uneven surface

HC r213 **RES** s10

4.4 How would Steve need to ride on this road surface?

Mark **one** answer

- [ ] With more care
- [ ] With lights on
- [ ] With more speed
- [ ] With brakes on

HC r288 **RES** s8

4.5 What should Steve do just before turning right?

Mark **one** answer

- [ ] Check over his right shoulder for overtaking vehicles
- [ ] A U-turn, to pull up on the other side of the road
- [ ] Sound the horn and flash headlights at other traffic
- [ ] Get off the motorcycle and wheel it across the road

HC r180 **RES** s3

Hazard awareness

In this section, you'll learn about

- static hazards, eg parked cars, junctions, roundabouts
- moving hazards, eg pedestrians, cyclists, drivers
- road and weather conditions
- physical conditions that make someone unfit to ride.

Hazard awareness

When you start your compulsory basic training (CBT) to learn to ride, you'll be concentrating on the basic controls of your motorcycle. As your skills improve, so will your ability to recognise hazards on the road.

A hazard is a situation that may require you, as a rider, to respond by taking action, such as braking or steering.

Hazards can be …

static, such as parked cars, junctions or roundabouts

moving, such as pedestrians, cyclists or drivers

road and weather conditions

you, if you aren't alert and fit to ride

The 'Perfect day' video shows what riding would be like in an ideal world.

> **youtube.com/thinkuk**

> Static hazards

There are many types of static hazard, including

- bends
- junctions
- roundabouts
- parked vehicles and obstructions in the road
- roadworks
- road surfaces
- different types of crossings
- traffic lights.

HC r153 **RES** s8, 9, 10

All of these may require you to respond in some way, so

- be aware that they're there
- slow down and be ready to stop if necessary.

At level crossings with traffic light signals, you **MUST** stop before the barrier when the red lights are flashing, even if the barrier isn't yet down.

HC r293

Road signs

Road signs and markings are there to give you clues about possible hazards, so it's vital that you learn their meanings. You can find them in *The Official Highway Code* (book, eBook, interactive CD-ROM, app and online) and *Know Your Traffic Signs* (book and online).

Watch out for signs and markings so that you can slow down in good time and are prepared for any action you may need to take. For example, if you see a sign for a bend, ask yourself, 'What if there's a pedestrian or an obstruction just around the bend – could I stop in time? Could I do it safely?'

HC p106–116 **RES** s7 **KYTS** p10–71, 77–93

Parked vehicles

In busy areas, parked cars can cause a hazard – especially if they're parked illegally, for example on the zigzag lines by a pedestrian crossing.

Watch out for

- children running out from between vehicles
- vehicle doors opening
- vehicles moving away.

Would you be able to stop, or safely avoid them, in time?

HC r205–206 **RES** s8, 10

Junctions

Your view is often reduced at junctions, especially in built-up areas (for example, in towns). Take extra care and pull forward slowly until you can see down the road. You may also be able to see reflections of traffic in the windows of buildings, such as shops.

Be careful not to block a junction; leave it clear so that other vehicles can enter and emerge.

Where lanes are closed, be ready for vehicles cutting in front of you and keep a safe distance from the vehicle in front.

HC r151 **RES** s10

At a traffic light-controlled junction where the lights aren't working, treat it as an unmarked junction and be prepared to stop. There may be police officers controlling traffic in these circumstances – make sure that you know and understand their signals.

HC r105, 176, p105 **RES** s10

Motorways and dual carriageways

If you're riding on a motorway or dual carriageway and see a hazard or obstruction ahead, you may use your hazard warning lights briefly to warn the traffic behind.

Slow-moving or stationary vehicles with a large arrow displayed on the back show where you need to change lanes when approaching roadworks.

Breakdowns

If your motorcycle breaks down and is causing an obstruction, switch on your hazard warning lights to warn other road users.

HC r116 **RES** s9, 11

Find out more about what to do if you break down on a motorway at this link.

> **direct.gov.uk/en/ TravelAndTransport/ Usingmotorwaysandroads/ Breakdownsdrivingconditions/ DG_185052**

> Moving hazards

Moving hazards tend to be hazards caused by other types of road user.

Road user	What to do
Pedestrians 	If you see pedestrians in the road, be patient and wait for them to finish crossing. On country roads there may be no pavement, so look out for pedestrians in the road. They may be walking towards you on your side of the road. **HC** r205–206 **RES** s8, 10
Cyclists	Be aware of cyclists and give them plenty of room. They may wobble or swerve to avoid drains or potholes. At junctions or traffic lights, give cyclists time to turn or pull away. When travelling in slow traffic, before you turn left, check for cyclists filtering through the traffic on your left. **HC** r211–213 **RES** s10

Road user	What to do
Horse riders 	Horses can be unpredictable and easily spooked. Reduce your speed and give them plenty of room when overtaking. **HC** r215 **RES** s10
Drivers of large vehicles 	If you see a bus at a bus stop, remember that • people may get off and then cross the road • the bus may be about to move off. **HC** r223 **RES** s10 School buses might stop at places other than bus stops. At some bridges, high vehicles may need to use the centre of the road to be able to pass underneath. **HC** r221 **RES** s10 Large goods vehicles over 13 metres long have red and yellow markings at the back of the vehicle. **HC** p117
Drivers of vehicles carrying hazardous loads 	Some vehicles have information signs on the back, to show that they contain a hazardous load. Learn what the signs mean. **HC** p117
Drivers overtaking you	Watch out for vehicles, especially other motorcyclists, overtaking and cutting in front of you. If you need to, drop back to keep a safe distance from the vehicle in front. When turning right, don't forget the 'lifesaver' look to your right to check for vehicles overtaking you before you make the turn. **HC** r211–213 **RES** s10

Road user	What to do
Disabled people using powered vehicles 	Reduce your speed and be careful. These small vehicles are extremely vulnerable on the road because • they're difficult to see • they travel slowly.
Older drivers 	Older drivers may not react very quickly, so be patient with them. **HC** r216 **RES** s10

A vehicle driving too closely behind you can be dangerous and intimidating. Move over and let the vehicle through if you can. If there's no room and the driver behind seems to be 'pushing' you, increase your distance from the vehicle in front. This will make an incident involving several vehicles less likely.

RES s10

 If it looks like the road user in front has forgotten to cancel their right indicator, be careful. Stay behind and don't overtake – they may be unsure of the position of a junction and turn suddenly.

HC r104

Find out about the hazard perception test on DSA's YouTube channel.

youtube.com/dsagov

If you have a provisional licence, you **MUST NOT**

- ride on public roads until you've successfully completed compulsory basic training (CBT)
- carry a pillion passenger
- tow a trailer
- ride on a motorway.

Until you've passed your practical riding tests, you can only ride unaccompanied on a motorcycle displaying red L plates, with an engine capacity less than 125 cc. To ride a larger machine displaying red L plates you must be

- at least 21 years of age
- accompanied by a Direct Access Scheme (DAS) trainer who's in radio contact with you
- wearing fluorescent safety clothing.

`HC` r253, p118–120

Road and weather conditions

Different types of weather – rain, ice, fog and even bright sunlight – can create extra hazards by making it harder to see the road or affecting your control of the vehicle. Change the way you ride to suit the weather conditions, and be aware of the added dangers.

 Find out more about how to ride in extreme weather conditions at this link.

> **direct.gov.uk/en/ TravelAndTransport/ Usingmotorwaysandroads/ Breakdownsdrivingconditions/ DG_185021**

In these conditions ...	remember to do this
Rain	Double your distance from the vehicle in front to four seconds.
Ice	Increase your distance from the vehicle in front to 20 seconds.
FOG **Fog**	Slow down and use dipped headlights.
Bright sunlight	Be aware that sunlight can dazzle you or other drivers.

HC r227 **RES** s12

Remember that if you're wet and cold, you could lose concentration and it may take you longer to react to a hazard. Always wear proper protective clothing and footwear when riding.

> Yourself

Don't allow yourself to become a hazard on the road. You need to be alert and concentrate on your riding at all times.

Awareness

Make sure you use your mirrors so that you're aware of what's going on around you at all times. These may be convex (curved outwards slightly) to give a wider field of vision.

HC r161

Tiredness

Don't ride if you're tired. Plan your journey so that you have enough rest and refreshment breaks. Try to stop at least once every two hours.

If you feel tired,

- pull over at a safe and legal place to rest
- on a motorway, leave at the next exit or services.

HC r91 **RES** s1, 11

See the GEM Motoring Assist website for more information about riding and tiredness.

❯ **motoringassist.com/fatigue**

Distractions

Your concentration can be affected by

- using a hands-free phone headset
- listening to loud music
- looking at navigation equipment
- how you're feeling.

It's important to avoid being distracted by these things while you're riding.

- Turn off your mobile phone or switch it to voicemail.
- Before looking at navigation equipment or using your phone, find somewhere safe and legal to stop.
- Keep music at a reasonable volume.
- If you're upset or angry, take time to calm down before you begin riding.

When you're riding for long distances at speed, noise can make you feel tired and can damage your hearing. It's a good idea to wear ear plugs to protect your hearing when you ride.

HC r148–150 **RES** s1, 11

Alcohol

Never ride if you've been drinking alcohol: it's not worth taking the chance. If you ride to a social event, don't drink alcoholic drinks. If you've had a drink, find another way to get home, such as public transport, taxi, walking or getting a lift.

HC r95

Did you know?

Alcohol can

- reduce your concentration, coordination and control
- give you a false sense of confidence
- reduce your judgement of speed
- slow down your reactions.

See the Think! road safety information on drink-driving.

❯ **http://think.direct.gov.uk/ drink-driving.html**

See the Think! road safety information on drug driving.

❯ **http://drugdrive.direct.gov.uk**

Medicines and drugs

You must be fit to ride. Some medicines can make you sleepy: check the label or ask your doctor or pharmacist if it's safe for you to ride your motorcycle after taking any medication that may affect your riding.

HC r90, 95–96 **RES** s1

Using illegal drugs is highly dangerous and the effects of some can last up to 72 hours. Never take them before riding.

If you've been convicted of riding while unfit through drink or drugs, the cost of your insurance will rise considerably. Riding while under the influence of drink or drugs may even invalidate your insurance.

RES s1

Eyesight

Your eyesight **MUST** be of the required legal standard; if you need glasses or contact lenses to bring your eyesight up to this standard, you **MUST** wear them every time you ride. Tinted glasses, visors and goggles can restrict your vision, so you mustn't wear them for riding at night.

You **MUST** tell the licensing authority if you suffer from any medical condition that may affect your ability to ride a motorcycle.

HC r90, 92–94 **RES** s1

Find out about the eyesight requirements for riding at this link.

❯ **direct.gov.uk/en/Motoring/
LearnerAndNewDrivers/
LearningToDriveOrRide/
DG_4022529**

Meeting the standards

You must be able to

use visual clues to prepare you for possible hazards. For example, reflections in shop windows

judge which possible hazards are most likely to affect you, so that you can plan what to do

respond to hazards safely.

You must know and understand

methods that you can use to scan around you, both close and into the distance

which kinds of hazard you may find on different roads. For example

- tractors on country roads
- deer on forest roads
- children crossing near schools.

155

> Notes

You can use this page to make your own notes or diagrams about the key points you need to remember.

Think about

- What are some examples of static hazards and why are they potentially dangerous?
- What kinds of moving hazards do you need to look out for when riding?
- What types of weather conditions can be hazardous and what can you do to reduce the risks?
- Think of the physical conditions that can make you unfit to ride. Have you experienced any? How did it affect you?

Your notes

_____

_____

_____

_____

_____

_____

_____

_____

_____

Things to discuss and practise with your trainer

These are just a few examples of what you could discuss and practise with your trainer. Read more about hazard awareness to come up with your own ideas.

Discuss with your trainer

- the effects that alcohol and drugs can have on your riding
- how your riding is affected by tiredness and what you can do to help stay alert
- how to deal with other people's bad driving and riding behaviour.

Practise with your trainer

- riding through a busy town centre and identifying all the potential hazards, eg wobbling cyclists, pedestrians, vans pulling out of junctions, etc. Discuss these after your lesson.
- riding
  - up to blind junctions
  - along roads where many vehicles are parked
- identifying road markings.

You get cold and wet when riding. Which TWO are likely to happen?

☐ You may lose concentration

☐ You may slide off the seat

☐ Your visor may freeze up

☐ Your reaction times may be slower

☐ Your helmet may loosen

When you're riding a motorcycle make sure you're wearing suitable clothing. If you become cold and uncomfortable this could cause you to lose concentration and could slow down your reaction time.

You are riding up to a zebra crossing. You intend to stop for waiting pedestrians. How could you let them know you are stopping?

☐ By signalling with your left arm

☐ By waving them across

☐ By flashing your headlight

☐ By signalling with your right arm

Giving the correct arm signal would indicate to approaching vehicles, as well as pedestrians, that you are stopping at the pedestrian crossing.

You are about to ride home. You cannot find the glasses you need to wear. You should

☐ ride home slowly, keeping to quiet roads

☐ borrow a friend's glasses and use those

☐ ride home at night, so that the lights will help you

☐ find a way of getting home without riding

Don't be tempted to ride if you've lost or forgotten your glasses. You must be able to see clearly when riding. If you can't you will be endangering yourself and other road users.

Which THREE of these are likely effects of drinking alcohol?

☐ Reduced coordination

☐ Increased confidence

☐ Poor judgement

☐ Increased concentration

☐ Faster reactions

☐ Colour blindness

Alcohol can increase confidence to a point where a rider's behaviour might become 'out of character'. Someone who normally behaves sensibly suddenly takes risks and could endanger themselves and others. Never drink and ride, or accept a ride from anyone who's been drinking.

5.5

Mark one answer RES s4, HC r92

You find that you need glasses to read vehicle number plates at the required distance. When MUST you wear them?

- ☐ Only in bad weather conditions
- ☐ At all times when riding
- ☐ Only when you think it necessary
- ☐ Only in bad light or at night time

Have your eyesight tested before you start your practical training. Then, throughout your riding life, have periodical checks to ensure that your eyesight hasn't deteriorated.

5.6

Mark three answers RES s1, HC r95

Drinking any amount of alcohol is likely to

- ☐ slow down your reactions to hazards
- ☐ increase the speed of your reactions
- ☐ worsen your judgement of speed
- ☐ improve your awareness of danger
- ☐ give a false sense of confidence

Never drink if you are going to ride. It's always the safest option not to drink at all. Don't take risks, it's not worth it.

5.7

Mark one answer RES s4, HC r94

Which of the following types of glasses should NOT be worn when riding at night?

- ☐ Half-moon
- ☐ Round
- ☐ Bi-focal
- ☐ Tinted

If you are riding at night or in poor visibility, tinted lenses or a tinted visor will reduce the amount of available light reaching your eyes, making you less able to see clearly.

5.8

Mark one answer HC r116

For which of these may you use hazard warning lights?

- ☐ When riding on a motorway to warn traffic behind of a hazard ahead
- ☐ When you are double parked on a two way road
- ☐ When your direction indicators are not working
- ☐ When warning oncoming traffic that you intend to stop

Hazard warning lights are an important safety feature. Use them when riding on a motorway to warn following traffic of danger ahead. You should also use them if your motorcycle has broken down and is causing an obstruction.

Why should you wear ear plugs when riding a motorcycle?

☐ To help to prevent ear damage

☐ To make you less aware of traffic

☐ To help to keep you warm

☐ To make your helmet fit better

The use of ear plugs is recommended to reduce the effect of noise levels and protect your hearing.

You are going out to a social event and alcohol will be available. You will be riding your motorcycle shortly afterwards. What is the safest thing to do?

☐ Stay just below the legal limit

☐ Have soft drinks and alcohol in turn

☐ Don't go beyond the legal limit

☐ Stick to non-alcoholic drinks

The legal limit of alcohol is 80 milligrams per 100 millilitres of blood. However, drinking even the smallest amount of alcohol can affect your judgement and reactions. The safest and best option is to avoid any alcohol at all when riding or driving.

You are convicted of riding after drinking too much alcohol. How could this affect your insurance?

☐ Your insurance may become invalid

☐ The amount of excess you pay will be reduced

☐ You will only be able to get third-party cover

☐ Cover will only be given for riding smaller motorcycles

Riding while under the influence of drink or drugs can invalidate your insurance. This also endangers yourself and others. It's not a risk worth taking.

Why should you check over your shoulder before turning right into a side road?

☐ To make sure the side road is clear

☐ To check for emerging traffic

☐ To check for overtaking vehicles

☐ To confirm your intention to turn

Take a last check over your shoulder before committing yourself to a manoeuvre. This is especially important when turning right, as other road users may not have seen your signal or may not understand your intentions.

5.13 — Mark two answers — RES s1, HC r96

You are not sure if your cough medicine will affect you. What TWO things should you do?

- ☐ Ask your doctor
- ☐ Check the medicine label
- ☐ Ride if you feel alright
- ☐ Ask a friend or relative for advice

If you're taking medicine or drugs prescribed by your doctor, check to ensure that they won't make you drowsy. If you forget to ask when you're at the surgery, check with your pharmacist.

5.14 — Mark one answer — HC r116

When should you use hazard warning lights?

- ☐ When you are double-parked on a two-way road
- ☐ When your direction indicators are not working
- ☐ When warning oncoming traffic that you intend to stop
- ☐ When your motorcycle has broken down and is causing an obstruction

Hazard warning lights are an important safety feature and should be used if you have broken down and are causing an obstruction. Don't use them as an excuse to park illegally, such as when using a cash machine or post box. You may also use them on motorways to warn following traffic of danger ahead.

5.15 — Mark one answer — RES s12

It is a very hot day. What would you expect to find?

- ☐ Mud on the road
- ☐ A soft road surface
- ☐ Roadworks ahead
- ☐ Banks of fog

In very hot weather the road surface can become soft and may melt. Take care when braking and cornering on soft tarmac, as this can lead to reduced grip and cause skidding.

5.16 — Mark one answer — RES s9, HC r167

You see this road marking in between queuing traffic. What should you look out for?

KEEP
CLEAR

- ☐ Overhanging trees
- ☐ Roadworks
- ☐ Traffic wardens
- ☐ Traffic emerging

'Keep clear' markings should not be obstructed. They can be found in congested areas to help traffic waiting to emerge onto a busy road.

Where would you expect to see these markers?

These markers must be fitted to vehicles over 13 metres long, large goods vehicles, and rubbish skips placed in the road. They are reflective to make them easier to see in the dark.

☐ On a motorway sign
☐ At the entrance to a narrow bridge
☐ On a large goods vehicle
☐ On a builder's skip placed on the road

What is the main hazard shown in this picture?

Look at the picture carefully and try to imagine you're there. The cyclist in this picture appears to be trying to cross the road. You must be able to deal with the unexpected, especially when you're approaching a hazardous junction. Look well ahead to give yourself time to deal with any hazards.

☐ Vehicles turning right
☐ Vehicles doing U-turns
☐ The cyclist crossing the road
☐ Parked cars around the corner

Which road user has caused a hazard?

The car arrowed A is parked within the area marked by zigzag lines at the pedestrian crossing. Parking here is illegal. It also

- blocks the view for pedestrians wishing to cross the road
- restricts the view of the crossing for approaching traffic.

☐ The parked car (arrowed A)
☐ The pedestrian waiting to cross (arrowed B)
☐ The moving car (arrowed C)
☐ The car turning (arrowed D)

5.20 Mark one answer — RES s8, HC r195

What should the driver of the car approaching the crossing do?

☐ Continue at the same speed

☐ Sound the horn

☐ Drive through quickly

☐ Slow down and get ready to stop

Look well ahead to see if any hazards are developing. This will give you more time to deal with them in the correct way. The man in the picture is clearly intending to cross the road. You should be travelling at a speed that allows you to check your mirror, slow down and stop in good time. You shouldn't have to brake harshly.

5.21 Mark three answers — RES s8, 10, HC r205–206

What THREE things should the driver of the grey car (arrowed) be especially aware of?

☐ Pedestrians stepping out between cars

☐ Other cars behind the grey car

☐ Doors opening on parked cars

☐ The bumpy road surface

☐ Cars leaving parking spaces

☐ Empty parking spaces

You need to be aware that other road users may not have seen you. Always be on the lookout for hazards that may develop suddenly and need you to take avoiding action.

5.22 Mark one answer — RES s7, HC p109, KYTS p11

You see this sign ahead. You should expect the road to

☐ go steeply uphill

☐ go steeply downhill

☐ bend sharply to the left

☐ bend sharply to the right

Adjust your speed in good time and select the correct gear for your speed. Going too fast into the bend could cause you to lose control.

Braking late and harshly while changing direction reduces your vehicle's grip on the road, and is likely to cause a skid.

You are approaching this cyclist. You should

Keep well back and allow the cyclist room to take up the correct position for the turn. Don't get too close behind or try to squeeze past.

☐ overtake before the cyclist gets to the junction

☐ flash your headlights at the cyclist

☐ slow down and allow the cyclist to turn

☐ overtake the cyclist on the left-hand side

Why must you take extra care when turning right at this junction?

You may have to pull forward slowly until you can see up and down the road. Be aware that the traffic approaching the junction can't see you either. If you don't know that it's clear, don't go.

☐ Road surface is poor

☐ Footpaths are narrow

☐ Road markings are faint

☐ There is reduced visibility

When approaching this bridge you should give way to

A double-deck bus or high-sided lorry will have to take up a position in the centre of the road so that it can clear the bridge. There is normally a sign to indicate this.

Look well down the road, through the bridge and be aware you may have to stop and give way to an oncoming large vehicle.

☐ bicycles

☐ buses

☐ motorcycles

☐ cars

5.26 | Mark one answer | RES s7, KYTS p24

What type of vehicle could you expect to meet in the middle of the road?

The highest point of the bridge is in the centre so a large vehicle might have to move to the centre of the road to allow it enough room to pass under the bridge.

☐ Lorry

☐ Bicycle

☐ Car

☐ Motorcycle

5.27 | Mark one answer | RES s7, HC r171

At this blind junction you must stop

The 'stop' sign has been put here because there is a poor view into the main road. You must stop because it will not be possible to assess the situation on the move, however slowly you are travelling.

☐ behind the line, then edge forward to see clearly

☐ beyond the line at a point where you can see clearly

☐ only if there is traffic on the main road

☐ only if you are turning to the right

5.28 | Mark one answer | RES s1, HC r147

A driver pulls out of a side road in front of you. You have to brake hard. You should

☐ ignore the error and stay calm

☐ flash your lights to show your annoyance

☐ sound your horn to show your annoyance

☐ overtake as soon as possible

Where there are a number of side roads, be alert. Be especially careful if there are a lot of parked vehicles because they can make it more difficult for drivers emerging to see you. Try to be tolerant if a vehicle does emerge and you have to brake quickly. Don't react aggressively.

Mark one answer

An elderly person's driving ability could be affected because they may be unable to

☐ obtain car insurance

☐ understand road signs

☐ react very quickly

☐ give signals correctly

Be tolerant of older drivers. Poor eyesight and hearing could affect the speed with which they react to a hazard and may cause them to be hesitant.

Mark one answer

You have just passed these warning lights. What hazard would you expect to see next?

These lights warn that children may be crossing the road to a nearby school. Slow down so that you're ready to stop if necessary.

☐ A level crossing with no barrier

☐ An ambulance station

☐ A school crossing patrol

☐ An opening bridge

Mark one answer

You are planning a long journey. Do you need to plan rest stops?

☐ Yes, you should plan to stop every half an hour

☐ Yes, regular stops help concentration

☐ No, you will be less tired if you get there as soon as possible

☐ No, only fuel stops will be needed

Try to plan your journey so that you can take rest stops. It's recommended that you take a break of at least 15 minutes after every two hours of driving. This should help to maintain your concentration.

5.32 — Mark one answer — RES s7, HC r291–299

The red lights are flashing. What should you do when approaching this level crossing?

At level crossings the red lights flash before and when the barrier is down. At most crossings an amber light will precede the red lights. You must stop behind the white line unless you have already crossed it when the amber light comes on. NEVER zigzag around half-barriers.

- ☐ Go through quickly
- ☐ Go through carefully
- ☐ Stop before the barrier
- ☐ Switch on hazard warning lights

5.33 — Mark one answer — RES s7, HC r176

You are approaching crossroads. The traffic lights have failed. What should you do?

- ☐ Brake and stop only for large vehicles
- ☐ Brake sharply to a stop before looking
- ☐ Be prepared to brake sharply to a stop
- ☐ Be prepared to stop for any traffic

When approaching a junction where the traffic lights have failed, you should proceed with caution. Treat the situation as an unmarked junction and be prepared to stop.

5.34 — Mark one answer — RES s10, HC r206–207

What should the driver of the red car (arrowed) do?

Some people might take longer to cross the road. They may be older or have a disability. Be patient and don't hurry them by showing your impatience. They might have poor eyesight or not be able to hear traffic approaching. If pedestrians are standing at the side of the road, don't signal or wave them to cross. Other road users may not have seen your signal and this could lead the pedestrians into a hazardous situation.

- ☐ Wave the pedestrians who are waiting to cross
- ☐ Wait for the pedestrian in the road to cross
- ☐ Quickly drive behind the pedestrian in the road
- ☐ Tell the pedestrian in the road she should not have crossed

You are following a slower-moving vehicle on a narrow country road. There is a junction just ahead on the right. What should you do?

☐ Overtake after checking your mirrors and signalling

☐ Stay behind until you are past the junction

☐ Accelerate quickly to pass before the junction

☐ Slow down and prepare to overtake on the left

You should never overtake as you approach a junction. If a vehicle emerged from the junction while you were overtaking, a dangerous situation could develop very quickly.

What should you do as you approach this overhead bridge?

Oncoming large vehicles may need to move to the middle of the road so that they can pass safely under the bridge. There will not be enough room for you to continue and you should be ready to stop and wait.

☐ Move out to the centre of the road before going through

☐ Find another route, this is only for high vehicles

☐ Be prepared to give way to large vehicles in the middle of the road

☐ Move across to the right-hand side before going through

5.37 | **Mark one answer** | **RES s5**

Why are mirrors often slightly curved (convex)?

☐ They give a wider field of vision

☐ They totally cover blind spots

☐ They make it easier to judge the speed of following traffic

☐ They make following traffic look bigger

Although a convex mirror gives a wide view of the scene behind, you should be aware that it will not show you everything behind or to the side of the vehicle. Before you move off you will need to check over your shoulder to look for anything not visible in the mirrors.

5.38 | **Mark one answer** | **RES s11, HC p113, 117, KYTS p135**

You see this sign on the rear of a slow-moving lorry that you want to pass. It is travelling in the middle lane of a three-lane motorway. You should

This sign is found on slow-moving or stationary works vehicles. If you wish to overtake, do so on the left, as indicated. Be aware that there might be workmen in the area.

☐ cautiously approach the lorry then pass on either side

☐ follow the lorry until you can leave the motorway

☐ wait on the hard shoulder until the lorry has stopped

☐ approach with care and keep to the left of the lorry

5.39 | **Mark one answer** | **HC r104**

You think the driver of the vehicle in front has forgotten to cancel their right indicator. You should

☐ flash your lights to alert the driver

☐ sound your horn before overtaking

☐ overtake on the left if there is room

☐ stay behind and not overtake

The driver may be unsure of the location of a junction and turn suddenly. Be cautious and don't attempt to overtake.

What is the main hazard the driver of the red car (arrowed) should be aware of?

If you can do so safely give way to buses signalling to move off at bus stops. Try to anticipate the actions of other road users around you. The driver of the red car should be prepared for the bus pulling out. As you approach a bus stop look to see how many passengers are waiting to board. If the last one has just got on, the bus is likely to move off.

☐ Glare from the sun may affect the driver's vision

☐ The black car may stop suddenly

☐ The bus may move out into the road

☐ Oncoming vehicles will assume the driver is turning right

This yellow sign on a vehicle indicates this is

Buses which carry children to and from school may stop at places other than scheduled bus stops. Be aware that they might pull over at any time to allow children to get on or off. This will normally be when traffic is heavy during rush hour.

☐ a broken-down vehicle

☐ a school bus

☐ an ice cream van

☐ a private ambulance

5.42   Mark two answers   RES s10, HC r205–206

What TWO main hazards should you be aware of when going along this street?

- ☐ Glare from the sun
- ☐ Car doors opening suddenly
- ☐ Lack of road markings
- ☐ The headlights on parked cars being switched on
- ☐ Large goods vehicles
- ☐ Children running out from between vehicles

On roads where there are many parked vehicles you should take extra care. You might not be able to see children between parked cars and they may run out into the road without looking.

People may open car doors without realising the hazard this can create. You will also need to look well down the road for oncoming traffic.

5.43   Mark one answer   RES s10, HC r213

What is the main hazard you should be aware of when following this cyclist?

- ☐ The cyclist may move to the left and dismount
- ☐ The cyclist may swerve out into the road
- ☐ The contents of the cyclist's carrier may fall onto the road
- ☐ The cyclist may wish to turn right at the end of the road

When following a cyclist be aware that they have to deal with the hazards around them. They may wobble or swerve to avoid a pothole in the road or see a potential hazard and change direction suddenly. Don't follow them too closely or rev your engine impatiently.

5.44   Mark one answer   RES s1, HC r147

A driver's behaviour has upset you. It may help if you

- ☐ stop and take a break
- ☐ shout abusive language
- ☐ gesture to them with your hand
- ☐ follow their car, flashing your headlights

Tiredness may make you more irritable than you would be normally. You might react differently to situations because of it. If you feel yourself becoming tense, take a break.

5.45   Mark one answer   RES s7, HC r153

In areas where there are 'traffic calming' measures you should

☐ travel at a reduced speed

☐ always travel at the speed limit

☐ position in the centre of the road

☐ only slow down if pedestrians are near

Traffic calming measures such as road humps, chicanes and narrowings are intended to slow you down. Maintain a reduced speed until you reach the end of these features. They are there to protect pedestrians. Kill your speed!

5.46   Mark two answers   RES s7, HC r291–299, p108–109

When approaching this hazard why should you slow down?

There are two hazards clearly signed in this picture. You should be preparing for the bend by slowing down and selecting the correct gear. You might also have to stop at the level crossing, so be alert and be prepared to stop if necessary.

☐ Because of the bend

☐ Because it's hard to see to the right

☐ Because of approaching traffic

☐ Because of animals crossing

☐ Because of the level crossing

5.47   Mark one answer   RES s7, HC p116, KYTS p70–71

Why are place names painted on the road surface?

☐ To restrict the flow of traffic

☐ To warn you of oncoming traffic

☐ To enable you to change lanes early

☐ To prevent you changing lanes

The names of towns and cities may be painted on the road at busy junctions and complex road systems. Their purpose is to let you move into the correct lane in good time, allowing traffic to flow more freely.

5.48   Mark one answer   HC r135

Some two-way roads are divided into three lanes. Why are these particularly dangerous?

☐ Traffic in both directions can use the middle lane to overtake

☐ Traffic can travel faster in poor weather conditions

☐ Traffic can overtake on the left

☐ Traffic uses the middle lane for emergencies only

If you intend to overtake you must consider that approaching traffic could be planning the same manoeuvre. When you have considered the situation and have decided it is safe, indicate your intentions early. This will show the approaching traffic that you intend to pull out.

5.49   Mark one answer   RES s10, HC r220

You are on a dual carriageway. Ahead you see a vehicle with an amber flashing light. What could this be?

☐ An ambulance

☐ A fire engine

☐ A doctor on call

☐ A disabled person's vehicle

An amber flashing light on a vehicle indicates that it is slow-moving. Battery powered vehicles used by disabled people are limited to 8 mph. It's not advisable for them to be used on dual carriageways where the speed limit exceeds 50 mph. If they are then an amber flashing light must be used.

5.50   Mark one answer   HC p104

What does this signal from a police officer mean to oncoming traffic?

☐ Go ahead

☐ Stop

☐ Turn left

☐ Turn right

Police officers may need to direct traffic, for example, at a junction where the traffic lights have broken down. Check your copy of The Highway Code for the signals that they use.

5.51 — Mark two answers — RES s10, HC r223

Why should you be especially cautious when going past this stationary bus?

A stationary bus at a bus stop can hide pedestrians just in front of it who might be about to cross the road. Only go past at a speed that will enable you to stop safely if you need to.

☐ There is traffic approaching in the distance
☐ The driver may open the door
☐ It may suddenly move off
☐ People may cross the road in front of it
☐ There are bicycles parked on the pavement

5.52 — Mark three answers — RES s8, HC r162–167

Overtaking is a major cause of collisions. In which THREE of these situations should you NOT overtake?

☐ If you are turning left shortly afterwards
☐ When you are in a one-way street
☐ When you are approaching a junction
☐ If you are travelling up a long hill
☐ When your view ahead is blocked

You should not overtake unless it is really necessary. Arriving safely is more important than taking risks. Also look out for road signs and markings that show it is illegal or would be unsafe to overtake. In many cases overtaking is unlikely to significantly improve journey times.

5.53 — Mark three answers — HC r95

Which THREE result from drinking alcohol?

☐ Less control
☐ A false sense of confidence
☐ Faster reactions
☐ Poor judgement of speed
☐ Greater awareness of danger

You must understand the serious dangers of mixing alcohol with driving or riding. Alcohol will severely reduce your ability to drive or ride safely. Just one drink could put you over the limit. Don't risk people's lives – DON'T DRINK AND DRIVE OR RIDE!

Case study practice – 5 Hazard awareness

You've had new mirrors fitted to your motorcycle. They're slightly curved and give a wider field of vision.

You're travelling to a local pub to see some friends and stay for several hours.

At the end of the evening, you ride home. The weather has changed and it's raining steadily.

There's a skip parked on the road ahead, showing parking lights and hazard warning plates.

5.1 What word describes these slightly curved mirrors?

Mark **one** answer

- ☐ Convenient
- ☐ Concourse
- ☐ Convex
- ☐ Concentric

RES s5

5.2 What's the safest thing to do, during your stay at the pub?

Mark **one** answer

- ☐ Only drink pints of shandy
- ☐ Alternate soft drinks with alcohol
- ☐ Drink shorts with lots of water
- ☐ Stick to soft drinks the whole time

HC r95 **RES** s1

5.3 How could the conditions affect your visibility during your journey home?

Mark **one** answer

☐ By making you less visible to others
☐ By making it easier for you to see others
☐ By making the street lights seem brighter
☐ By making other road users take care

`HC` `r227` `RES` `s10`

5.4 What colour hazard warning plates would you see on skips and long vehicles?

Mark **one** answer

☐ Red and yellow
☐ Blue and yellow
☐ Green and yellow
☐ White and yellow

`HC` `p117`

5.5 In this weather, how much time should you leave between your vehicle and the one in front?

Mark **one** answer

☐ Two seconds
☐ Three seconds
☐ Four seconds
☐ Five seconds

`HC` `r227` `RES` `s11`

Vulnerable road users

In this section, you'll learn about

> who is particularly vulnerable on the road

> how to help keep other road users safe.

Vulnerable road users

As a motorcyclist, you'll share the road with many other road users. Some of these are more vulnerable than you, because of their

- inexperience or lack of judgement
- size
- speed
- unpredictable behaviour.

Among the most vulnerable road users are

- pedestrians – especially children and older people
- cyclists
- other motorcyclists
- horse riders.

Remember to treat all road users with courtesy and consideration. It's particularly important to be patient when there are children, older or disabled people using the road.

The most vulnerable drivers and riders are those who are still learning, inexperienced or older. Keep calm and make allowances for them.

> Pedestrians

People walking on or beside the road – pedestrians – are vulnerable because they move more slowly than other road users and have no protection if they're involved in a collision. Everybody is a pedestrian at some time, but not every pedestrian has the understanding of how to use roads safely.

Pedestrians normally use a pavement or footpath. Take extra care if they have to walk in the road – for example, when the pavement is closed for repairs or on country roads where there's no pavement. Always check for road signs that indicate people may be walking in the road.

No footpath for 310 yds

HC r206 **RES** s10 **KYTS** p13

On country roads, it's usually safest for pedestrians to walk on the right-hand side of the road, so that they're facing oncoming traffic and can see the vehicles approaching.

HC r2

A large group of people, such as those on an organised walk, may walk on the left-hand side. At night, the person at the front of the group should show a white light while the person at the back of the group should show a bright red light to help approaching drivers to see them.

HC r5

Watch out for pedestrians already crossing when you're turning into a side road. They have priority, so allow them to finish crossing.

HC r170 **RES** s9

When you see a bus stopped on the other side of the road, watch out for pedestrians who may come from behind the bus and cross the road, or dash across the road from your left to catch the bus.

HC r223 **RES** s10

Pedestrian crossings

Pedestrian crossings allow people to cross the road safely: be ready to slow down and stop as you approach them. Make sure you know how different types of crossing work. See section 2, Attitude, for more details.

Remember that you should never park on or near a pedestrian crossing; for example, on the zigzag lines either side of a zebra crossing.

HC r195–199 **RES** s8

Look for tell-tale signs that someone is going to cross the road between parked cars, such as

- seeing their feet when looking between the wheels of the parked cars
- a ball bouncing out into the road
- a bicycle wheel sticking out between cars.

Slow down and be prepared to stop.

HC r205 **RES** s10

Children

Children are particularly vulnerable as road users because they can be unpredictable. They're less likely than other pedestrians to look before stepping into the road.

 See this link for information on teaching road safety to children.

▸ **direct.gov.uk/en/Parents/ Yourchildshealthandsafety/ Roadandtravelsafety/DG_194513**

Ride carefully near schools.

 There may be flashing amber lights under a school warning sign, to show that children are likely to be crossing the road on their way to or from school. Slow down until you're clear of the area.

 Be prepared for a school crossing patrol to stop the traffic by stepping out into the road with a stop sign. You **MUST** obey the stop signal given by a school crossing patrol.

 Don't wait or park on yellow zigzag lines outside a school. A clear view of the crossing area outside the school is needed by

- drivers and riders on the road
- pedestrians on the pavement.

HC r208–210, 238 **RES** s7, 10 **KYTS** p56

Buses and coaches carrying schoolchildren show a special sign in the back. This tells you that they may stop often, and not just at normal bus stops.

HC r209, p117 **RES** s10

Older and disabled pedestrians

If you see older people about to cross the road ahead, be careful as they may have misjudged your speed.

If they're crossing, be patient and allow them to cross in their own time: they may need extra time to cross the road.

HC r207 RES s10

A pedestrian with hearing difficulties may have a dog with a distinctive yellow or burgundy coat.

Take extra care as they may not be aware of vehicles approaching.

A person carrying a white stick with a red band is both deaf and blind. They may also have a guide dog with a red and white checked harness.

HC r207 RES s10

> Cyclists

Cyclists should normally follow the same rules of the road as drivers, but they're slower and more vulnerable than other vehicles.

Find out about cycling safely at this link.

> **direct.gov.uk/en/ TravelAndTransport/Cycling/ DG_10026401**

Cycle routes

In some areas there may be special cycle or shared cycle and pedestrian routes, which are marked by signs.

KYTS p35–36

At traffic lights, advanced stop lines are sometimes marked on the road so that cyclists can stop in front of other traffic. When the lights are red or about to become red, you should stop at the first white line.

HC r178

Overtaking cyclists

If you're overtaking a cyclist, give them as much room as you would a car. They may swerve

- to avoid an uneven road surface
- if a gust of wind blows them off course.

HC r211–213 **RES** s8, 10

A cyclist travelling at a low speed, or glancing over their shoulder to check for traffic, may be planning to turn right. Stay behind and give them plenty of room.

Never overtake a slow-moving vehicle just before you turn left. Hold back and wait until it has passed the junction before you turn.

Cyclists at junctions

When you're emerging from a junction, look carefully for cyclists. They're not as easy to see as larger vehicles. Also look out for cyclists emerging from junctions.

HC r77, 187 **RES** s9

Be aware of cyclists at a roundabout. They travel at lower speeds and are more vulnerable than other road users, and may decide to stay in the left-hand lane whichever direction they're planning to take. Hold back and allow plenty of room.

> Other motorcyclists

As you'll know, motorcyclists can be hard to see because their vehicles are smaller than cars. They're usually fast-moving too, so they can be very vulnerable in a collision.

Remember to leave enough room while overtaking another motorcycle; the rider may swerve to avoid an uneven surface or be affected by a gust of wind. Look carefully for motorcyclists at junctions too, as they may be easily hidden by other vehicles, **street furniture** or other roadside features, such as trees.

Definition

street furniture
objects and pieces of equipment on roads and pavements; for example, street lights and signs, bus stops, benches, bollards, etc

Before you turn right, always check for other traffic, especially motorcyclists, who may be overtaking. Always use the 'lifesaver' look before making your manoeuvre.

HC r180

 See the Think! road safety information about riding safely near motorcyclists.

❯ **http://think.direct.gov.uk/ motorcycles.html**

When you're moving in queues of traffic, be aware that other motorcyclists may also

- filter between lanes
- cut in just in front of you
- pass very close to you.

Keep checking your mirrors for motorcycles approaching from behind and give them space if possible.

If there's a slow-moving motorcyclist ahead and you're not sure what the rider is going to do, stay behind them in case they change direction suddenly.

HC r180 **RES** s9

If a motorcyclist is injured in an incident, get medical assistance. Don't remove their helmet unless it's essential.

HC r283 **RES** s16

If you have a collision, you **MUST** stop. By law, you **MUST** stop at the scene of the incident if damage or injury is caused to any other person, vehicle, animal or property.

HC r286 RES s16

> Animals

Horses and other animals can behave in unpredictable ways on the road because they get frightened by the noise and speed of vehicles. Always ride carefully if there are animals on the road.

- Stay well back.
- Don't rev your engine or sound your horn near horses as this may startle them.
- Go very slowly and be ready to stop.

When it's safe to overtake,

- ride past slowly
- leave plenty of room.

HC r214–215 RES s10

Take extra care when approaching a roundabout. Horse riders, like cyclists, may keep to the left, even if they're signalling right. Stay well back.

HC r187, 215 RES s9

See the Think! road safety advice about horses on the road.

> **http://think.direct.gov.uk/horses.html**

> Drivers

Drivers, especially those who are inexperienced or older, may not react as quickly as you to what's happening on the road. Learner drivers and riders may make mistakes, such as stalling at a junction. Be patient and be ready to slow down or stop if necessary.

HC r216–217 **RES** s1

A flashing amber beacon on the top of a vehicle means it's a slow-moving vehicle. A powered wheelchair or mobility scooter used by a disabled person **MUST** have a flashing amber light when travelling on a dual carriageway with a speed limit that exceeds 50 mph.

HC r220

If you find another vehicle is following you too closely in fast-moving traffic, slow down gradually to increase your distance from the vehicle in front. This gives you more room to slow down or stop if necessary, and so reduces the risk of the vehicle behind crashing into you because the driver hasn't left enough room to stop safely.

Learner riders and drivers, and newly qualified riders and drivers

Statistics show that 17- to 25-year-olds are the most likely to be involved in a road traffic incident. Over-confidence and lack of experience and judgement are the main causes of incidents for young and new drivers and riders.

Newly qualified riders can decrease their risk of being involved in road traffic incidents, particularly on the motorway, by taking further training; for example, under the Enhanced Rider Scheme.

HC p134 **RES** s11

 Find out more about the Enhanced Rider Scheme online.

❯ **direct.gov.uk/ERS**

Meeting the standards

You must be able to

look out for the effect of starting your engine near vulnerable road users. Passing cyclists or pedestrians may be affected

look for vulnerable road users at junctions, roundabouts and crossings. For example

- cyclists
- other motorcyclists
- horse riders.

You must know and understand

when other road users are vulnerable and how to allow for them

the rules that apply to vulnerable road users, like cyclists, and the position that they may select on the road as a result

how vulnerable road users may act on the road. For example

- cyclists may wobble
- children may run out
- older people may take longer to cross the road.

> Notes

You can use this page to make your own notes or diagrams about the key points you need to remember.

Think about

- Which types of pedestrian crossing might you see, and what are the differences between them?
- When might you need to watch out for children near the road?
- Which disability might a person have if they're walking with a dog that has a red and white checked harness?
- What might a cyclist be about to do if they're checking over their shoulder?
- What mustn't you do when riding near horses or other animals on the road?

Your notes

_____

_____

_____

_____

_____

_____

_____

_____

_____

_____

_____

 ## Things to discuss and practise with your trainer

These are just a few examples of what you could discuss and practise with your trainer. Read more about vulnerable road users to come up with your own ideas.

Discuss with your trainer

- which sticks are used by people with different disabilities, eg a white stick with a red band
- what you think a cyclist's experience of riding through traffic may be? How can you make them feel safer?
- where pedestrians may have to walk in the road and what you should look out for.

Practise with your trainer

- riding near schools at times when students and parents are likely to be arriving or leaving
- riding up to different types of crossing to practise how to respond to their users and any lights
- identifying the signs warning you of vulnerable road users, eg a red triangle with a picture of a bicycle. Discuss these after your lesson.

You should not ride too closely behind a lorry because

☐ you will breathe in the lorry's exhaust fumes

☐ wind from the lorry will slow you down

☐ drivers behind you may not be able to see you

☐ it will reduce your view ahead

If you're following too close behind a large vehicle your view beyond it will be restricted. Drop back. This will help you to see more of the road ahead. It will also help the driver of the large vehicle to see you in the mirror and gives you a safe separation distance in which to take avoiding action if a hazardous situation arises.

You are riding on a country lane. You see cattle on the road. You should

☐ slow down

☐ stop if necessary

☐ give plenty of room

☐ rev your engine

☐ sound your horn

☐ ride up close behind them

Try not to startle the animals. They can be easily frightened by noise or by traffic passing too closely.

A learner driver has begun to emerge into your path from a side road on the left. You should

☐ be ready to slow down and stop

☐ let them emerge then ride close behind

☐ turn into the side road

☐ brake hard, then wave them out

If you see another vehicle begin to emerge into your path you should ride defensively. Always be ready to slow down or stop if necessary.

The vehicle ahead is being driven by a learner. You should

☐ keep calm and be patient

☐ ride up close behind

☐ put your headlight on full beam

☐ sound your horn and overtake

Learners might take longer to react to traffic situations. Don't unnerve them by riding up close behind or showing signs of impatience.

6.5

Mark one answer

RES s8, HC r126

You are riding in fast-flowing traffic. The vehicle behind is following too closely. You should

- ☐ slow down gradually to increase the gap in front of you
- ☐ slow down as quickly as possible by braking
- ☐ accelerate to get away from the vehicle behind you
- ☐ apply the brakes sharply to warn the driver behind

It is dangerous for vehicles to travel too close together. Visibility is reduced and there is a higher risk of collision if a vehicle brakes suddenly to avoid a hazard. By increasing the separation distance between you and the vehicle in front, you have a greater safety margin. It also gives space for the vehicles behind to overtake you if they wish.

6.6

Mark one answer

RES s8, HC r195

You are riding towards a zebra crossing. Waiting to cross is a person in a wheelchair. You should

- ☐ continue on your way
- ☐ wave to the person to cross
- ☐ wave to the person to wait
- ☐ be prepared to stop

As you would with an able-bodied person, you should prepare to slow down and stop. Don't wave them across, as other traffic may not stop.

6.7

Mark one answer

RES s12, HC r233

Why should you allow extra room when overtaking another motorcyclist on a windy day?

- ☐ The rider may turn off suddenly to get out of the wind
- ☐ The rider may be blown across in front of you
- ☐ The rider may stop suddenly
- ☐ The rider may be travelling faster than normal

On a windy day, be aware that the blustery conditions might blow you or other motorcyclists out of position. Think about this before deciding to overtake.

193

You have stopped at a pelican crossing. A disabled person is crossing slowly in front of you. The lights have now changed to green. You should

☐ allow the person to cross

☐ ride in front of the person

☐ ride behind the person

☐ sound your horn

☐ be patient

☐ edge forward slowly

At a pelican crossing the green light means you may proceed as long as the crossing is clear. If someone hasn't finished crossing, be patient and wait for them.

Where should you take particular care to look out for other motorcyclists and cyclists?

☐ On dual carriageways

☐ At junctions

☐ At zebra crossings

☐ On one-way streets

Other motorcyclists and cyclists may be difficult to see on the road, particularly at junctions. If your view is blocked by other traffic you may not be able to see them approaching.

Why is it vital for a rider to make a 'lifesaver' check before turning right?

☐ To check for any overtaking traffic

☐ To confirm that they are about to turn

☐ To make sure the side road is clear

☐ To check that the rear indicator is flashing

The 'lifesaver' glance makes you aware of what is happening behind and alongside you before altering your course. This glance must be timed so that you still have time to react if it isn't safe to carry out your manoeuvre.

6.11

Mark two answers

RES s10, HC r214

You are about to overtake horse riders. Which TWO of the following could scare the horses?

When passing horses allow them plenty of space and slow down. Animals can be frightened by sudden or loud noises, so don't sound your horn or rev the engine.

☐ Sounding your horn

☐ Giving arm signals

☐ Riding slowly

☐ Revving your engine

6.12

Mark one answer

RES s1

What is a main cause of road traffic incidents among young and new motorcyclists?

☐ Using borrowed equipment

☐ Lack of experience and judgement

☐ Riding in bad weather conditions

☐ Riding on country roads

Young and inexperienced motorcyclists are far more likely to be involved in incidents than more experienced riders. Reasons for this include natural exuberance, showing off, competitive behaviour and over confidence. Don't overestimate your abilities and never ride too fast for the conditions.

6.13

Mark one answer

RES s1

Which of the following is applicable to young motorcyclists?

☐ They are normally better than experienced riders

☐ They are usually less likely to have a crash

☐ They are often over-confident of their own ability

☐ They are more likely to get cheaper insurance

Young and inexperienced motorcyclists often have more confidence than ability. It takes time to gain experience and become a good rider. Make sure you have the right attitude and put safety first.

The road outside this school is marked with yellow zigzag lines. What do these lines mean?

Parking here will block the view of the school gates, endangering the lives of children on their way to and from school.

☐ You may park on the lines when dropping off schoolchildren

☐ You may park on the lines when picking up schoolchildren

☐ You should not wait or park your motorcycle here

☐ You must stay with your motorcycle if you park here

Which sign means that there may be people walking along the road?

Always check the road signs. Triangular signs are warning signs and they'll keep you informed of hazards ahead and help you to anticipate any problems. There are a number of different signs showing pedestrians. Learn the meaning of each one.

6.16

Mark one answer

RES s9, HC r170

You are turning left from a main road into a side road. People are already crossing the road into which you are turning. You should

Always check the road into which you are turning. Approaching at the correct speed will allow you enough time to observe and react.

Give way to any pedestrians already crossing the road.

- ☐ continue, as it is your right of way
- ☐ signal to them to continue crossing
- ☐ wait and allow them to cross
- ☐ sound your horn to warn them of your presence

6.17

Mark one answer

RES s9, HC r211

You intend to turn right into a side road. Just before turning you should check for motorcyclists who might be

- ☐ overtaking on your left
- ☐ following you closely
- ☐ emerging from the side road
- ☐ overtaking on your right

Never attempt to change direction to the right without first checking your right-hand mirror. A motorcyclist might not have seen your signal and could be hidden by the car behind you. This action should become a matter of routine.

6.18

Mark one answer

RES s8, HC r25

A toucan crossing is different from other crossings because

- ☐ moped riders can use it
- ☐ it is controlled by a traffic warden
- ☐ it is controlled by two flashing lights
- ☐ cyclists can use it

Toucan crossings are shared by pedestrians and cyclists and they are shown the green light together. Cyclists are permitted to cycle across.

The signals are push-button operated and there is no flashing amber phase.

How will a school crossing patrol signal you to stop?

☐ By pointing to children on the opposite pavement

☐ By displaying a red light

☐ By displaying a stop sign

☐ By giving you an arm signal

If a school crossing patrol steps out into the road with a stop sign you must stop. Don't wave anyone across the road and don't get impatient or rev your engine.

Which sign tells you that pedestrians may be walking in the road as there is no pavement?

Give pedestrians who are walking at the side of the road plenty of room when you pass them. They may turn around when they hear your engine and unintentionally step into the path of your vehicle.

What does this sign mean?

This sign shows a shared route for pedestrians and cyclists: when it ends, the cyclists will be rejoining the main road.

☐ No route for pedestrians and cyclists

☐ A route for pedestrians only

☐ A route for cyclists only

☐ A route for pedestrians and cyclists

6.22 — Mark one answer — RES s10, HC r207

You see a pedestrian with a white stick and red band. This means that the person is

☐ physically disabled
☐ deaf only
☐ blind only
☐ deaf and blind

If someone is deaf as well as blind, they may be carrying a white stick with a red reflective band. You can't see if a pedestrian is deaf. Don't assume everyone can hear you approaching.

6.23 — Mark one answer — RES s10, HC r207

What action would you take when elderly people are crossing the road?

☐ Wave them across so they know that you have seen them
☐ Be patient and allow them to cross in their own time
☐ Rev the engine to let them know that you are waiting
☐ Tap the horn in case they are hard of hearing

Be aware that older people might take a long time to cross the road. They might also be hard of hearing and not hear you approaching. Don't hurry older people across the road by getting too close to them or revving your engine.

6.24 — Mark one answer — RES s10, HC r207

You see two elderly pedestrians about to cross the road ahead. You should

☐ expect them to wait for you to pass
☐ speed up to get past them quickly
☐ stop and wave them across the road
☐ be careful, they may misjudge your speed

Older people may have impaired hearing, vision, concentration and judgement. They may also walk slowly and so could take a long time to cross the road.

6.25

You are coming up to a roundabout. A cyclist is signalling to turn right. What should you do?

☐ Overtake on the right

☐ Give a horn warning

☐ Signal the cyclist to move across

☐ Give the cyclist plenty of room

If you're following a cyclist who's signalling to turn right at a roundabout leave plenty of room. Give them space and time to get into the correct lane.

6.26

Which TWO should you allow extra room when overtaking?

☐ Motorcycles

☐ Tractors

☐ Bicycles

☐ Road-sweeping vehicles

Don't pass riders too closely as this may cause them to lose balance. Always leave as much room as you would for a car, and don't cut in.

6.27

Why should you look particularly for motorcyclists and cyclists at junctions?

☐ They may want to turn into the side road

☐ They may slow down to let you turn

☐ They are harder to see

☐ They might not see you turn

Cyclists and motorcyclists are smaller than other vehicles and so are more difficult to see. They can easily become hidden from your view by cars parked near a junction.

6.28

You are waiting to come out of a side road. Why should you watch carefully for motorcycles?

☐ Motorcycles are usually faster than cars

☐ Police patrols often use motorcycles

☐ Motorcycles are small and hard to see

☐ Motorcycles have right of way

If you're waiting to emerge from a side road watch out for motorcycles: they're small and can be difficult to see. Be especially careful if there are parked vehicles restricting your view, there might be a motorcycle approaching.

IF YOU DON'T KNOW, DON'T GO.

6.29
Mark one answer RES s4, HC r86

In daylight, an approaching motorcyclist is using a dipped headlight. Why?

☐ So that the rider can be seen more easily

☐ To stop the battery overcharging

☐ To improve the rider's vision

☐ The rider is inviting you to proceed

A motorcycle can be lost from sight behind another vehicle. The use of the headlight helps to make it more conspicuous and therefore more easily seen.

6.30
Mark one answer RES s4, HC r86

Motorcyclists should wear bright clothing mainly because

☐ they must do so by law

☐ it helps keep them cool in summer

☐ the colours are popular

☐ drivers often do not see them

Motorcycles are small vehicles and can be difficult to see. If the rider wears bright clothing it can make it easier for other road users to see them approaching, especially at junctions.

6.31
Mark one answer RES s8, HC r211–213

There is a slow-moving motorcyclist ahead of you. You are unsure what the rider is going to do. You should

☐ pass on the left

☐ pass on the right

☐ stay behind

☐ move closer

If a motorcyclist is travelling slowly it may be that they are looking for a turning or entrance. Be patient and stay behind them in case they need to make a sudden change of direction.

6.32
Mark one answer RES s8, HC r212

Motorcyclists will often look round over their right shoulder just before turning right. This is because

☐ they need to listen for following traffic

☐ motorcycles do not have mirrors

☐ looking around helps them balance as they turn

☐ they need to check for traffic in their blind area

If you see a motorcyclist take a quick glance over their shoulder, this could mean they are about to change direction. Recognising a clue like this helps you to be prepared and take appropriate action, making you safer on the road.

6.33 — Mark three answers — RES s10, HC r207, 211

At road junctions which of the following are most vulnerable?

☐ Cyclists

☐ Motorcyclists

☐ Pedestrians

☐ Car drivers

☐ Lorry drivers

Pedestrians and riders on two wheels can be harder to see than other road users. Make sure you keep a look-out for them, especially at junctions. Good effective observation, coupled with appropriate action, can save lives.

6.34 — Mark one answer — RES s10, HC r211

Motorcyclists are particularly vulnerable

☐ when moving off

☐ on dual carriageways

☐ when approaching junctions

☐ on motorways

Another road user failing to see a motorcyclist is a major cause of collisions at junctions. Wherever streams of traffic join or cross there's the potential for this type of incident to occur.

6.35 — Mark two answers — RES s9, HC r187, 215

You are approaching a roundabout. There are horses just ahead of you. You should

☐ be prepared to stop

☐ treat them like any other vehicle

☐ give them plenty of room

☐ accelerate past as quickly as possible

☐ sound your horn as a warning

Horse riders often keep to the outside of the roundabout even if they are turning right. Give them plenty of room and remember that they may have to cross lanes of traffic.

6.36 — Mark one answer — RES s8, HC r207

As you approach a pelican crossing the lights change to green. Elderly people are halfway across. You should

☐ wave them to cross as quickly as they can

☐ rev your engine to make them hurry

☐ flash your lights in case they have not heard you

☐ wait because they will take longer to cross

Even if the lights turn to green, wait for them to clear the crossing. Allow them to cross the road in their own time, and don't try to hurry them by revving your engine.

6.37
Mark one answer   RES s7, 8, 10, HC r208

There are flashing amber lights under a school warning sign. What action should you take?

☐ Reduce speed until you are clear of the area

☐ Keep up your speed and sound the horn

☐ Increase your speed to clear the area quickly

☐ Wait at the lights until they change to green

The flashing amber lights are switched on to warn you that children may be crossing near a school. Slow down and take extra care as you may have to stop.

6.38
Mark one answer   HC p117

Where would you see this sign?

Watch out for children crossing the road from the other side of the bus.

☐ Near a school crossing

☐ At a playground entrance

☐ On a school bus

☐ At a 'pedestrians only' area

6.39
Mark one answer   RES s9, HC r77, 187

You are following two cyclists. They approach a roundabout in the left-hand lane. In which direction should you expect the cyclists to go?

☐ Left

☐ Right

☐ Any direction

☐ Straight ahead

Cyclists approaching a roundabout in the left-hand lane may be turning right but may not have been able to get into the correct lane due to the heavy traffic. They may also feel safer keeping to the left all the way round the roundabout. Be aware of them and give them plenty of room.

You are travelling behind a moped. You want to turn left just ahead. You should

☐ overtake the moped before the junction

☐ pull alongside the moped and stay level until just before the junction

☐ sound your horn as a warning and pull in front of the moped

☐ stay behind until the moped has passed the junction

Passing the moped and turning into the junction could mean that you cut across the front of the rider. This might force them to slow down, stop or even lose control. Slow down and stay behind the moped until it has passed the junction and you can then turn safely.

You see a horse rider as you approach a roundabout. They are signalling right but keeping well to the left. You should

Allow the horse rider to enter and exit the roundabout in their own time. They may feel safer keeping to the left all the way around the roundabout. Don't get up close behind or alongside them. This is very likely to upset the horse and create a dangerous situation.

☐ proceed as normal

☐ keep close to them

☐ cut in front of them

☐ stay well back

How would you react to drivers who appear to be inexperienced?

☐ Sound your horn to warn them of your presence

☐ Be patient and prepare for them to react more slowly

☐ Flash your headlights to indicate that it is safe for them to proceed

☐ Overtake them as soon as possible

Learners might not have confidence when they first start to drive. Allow them plenty of room and don't react adversely to their hesitation. We all learn from experience, but new drivers will have had less practice in dealing with all the situations that might occur.

6.43
Mark one answer RES s1, HC r217

You are following a learner driver who stalls at a junction. You should

- ☐ be patient as you expect them to make mistakes
- ☐ stay very close behind and flash your headlights
- ☐ start to rev your engine if they take too long to restart
- ☐ immediately steer around them and drive on

Learning is a process of practice and experience. Try to understand this and tolerate those who are at the beginning of this process.

6.44
Mark one answer RES s10, HC r5, 154

You are on a country road. What should you expect to see coming towards you on YOUR side of the road?

- ☐ Motorcycles
- ☐ Bicycles
- ☐ Pedestrians
- ☐ Horse riders

On a quiet country road always be aware that there may be a hazard just around the next bend, such as a slow-moving vehicle or pedestrians. Pedestrians are advised to walk on the right-hand side of the road if there is no pavement, so they may be walking towards you on your side of the road.

6.45
Mark one answer RES s1, HC r216

You are following a car driven by an elderly driver. You should

- ☐ expect the driver to drive badly
- ☐ flash your lights and overtake
- ☐ be aware that the driver's reactions may not be as fast as yours
- ☐ stay very close behind but be careful

You must show consideration to other road users. The reactions of older drivers may be slower and they might need more time to deal with a situation. Be tolerant and don't lose patience or show your annoyance.

You are following a cyclist. You wish to turn left just ahead. You should

Make allowances for cyclists. Allow them plenty of room. Don't try to overtake and then immediately turn left. Be patient and stay behind them until they have passed the junction.

- ☐ overtake the cyclist before the junction
- ☐ pull alongside the cyclist and stay level until after the junction
- ☐ hold back until the cyclist has passed the junction
- ☐ go around the cyclist on the junction

A horse rider is in the left-hand lane approaching a roundabout. You should expect the rider to

- ☐ go in any direction
- ☐ turn right
- ☐ turn left
- ☐ go ahead

Horses and their riders will move more slowly than other road users. They might not have time to cut across heavy traffic to take up position in the offside lane. For this reason a horse and rider may approach a roundabout in the left-hand lane, even though they're turning right.

Powered vehicles used by disabled people are small and hard to see. How do they give early warning when on a dual carriageway?

- ☐ They will have a flashing red light
- ☐ They will have a flashing green light
- ☐ They will have a flashing blue light
- ☐ They will have a flashing amber light

Powered vehicles used by disabled people are small, low, hard to see and travel very slowly. On a dual carriageway a flashing amber light will warn other road users.

6.49 — Mark one answer — RES s8, HC r187, 212

You should never attempt to overtake a cyclist

- ☐ just before you turn left
- ☐ on a left-hand bend
- ☐ on a one-way street
- ☐ on a dual carriageway

If you want to turn left and there's a cyclist in front of you, hold back. Wait until the cyclist has passed the junction and then turn left behind them.

6.50 — Mark one answer — HC r225

Ahead of you there is a moving vehicle with a flashing amber beacon. This means it is

- ☐ slow moving
- ☐ broken down
- ☐ a doctor's car
- ☐ a school crossing patrol

As you approach the vehicle, assess the situation. Due to its slow progress you will need to judge whether it is safe to overtake.

6.51 — Mark one answer — HC p107, KYTS p35

What does this sign mean?

The picture of a cycle will also usually be painted on the road, sometimes with a different coloured surface. Leave these clear for cyclists and don't pass too closely when you overtake.

- ☐ Contraflow pedal cycle lane
- ☐ With-flow pedal cycle lane
- ☐ Pedal cycles and buses only
- ☐ No pedal cycles or buses

6.52 — Mark one answer — RES s10, HC r215

You notice horse riders in front. What should you do FIRST?

Be particularly careful when approaching horse riders – slow down and be prepared to stop. Always pass wide and slowly and look out for signals given by horse riders. Horses are unpredictable: always treat them as potential hazards and take great care when passing them.

- ☐ Pull out to the middle of the road
- ☐ Slow down and be ready to stop
- ☐ Accelerate around them
- ☐ Signal right

6.53
Mark one answer — RES s7, HC r208, 238, KYTS p56

You must not stop on these road markings because you may obstruct

These markings are found on the road outside schools. DO NOT stop (even to set down or pick up children) or park on them. The markings are to make sure that drivers, riders, children and other pedestrians have a clear view.

☐ children's view of the crossing area

☐ teachers' access to the school

☐ delivery vehicles' access to the school

☐ emergency vehicles' access to the school

6.54
Mark one answer — RES s10, HC r2, 206

The left-hand pavement is closed due to street repairs. What should you do?

☐ Watch out for pedestrians walking in the road

☐ Use your right-hand mirror more often

☐ Speed up to get past the roadworks quicker

☐ Position close to the left-hand kerb

Where street repairs have closed off pavements, proceed carefully and slowly as pedestrians might have to walk in the road.

6.55
Mark one answer — RES s10, HC r213

You are following a motorcyclist on an uneven road. You should

☐ allow less room so you can be seen in their mirrors

☐ overtake immediately

☐ allow extra room in case they swerve to avoid potholes

☐ allow the same room as normal because road surfaces do not affect motorcyclists

Potholes and bumps in the road can unbalance a motorcyclist. For this reason the rider might swerve to avoid an uneven road surface. Watch out at places where this is likely to occur.

6.56
Mark one answer   HC p109, KYTS p36

What does this sign tell you?

☐ No cycling
☐ Cycle route ahead
☐ Cycle parking only
☐ End of cycle route

With people's concern today for the environment, cycle routes are being created in our towns and cities. These are usually defined by road markings and signs.

Respect the presence of cyclists on the road and give them plenty of room if you need to pass.

6.57
Mark one answer   RES s9, HC r77, 187

You are approaching this roundabout and see the cyclist signal right. Why is the cyclist keeping to the left?

☐ It is a quicker route for the cyclist
☐ The cyclist is going to turn left instead
☐ The cyclist thinks The Highway Code does not apply to bicycles
☐ The cyclist is slower and more vulnerable

Cycling in today's heavy traffic can be hazardous. Some cyclists may not feel happy about crossing the path of traffic to take up a position in an outside lane. Be aware of this and understand that, although in the left-hand lane, the cyclist might be turning right.

6.58
Mark one answer   RES s8, HC r195–199

You are approaching this crossing. You should

☐ prepare to slow down and stop
☐ stop and wave the pedestrians across
☐ speed up and pass by quickly
☐ continue unless the pedestrians step out

Be courteous and prepare to stop. Do not wave people across as this could be dangerous if another vehicle is approaching the crossing.

You see a pedestrian with a dog. The dog has a yellow or burgundy coat. This especially warns you that the pedestrian is

Take extra care as the pedestrian may not be aware of vehicles approaching.

- ☐ elderly
- ☐ dog training
- ☐ colour blind
- ☐ deaf

At toucan crossings

- ☐ you only stop if someone is waiting to cross
- ☐ cyclists are not permitted
- ☐ there is a continuously flashing amber beacon
- ☐ pedestrians and cyclists may cross

There are some crossings where cycle routes lead the cyclists to cross at the same place as pedestrians. These are called toucan crossings. Always look out for cyclists, as they're likely to be approaching faster than pedestrians.

Some junctions controlled by traffic lights have a marked area between two stop lines. What is this for?

- ☐ To allow taxis to position in front of other traffic
- ☐ To allow people with disabilities to cross the road
- ☐ To allow cyclists and pedestrians to cross the road together
- ☐ To allow cyclists to position in front of other traffic

These are known as advanced stop lines. When the lights are red (or about to become red) you should stop at the first white line. However if you have crossed that line as the lights change you must stop at the second line even if it means you are in the area reserved for cyclists.

6.62
Mark one answer RES s8, HC r211–213

When you are overtaking a cyclist you should leave as much room as you would give to a car. What is the main reason for this?

☐ The cyclist might speed up

☐ The cyclist might get off the bike

☐ The cyclist might swerve

☐ The cyclist might have to make a left turn

Before overtaking assess the situation. Look well ahead to see if the cyclist will need to change direction. Be especially aware of the cyclist approaching parked vehicles as they will need to alter course. Do not pass too closely or cut in sharply.

6.63
Mark three answers RES s10, HC r214

Which THREE should you do when passing sheep on a road?

☐ Allow plenty of room

☐ Go very slowly

☐ Pass quickly but quietly

☐ Be ready to stop

☐ Briefly sound your horn

Slow down and be ready to stop if you see animals in the road ahead. Animals are easily frightened by noise and vehicles passing too close to them. Stop if signalled to do so by the person in charge.

6.64
Mark one answer HC r5

At night you see a pedestrian wearing reflective clothing and carrying a bright red light. What does this mean?

☐ You are approaching roadworks

☐ You are approaching an organised walk

☐ You are approaching a slow-moving vehicle

☐ You are approaching a traffic danger spot

The people on the walk should be keeping to the left, but don't assume this. Pass slowly, make sure you have time to do so safely. Be aware that the pedestrians have their backs to you and may not know that you're there.

6.65
Mark one answer HC p134

You have just passed your test. How can you reduce your risk of being involved in a collision?

☐ By always staying close to the vehicle in front

☐ By never going over 40 mph

☐ By staying only in the left-hand lane on all roads

☐ By taking further training

New drivers and riders are often involved in a collision or incident early in their driving career. Due to a lack of experience they may not react to hazards as quickly as more experienced road users. Approved training courses are offered by driver and rider training schools. The Pass Plus scheme has been created by DSA for new drivers who would like to improve their basic skills and safely widen their driving experience.

Case study practice – 6 Vulnerable road users

Daniel lives in a village and is riding his motorcycle to town. Sheep are being herded across the road ahead.

Once in town, traffic is heavy. At a pelican crossing, amber lights are flashing and people are still crossing.

Later, Daniel needs to turn left into a side road where pedestrians are just beginning to cross. Further along on Daniel's side of the road, there's a refuse collection vehicle with flashing amber beacons.

6.1 How should Daniel act while the sheep are crossing?

Mark **one** answer

- ☐ Turn the engine off and wait until the animals have crossed
- ☐ Get off the motorcycle and wheel it past the animals
- ☐ Move slowly forward and sound the horn until they move
- ☐ Flash the headlights and rev the engine to hurry them across

`HC` `r214` `RES` `s10`

6.2 At the pelican crossing, how should Daniel act?

Mark **one** answer

- ☐ Stop but keep revving the engine to hurry them up
- ☐ Stop and wait patiently until they've crossed
- ☐ Keep moving slowly forward with lights flashing
- ☐ Keep going and ride slowly past the pedestrians

`HC` `r196`

6.3 What should Daniel do at this left turn?

Mark **one** answer

☐ Get off and wheel the motorcycle on the pavement

☐ Indicate then ride slowly round the pedestrians

☐ Flash his headlights and use the horn before turning

☐ Wait until the pedestrians have crossed safely

HC r170 **RES** s9

6.4 Which of these vehicles might have an amber beacon?

Mark **one** answer

☐ A vehicle that's slow-moving

☐ A vehicle that's reversing

☐ A vehicle that has a puncture

☐ A vehicle that's pulling out

HC r225

6.5 How should Daniel overtake the vehicle?

Mark **one** answer

☐ By dismounting and wheeling the motorcycle

☐ By revving the engine until the vehicle moves over

☐ By waiting until the road is clear of oncoming traffic

☐ By riding quickly past, while sounding the horn

HC r162, 163 **RES** s8

Other types of vehicle

In this section, you'll learn about

- different types of vehicles
- safety when riding towards or following other types of vehicle.

Other types of vehicle

When you're riding towards or following another type of vehicle, such as a bus or a lorry, you need to be aware of that vehicle's capabilities and how they're different to those of your motorcycle.

> Other motorcycles

Windy weather has a big effect on motorcyclists. Other motorcyclists can be blown into your path, so

- if you're overtaking another motorcyclist, allow extra room
- if a motorcyclist in front of you is overtaking a high-sided vehicle, keep well back, as they could be blown off course
- be particularly aware of other motorcyclists where there are crosswind warning signs.

HC r232–233, p109 **RES** s12

>  **TIP**
>
> Crosswinds are likely to affect
>
> - cyclists
> - motorcyclists
> - drivers towing caravans or trailers
> - drivers of high-sided vehicles
>
> more than car drivers. If you're following or overtaking, be aware that these vehicles might be blown off course, and give them extra room.
>
> **RES** s12

Metal drain covers can become very slippery in wet weather and are particularly hazardous for two-wheeled vehicles. Take care to avoid uneven or slippery surfaces and watch out for other motorcyclists having to do so.

HC r213 **RES** s10

> Large vehicles

Large vehicles can make it difficult for you to see the road ahead. Keep well back if you're following a large vehicle, especially if you're planning to overtake. If another vehicle fills the gap you've left, drop back further. This will improve your view of the road ahead.

HC r164, 222 **RES** s8

Overtaking a large vehicle is risky because it takes more time to overtake than a car.

Keep well back until you can see that the road ahead is clear. This also helps the driver of the large vehicle to see you in their mirrors.

Never begin to overtake unless you're sure that you can complete the manoeuvre safely.

HC r164 **RES** s8, 12

In wet weather, large vehicles throw up a lot of spray. This can affect your view, and your vision, if your visor becomes smeared or dirty. Drop back further until you can see better. If the conditions make it difficult for you to see or be seen, use dipped headlights. If visibility is reduced to less than 100 metres (328 feet), you may use fog lights (if fitted).

If your visor or goggles mist up, stop and clean them to make sure that your vision isn't restricted before continuing.

HC r226 **RES** s11, 12

If you're riding downhill and a large vehicle coming uphill needs to move out to pass a parked car, slow down and give way if possible. It's much more difficult for large vehicles to stop and then start up again if they're going uphill.

RES s8

Stay well back and give large vehicles plenty of room as they approach or negotiate

- road junctions
- crossroads
- mini-roundabouts.

To get around a corner, long vehicles may need to move in the opposite direction to the one they're indicating. If they want to turn left, they may indicate left but move over to the right before making the turn, and vice versa.

HC r221 **RES** s9

If you're waiting to turn left from a minor road and a large vehicle is approaching from the right, think. It may seem as if there's time to turn but there could be an overtaking vehicle hidden from view.

> Buses

Bus drivers need to make frequent stops to pick up and set down passengers. If a bus pulls up at a bus stop, watch out for pedestrians who may get off and cross the road in front of or behind the bus. Be prepared to give way to a bus that's trying to move off from a bus stop, as long as it's safe to do so.

HC r223 **RES** s10

> Trams

Some cities have trams. Take extra care around them because they

- are very quiet
- move quickly
- can't steer to avoid you.

HC r223–224 **RES** s7, 8

In these cities there may be extra white light signals at some traffic lights, which are for tram drivers. When you're riding in an area where trams run, take care when crossing tram tracks, particularly in bad weather, as they can become very slippery.

RES s7, 8

> Powered vehicles used by disabled people

Powered vehicles used by disabled people, such as wheelchairs and mobility scooters, have a maximum speed limit of 8 mph (12 km/h) when used on the road.

HC r36, 220

Meeting the standards

You must be able to

look out for other road users and predict what they may do

monitor and manage your own reactions to other road users.

You must know and understand

the rules that apply to other road users and the positions they may select on the road as a result. For example

- drivers of large vehicles
- bus and coach drivers
- cyclists
- car drivers

the importance of predicting the actions of other road users, especially as many motorcycle crashes involve claims of, 'I just didn't see you!' from others.

> Notes

You can use this page to make your own notes or diagrams about the key points you need to remember.

Think about

- What conditions could make you or another motorcyclist swerve unexpectedly?
- When do you need to give large vehicles plenty of space?
- What should you watch out for when a bus has stopped at the side of the road?
- What do you need to be aware of when riding in an area that has trams?

Your notes

_____

_____

_____

_____

_____

_____

_____

_____

_____

Things to discuss and practise with your trainer

These are just a few examples of what you could discuss and practise with your trainer. Read more about other types of vehicle to come up with your own ideas.

Discuss with your trainer

- how windy weather can affect the way that motorcyclists ride. What can you do to allow for this when you encounter another motorcyclist in these conditions?
- the maximum speed of powered wheelchairs and how you should behave when you need to overtake one
- how trams operate and what to look out for if you encounter a tram system.

Practise with your trainer

- how to behave when you're following a large vehicle, particularly at junctions and roundabouts
- overtaking large vehicles and noting how this differs from overtaking a car
- how to react to buses in a busy town centre.

You are riding behind a long vehicle. There is a mini-roundabout ahead. The vehicle is signalling left, but positioned to the right. You should

☐ sound your horn

☐ overtake on the left

☐ keep well back

☐ flash your headlights

The long vehicle needs more room than other vehicles in order to make the left turn. Don't overtake on the left – the driver will not expect you to be there and may not see you. Staying well back will also give you a better view around the vehicle.

Why should you be careful when riding on roads where electric trams operate?

☐ They cannot steer to avoid you

☐ They move quickly and quietly

☐ They are noisy and slow

☐ They can steer to avoid you

☐ They give off harmful exhaust fumes

Electric trams run on rails and cannot steer to avoid you. Keep a lookout for trams as they move very quietly and can appear suddenly.

You are about to overtake a slow-moving motorcyclist. Which one of these signs would make you take special care?

☐

☐

☐

☐

In windy weather, watch out for motorcyclists and also cyclists as they can be blown sideways into your path. When you pass them, leave plenty of room and check their position in your mirror before pulling back in.

You are waiting to emerge left from a minor road. A large vehicle is approaching from the right. You have time to turn, but you should wait. Why?

☐ The large vehicle can easily hide an overtaking vehicle

☐ The large vehicle can turn suddenly

☐ The large vehicle is difficult to steer in a straight line

☐ The large vehicle can easily hide vehicles from the left

Large vehicles can hide other vehicles that are overtaking, especially motorcycles which may be filtering past queuing traffic. You need to be aware of the possibility of hidden vehicles and not assume that it is safe to emerge.

You are following a long vehicle. It approaches a crossroads and signals left, but moves out to the right. You should

A lorry may swing out to the right as it approaches a left turn. This is to allow the rear wheels to clear the kerb as it turns. Don't try to filter through if you see a gap on the nearside.

☐ get closer in order to pass it quickly

☐ stay well back and give it room

☐ assume the signal is wrong and it is really turning right

☐ overtake as it starts to slow down

You are following a long vehicle approaching a crossroads. The driver signals right but moves close to the left-hand kerb. What should you do?

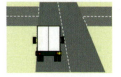

When a long vehicle is going to turn right it may need to keep close to the left-hand kerb. This is to prevent the rear end of the trailer cutting the corner. You need to be aware of how long vehicles behave in such situations. Don't overtake the lorry because it could turn as you're alongside. Stay behind and wait for it to turn.

☐ Warn the driver of the wrong signal

☐ Wait behind the long vehicle

☐ Report the driver to the police

☐ Overtake on the right-hand side

You are approaching a mini-roundabout. The long vehicle in front is signalling left but positioned over to the right. You should

At mini-roundabouts there isn't much room for a long vehicle to manoeuvre. It will have to swing out wide so that it can complete the turn safely. Keep well back and don't try to move up alongside it.

☐ sound your horn

☐ overtake on the left

☐ follow the same course as the lorry

☐ keep well back

7.8

Mark one answer | RES s10, HC r164, 222

Before overtaking a large vehicle you should keep well back. Why is this?

☐ To give acceleration space to overtake quickly on blind bends

☐ To get the best view of the road ahead

☐ To leave a gap in case the vehicle stops and rolls back

☐ To offer other drivers a safe gap if they want to overtake you

When following a large vehicle keep well back. If you're too close you won't be able to see the road ahead and the driver of the long vehicle might not be able to see you in their mirrors.

7.9

Mark two answers | RES s10, HC r223

You are travelling behind a bus that pulls up at a bus stop. What should you do?

☐ Accelerate past the bus sounding your horn

☐ Watch carefully for pedestrians

☐ Be ready to give way to the bus

☐ Pull in closely behind the bus

There might be pedestrians crossing from in front of the bus. Look out for them if you intend to pass. Consider staying back and waiting.

How many people are waiting to get on the bus? Check the queue if you can. The bus might move off straight away if there is no one waiting to get on.

If a bus is signalling to pull out, give it priority as long as it is safe to do so.

You are following a large lorry on a wet road. Spray makes it difficult to see. You should

☐ drop back until you can see better

☐ put your headlights on full beam

☐ keep close to the lorry, away from the spray

☐ speed up and overtake quickly

Large vehicles may throw up a lot of spray when the roads are wet. This will make it difficult for you to see ahead. Dropping back further will

- move you out of the spray and allow you to see further
- increase your separation distance. It takes longer to stop when the roads are wet and you need to allow more room.

Don't

- follow the vehicle in front too closely
- overtake, unless you can see and are sure that the way ahead is clear.

You keep well back while waiting to overtake a large vehicle. A car fills the gap. You should

☐ sound your horn

☐ drop back further

☐ flash your headlights

☐ start to overtake

It's very frustrating when your separation distance is shortened by another vehicle. React positively, stay calm and drop further back.

You are following a long lorry. The driver signals to turn left into a narrow road. What should you do?

☐ Overtake on the left before the lorry reaches the junction

☐ Overtake on the right as soon as the lorry slows down

☐ Do not overtake unless you can see there is no oncoming traffic

☐ Do not overtake, stay well back and be prepared to stop

When turning into narrow roads articulated and long vehicles will need more room. Initially they will need to swing out in the opposite direction to which they intend to turn. They could mask another vehicle turning out of the same junction. DON'T be tempted to overtake them or pass on the inside.

7.13

Mark one answer

RES s10, HC r223

When you approach a bus signalling to move off from a bus stop you should

☐ get past before it moves

☐ allow it to pull away, if it is safe to do so

☐ flash your headlights as you approach

☐ signal left and wave the bus on

Try to give way to buses if you can do so safely, especially when they signal to pull away from bus stops. Look out for people who've stepped off the bus or are running to catch it, and may try to cross the road without looking. Don't try to accelerate past before it moves away or flash your lights as other road users may be misled by this signal.

7.14

Mark one answer

RES s10, HC r164

You wish to overtake a long, slow-moving vehicle on a busy road. You should

☐ follow it closely and keep moving out to see the road ahead

☐ flash your headlights for the oncoming traffic to give way

☐ stay behind until the driver waves you past

☐ keep well back until you can see that it is clear

If you want to overtake a long vehicle, stay well back so that you can get a better view of the road ahead. The closer you get the less you will be able to see of the road ahead. Be patient, overtaking calls for sound judgement. DON'T take a gamble, only overtake when you are certain that you can complete the manoeuvre safely.

7.15

Mark one answer

RES s12, HC r232–233

Which of these is LEAST likely to be affected by crosswinds?

☐ Cyclists

☐ Motorcyclists

☐ High-sided vehicles

☐ Cars

Although cars are the least likely to be affected, crosswinds can take anyone by surprise. This is most likely to happen after overtaking a large vehicle, when passing gaps between hedges or buildings, and on exposed sections of road.

What should you do as you approach this lorry?

When turning, long vehicles need much more room on the road than other vehicles. At junctions they may take up the whole of the road space, so be patient and allow them the room they need.

- ☐ Slow down and be prepared to wait
- ☐ Make the lorry wait for you
- ☐ Flash your lights at the lorry
- ☐ Move to the right-hand side of the road

You are following a large vehicle approaching crossroads. The driver signals to turn left. What should you do?

- ☐ Overtake if you can leave plenty of room
- ☐ Overtake only if there are no oncoming vehicles
- ☐ Do not overtake until the vehicle begins to turn
- ☐ Do not overtake when at or approaching a junction

Hold back and wait until the vehicle has turned before proceeding. Do not overtake because the vehicle turning left could hide a vehicle emerging from the same junction.

Powered vehicles, such as wheelchairs or scooters, used by disabled people have a maximum speed of

- ☐ 8 mph
- ☐ 12 mph
- ☐ 16 mph
- ☐ 20 mph

These are small battery powered vehicles and include wheelchairs and mobility scooters. Some are designed for use on the pavement only and have an upper speed limit of 4 mph (6 km/h). Others can go on the road as well and have a speed limit of 8 mph (12 km/h). They are now very common and are generally used by the elderly, disabled or infirm. Take great care as they are extremely vulnerable because of their low speed and small size.

Why is it more difficult to overtake a large vehicle than a car?

☐ It takes longer to pass one

☐ They may suddenly pull up

☐ Their brakes are not as good

☐ They climb hills more slowly

Depending on relevant speed, it will usually take you longer to pass a lorry than other vehicles. Some hazards to watch for include oncoming traffic, junctions ahead, bends or dips which could restrict your view, and signs or road markings that prohibit overtaking. Make sure you can see that it's safe to complete the manoeuvre before you start to overtake.

Case study practice – 7
Other types of vehicle

Susan travels to work in the town centre on her motorcycle. It's a dull, wet day.

There are many trams and tramlines in the town area, and a bus is indicating to pull out from a bus stop.

At one junction, Susan has to cross the tramlines.

On the main high street, there are specifically shaped signs for trams.

Ahead, Susan sees a large vehicle indicating to turn left.

7.1 How can Susan improve her visibility in this weather?
Mark **one** answer

☐ By using main beam headlights
☐ By using hazard warning lights
☐ By using dipped headlights
☐ By using front and rear fog lights

HC r86 **RES** s4

7.2 How should Susan react to the bus?
Mark **one** answer

☐ Rev the engine and sound the horn
☐ Keep going past but slow down a little
☐ Speed up quickly to get past the bus
☐ Allow it to pull out if it's safe to do so

HC r223

7.3 Why should Susan take care when crossing the tramlines?

Mark **one** answer

- ☐ The tyres could get stuck between the tracks
- ☐ The lines could be very slippery in wet weather
- ☐ The motorcycle's tyres could stick to the metal
- ☐ The gaps in the lines could be full of water

HC r306 **RES** s8

7.4 What shape forms the tram signs that Susan sees?

Mark **one** answer

- ☐ Triangle
- ☐ Diamond
- ☐ Hexagon
- ☐ Rectangle

KYTS p31

7.5 What might this large vehicle do next?

Mark **one** answer

- ☐ Pull a little over to the right
- ☐ Use the horn to warn others
- ☐ Pull a little over to the left
- ☐ Run over the pavement area

HC r170, 221 **RES** s9

> **Section eight**

Road conditions and motorcycle handling

In this section, you'll learn about

- how to ride safely in different weather conditions
- riding at night
- keeping control of your motorcycle
- traffic-calming measures and different road surfaces.

Road conditions and motorcycle handling

As well as being aware of other road users, you need to think about the conditions you're riding in and how they might affect your safety. The weather, the time of day, hills, traffic calming and different road surfaces can all change the way you need to ride.

> Weather conditions

The weather makes a big difference to how you ride and how your motorcycle will handle.

Rain and wet conditions

When it's raining or the road is wet, leave at least double the normal stopping distance between you and the vehicle in front. If you're following a vehicle at a safe distance and another vehicle pulls into the gap you've left, drop back until you're at a safe distance again. See section 4, Safety margins, for more information on stopping distances.

If visibility becomes seriously reduced you **MUST** use dipped headlights. 'Seriously reduced' means you can't see for more than about 100 metres (328 feet).

`HC` `r226` `RES` `s12`

When there's been heavy rainfall, a ford is likely to flood and become difficult to cross. There may be a depth gauge to help you decide whether you should go through. If you decide to cross it,

- use a low gear
- ride through slowly
- test your brakes afterwards: wet brakes are less effective.

`HC` `r121` `RES` `s12`

Fog

When visibility is seriously reduced, you **MUST** use headlights and you may also use fog lights if you have them.

Remember to switch off your fog lights when conditions improve. Never use front or rear fog lights unless visibility is seriously reduced because

- they can dazzle other road users
- road users behind you won't be able to see your brake lights clearly
- road users behind you may mistake your fog lights for brake lights and slow unnecessarily
- road users behind you may mistake your brake lights for fog lights and not react in time to stop safely.

It's hard to see what's happening ahead in foggy weather, so always keep your speed down. Increase your distance from the vehicle in front in case it stops or slows suddenly.

HC r114, 226 **RES** s11, 12

Always allow more time for your journey in bad weather.

When riding on motorways in fog, reflective studs help you to see the road ahead.

- Red studs mark the left-hand edge of the carriageway.
- Amber studs mark the central reservation.

For more details, see section 9, Motorway riding.

HC r132 **RES** s7, 11

If you're parking on the road in foggy conditions, leave the parking lights switched on.

Very bad weather

In very bad weather, such as heavy snow or thick fog, don't travel unless your journey is essential. If you must travel, take great care and allow plenty of time.

Before you start your journey, make sure

- your lights are working
- your screen (if fitted) and visor are clean.

HC r228–235 **RES** s11, 12

When you're on the road, keep well back from the vehicle in front in case it stops suddenly. In icy conditions your stopping distance can be 10 times what it would be in dry conditions.

 **TIP** If the road looks wet and your tyres are making hardly any noise, you could be on black ice. Keep your speed down and use the highest gear possible to reduce the risk of skidding.

 See this website for advice on riding in extreme weather conditions.

> **bikesafe.co.uk/Advice-Centre/ Article/Winter-Riding.aspx**

Windy weather

Windy weather can affect all vehicles, but high-sided vehicles, cyclists, motorcyclists and cars towing caravans are likely to be the worst affected. A sudden gust may catch your motorcycle when you're

- passing a large vehicle on a dual carriageway or motorway
- riding on an exposed stretch of road
- passing gaps between buildings or hedges.

Look out for other vehicles that may also be affected by the wind and make allowances for them.

HC r232 **RES** s11, 12

> Riding at night

When you're riding at night, you need to think about how clearly you can see and be seen, as well as how your lights might affect other road users.

Make sure that your headlights don't dazzle the vehicle you're following or any oncoming traffic. If you're dazzled by the headlights of an oncoming vehicle, slow down or stop if necessary.

HC r114–115 **RES** s13

If you meet other road users at night, including cyclists and pedestrians, dip your headlights so that you don't dazzle them.

When you overtake at night, you can't see a long way ahead and there may be bends in the road or other unseen hazards.

On a motorway, use

- dipped headlights, even if the road is well lit
- sidelights if you've broken down and are parked on the hard shoulder. This will help other road users to see you.

RES s11, 12, 13

> Keeping control of your motorcycle

For safety, before starting your engine, push the motorcycle forward to check that the rear wheel turns freely: this shows that the gear selector is in neutral. Check that the neutral light on your instrument panel is showing too.

Apply the front brake before you get on the motorcycle. If you're parked on a two-way road, you should get on from the left.

When you're astride your motorcycle, you should be able to put both feet on the ground comfortably, to support yourself and your machine. Never ride with the side stand in the down position – this can be dangerous, especially when cornering. Always fold the stand away safely before setting off.

Once you're moving, the normal riding position should be about central in the lane you're using. Try not to look down at the front wheel as this can affect your balance.

RES s6

You need to have full control of your motorcycle at all times. Riding with the clutch disengaged or in neutral for any length of time (called coasting) reduces your control of the motorcycle, especially steering and braking. This is particularly dangerous when you're travelling downhill, as your motorcycle will speed up when there's no **engine braking**.

HC r122 **RES** s6, 8

Definition

engine braking
using the engine's resistance to help slow the vehicle

You can use your motorcycle's engine to help control your speed: for example, if you select a lower gear when you're riding down a steep hill, the engine will act as a brake. This helps avoid your brakes overheating and becoming less effective.

When you're riding up a steep hill, the engine has to work harder. If you close the throttle to reduce speed, you'll slow down sooner than usual. Changing down to a lower gear will help prevent the engine struggling as it delivers the power needed to climb the hill.

RES s8

On single-track roads, be aware of the limited space available. If you see a vehicle coming towards you, pull into (or opposite) a passing place.

HC r155

See the Don't Risk It website for advice on riding on country roads.

▶ **dontriskit.info/country-roads/ cinema-adverts/#3**

Always match your riding to the road and weather conditions. Your stopping distance will be affected by several factors, including

- your speed
- the condition of your tyres
- the road surface
- the weather.

HC r155 **RES** s8, 10

When riding normally, you should brake when the motorcycle is upright and moving in a straight line. Apply both brakes smoothly, the front brake just before the rear brake. If your motorcycle has linked brakes, check the motorcycle handbook for more details.

When stopping in an emergency, or on a wet road, there's an increased risk of skidding. Try to avoid braking so hard that you cause a skid as it can be hard to get your motorcycle back under control once you've started skidding.

The main causes of a motorcycle skidding are

- changing direction suddenly or travelling too fast
- too much acceleration
- heavy or sharp braking
- any combination of the above.

If you don't have anti-lock brakes and your motorcycle begins to skid when you're braking on a wet road,

- release the brake(s) causing the skid to allow the wheel(s) to turn
- re-apply the brakes, but avoid braking so hard that you skid again.

HC r119 **RES** s6, 8, 10

> Traffic calming and road surfaces

Traffic calming is used to slow traffic and make the roads safer for vulnerable road users, especially pedestrians. One of the most common measures is road humps (sometimes called speed humps). Make sure that you stay within the speed limit and don't overtake other moving vehicles within traffic-calmed areas.

HC r153 **RES** s7

Rumble devices (raised markings across the road) may be used to warn you of a hazard, such as a roundabout, and to encourage you to reduce your speed.

KYTS p68, 75

In cities where trams operate, the areas used by the trams may have a different surface texture or colour, which may be edged with white line markings.

HC r300 **KYTS** p31

If it rains after a long dry hot spell, the road surface can become unusually slippery. Loose chippings can also increase the risk of skidding, so slow down and be aware of the increased skid risk in these conditions.

HC r237 **RES** s12

Painted road markings, tar banding, tram rails and drain covers can all become very slippery in wet weather. Keep your motorcycle upright and avoid braking while riding over them. If this isn't possible, take great care as your tyres have very little grip on these surfaces.

Spilt diesel fuel is very slippery. It spills from overfilled fuel tanks and poorly fitting or missing filler caps. It's often found near filling stations, at roundabouts and on bends. If you see a rainbow pattern on the road surface, slow down in good time and avoid the area if possible.

HC r213, 306 **RES** s8, 12

Some motorcycles are fitted with traction control systems (TCS), which help to prevent the rear wheel spinning while accelerating. Slippery surfaces increase the risk of this happening.

Meeting the standards

You must be able to

use the throttle smoothly to reach and keep to a suitable speed

change gear smoothly and in good time

coordinate

- steering
- leaning
- the use of the brakes
- the use of the throttle

steer the machine safely and responsibly in all road and traffic conditions.

You must know and understand

why it's best not to over-rev your engine when moving away and while stationary

the benefits of changing gear at the right time when going up and down hills

that different machines may have different numbers of gears with different ratios

how to change the direction of the machine by coordinating

- throttle
- lean
- steering input.

> Notes

You can use this page to make your own notes or diagrams about the key points you need to remember.

Think about

- By how much must visibility be reduced before you can use fog lights?
- Why must you make sure that your fog lights are turned off when visibility improves again?
- In which weather conditions should you increase the distance between your motorcycle and the one in front?
- Which road users are most likely to be affected by very windy weather?
- When can you use engine braking, and why is it a good idea?
- What are rumble devices used for?

Your notes

Things to discuss and practise with your trainer

These are just a few examples of what you could discuss and practise with your trainer. Read more about motorcycle handling to come up with your own ideas.

Discuss with your trainer

- your stopping distances in different weather conditions
- how to use your front and back brakes in different situations and weather conditions
- what you should do if you get a sudden puncture.

Practise with your trainer

- positioning your motorcycle correctly in various situations, eg when turning right or left, and riding straight ahead
- going out at night to get used to riding with reduced visibility
- your gear selection and clutch control while riding downhill.

As a safety measure before starting your engine, you should

☐ push the motorcycle forward to check the rear wheel turns freely

☐ engage first gear and apply the rear brake

☐ engage first gear and apply the front brake

☐ glance at the neutral light on your instrument panel

Before starting the engine you should ensure the motorcycle is in neutral. This can be done by, moving the motorcycle to check that the rear wheel turns freely and making sure the neutral warning light is lit when the ignition is turned on.

You are approaching this junction. As the motorcyclist you should

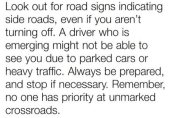

Look out for road signs indicating side roads, even if you aren't turning off. A driver who is emerging might not be able to see you due to parked cars or heavy traffic. Always be prepared, and stop if necessary. Remember, no one has priority at unmarked crossroads.

☐ prepare to slow down

☐ sound your horn

☐ keep near the left kerb

☐ speed up to clear the junction

☐ stop, as the car has right of way

What can you do to improve your safety on the road as a motorcyclist?

☐ Anticipate the actions of others

☐ Stay just above the speed limits

☐ Keep positioned close to the kerbs

☐ Remain well below speed limits

Always ride defensively. This means looking and planning ahead as well as anticipating the actions of other road users.

8.4

Which THREE of these can cause skidding?

☐ Braking too gently

☐ Leaning too far over when cornering

☐ Staying upright when cornering

☐ Braking too hard

☐ Changing direction suddenly

In order to keep control of your motorcycle and prevent skidding you must plan well ahead to prevent harsh, late braking. Try to avoid braking while changing direction, as this reduces the tyres' grip on the road. Take the road and weather conditions into consideration and adjust your speed if necessary.

8.5

It is very cold and the road looks wet. You cannot hear any road noise. You should

☐ continue riding at the same speed

☐ ride slower in as high a gear as possible

☐ ride in as low a gear as possible

☐ keep revving your engine

☐ slow down as there may be black ice

Rain freezing on roads is called black ice. It can be hard to see. Indications of black ice are when you can't hear tyre noise and the steering becomes very light. You need to keep your speed down and avoid harsh steering, braking and acceleration. Riding in as high a gear as possible will help to reduce the risk of wheel-spin.

8.6

When riding a motorcycle you should wear full protective clothing

☐ at all times

☐ only on faster, open roads

☐ just on long journeys

☐ only during bad weather

Protective clothing is designed to protect you from the cold and wet and also gives some protection from injury.

8.7

You have to make a journey in fog. What are the TWO most important things you should do before you set out?

☐ Fill up with fuel

☐ Make sure that you have a warm drink with you

☐ Check that your lights are working

☐ Check the battery

☐ Make sure that your visor is clean

When you're riding a motorcycle, keep your visor as clean as possible to give you a clear view of the road. It's a good idea to carry a clean, damp cloth in a polythene bag for this purpose.

You need to ensure that your lights are clean and can be seen clearly by other road users. This is especially important when visibility is reduced, for example in fog or heavy rain.

Mark one answer

The best place to park your motorcycle is

☐ on soft tarmac

☐ on bumpy ground

☐ on grass

☐ on firm, level ground

Parking your motorcycle on soft ground might cause the stand to sink and the bike to fall over. The ground should also be level to ensure that the bike is stable. Where off-road parking or motorcycle parking areas are available, use them.

Mark one answer

When riding in windy conditions, you should

☐ stay close to large vehicles

☐ keep your speed up

☐ keep your speed down

☐ stay close to the gutter

Strong winds can blow motorcycles off course and even across the road. In windy conditions you need to, slow down, avoid riding on exposed roads and watch for gaps in buildings and hedges where you may be affected by a sudden blast of wind.

Mark one answer

In normal riding your position on the road should be

☐ about a foot from the kerb

☐ about central in your lane

☐ on the right of your lane

☐ near the centre of the road

If you're riding a motorcycle it's very important to ride where other road users can see you. In normal weather you should ride in the centre of your lane. This will help you to avoid uneven road surfaces in the gutter and allow others to overtake on the right if they wish.

Mark one answer

Your motorcycle is parked on a two-way road. You should get on from the

☐ right and apply the rear brake

☐ left and leave the brakes alone

☐ left and apply the front brake

☐ right and leave the brakes alone

When you get onto a motorcycle you should get on from the left side to avoid putting yourself in danger from passing traffic. Also apply the front brake to prevent the motorcycle rolling either forwards or backwards.

8.12 — Mark one answer — RES s2

To gain basic skills in how to ride a motorcycle you should

- ☐ practise off-road with an approved training body
- ☐ ride on the road on the first dry day
- ☐ practise off-road in a public park or in a quiet cul-de-sac
- ☐ ride on the road as soon as possible

All new motorcyclists must complete a course of basic training with an approved training body before going on the road. This training is given on a site which has been authorised by the Driving Standards Agency as being suitable for off-road training.

8.13 — Mark one answer — RES s6

You should not ride with your clutch lever pulled in for longer than necessary because it

- ☐ increases wear on the gearbox
- ☐ increases petrol consumption
- ☐ reduces your control of the motorcycle
- ☐ reduces the grip of the tyres

Riding with the clutch lever pulled in is known as coasting. It gives you less steering control, reduces traction, and can cause you to pick up speed. When you're travelling downhill your motorcycle will pick up speed quickly. If you are coasting the engine won't be able to assist the braking.

8.14 — Mark one answer — RES s8

You are approaching a road with a surface of loose chippings. What should you do?

- ☐ Ride normally
- ☐ Speed up
- ☐ Slow down
- ☐ Stop suddenly

The handling of your motorcycle will be greatly affected by the road surface. Look well ahead and be especially alert if the road looks uneven or has loose chippings. Slow down in good time as braking harshly in these conditions will cause you to skid. Avoid making sudden changes of direction for the same reason.

8.15 — Mark three answers — RES s8

The main causes of a motorcycle skidding are

- ☐ heavy and sharp braking
- ☐ excessive acceleration
- ☐ leaning too far when cornering
- ☐ riding in wet weather
- ☐ riding in the winter

Skids are a lot easier to get into than they are to get out of.

Riding at a speed that suits the conditions, looking ahead for hazards and braking in good time will all help you to avoid skidding or losing control of your vehicle.

To stop your motorcycle quickly in an emergency you should apply

☐ the rear brake only

☐ the front brake only

☐ the front brake just before the rear

☐ the rear brake just before the front

You should plan ahead to avoid the need to stop suddenly. But if an emergency should arise you must be able to stop safely. Applying the correct amount of braking effort to each wheel will help you to stop safely and in control.

You leave the choke on for too long. This causes the engine to run too fast. When is this likely to make your motorcycle most difficult to control?

☐ Accelerating

☐ Going uphill

☐ Slowing down

☐ On motorways

Forgetting to switch the choke off will cause the engine to run too fast. This makes it difficult to control the motorcycle, especially when slowing down, for example when approaching junctions and bends.

You should NOT look down at the front wheel when riding because it can

☐ make your steering lighter

☐ improve your balance

☐ use less fuel

☐ upset your balance

When riding look ahead and around you, but don't look down at the front wheel as this can severely upset your balance.

8.19
Mark one answer
RES s6

In normal riding conditions you should brake

☐ by using the rear brake first and then the front

☐ when the motorcycle is being turned or ridden through a bend

☐ by pulling in the clutch before using the front brake

☐ when the motorcycle is upright and moving in a straight line

A motorcycle is most stable when it's upright and moving in a straight line. This is the best time to brake. Normally both brakes should be used, with the front brake being applied just before the rear.

8.20
Mark three answers
RES s8, HC r126

Which THREE of the following will affect your stopping distance?

☐ How fast you are going

☐ The tyres on your motorcycle

☐ The time of day

☐ The weather

☐ The street lighting

There are several factors that can affect the distance it takes to stop your motorcycle. In wet weather you should double the separation distance from the vehicle in front. Your tyres will have less grip on the road and you therefore need to allow more time to stop. Always ride in accordance with the conditions.

8.21
Mark one answer
RES s11

You are on a motorway at night. You MUST have your headlights switched on unless

☐ there are vehicles close in front of you

☐ you are travelling below 50 mph

☐ the motorway is lit

☐ your motorcycle is broken down on the hard shoulder

Always use your headlights at night on a motorway unless you have stopped on the hard shoulder. If you have to use the hard shoulder, switch off the headlights but leave the parking lights on so that other road users can see your motorcycle.

8.22
Mark one answer
RES s12

You have to park on the road in fog. You should

☐ leave parking lights on

☐ leave no lights on

☐ leave dipped headlights on

☐ leave main beam headlights on

If you have to park on the road in foggy conditions it's important that your motorcycle can be seen by other road users. Try to find a place to park off the road. If this isn't possible leave your motorcycle facing in the same direction as the traffic. Make sure that your lights are clean and that you leave your parking lights on.

Mark one answer

You ride over broken glass and get a sudden puncture. What should you do?

☐ Close the throttle and roll to a stop

☐ Brake to a stop as quickly as possible

☐ Release your grip on the handlebars

☐ Steer from side to side to keep your balance

Your motorcycle will be very unstable if a tyre bursts. Try to keep a straight course and stop as gently as possible.

Mark one answer

Spilt fuel on the road can be very dangerous for you as a motorcyclist. How can this hazard be seen?

☐ By a rainbow pattern on the surface

☐ By a series of skid marks

☐ By a pitted road surface

☐ By a highly polished surface

This rainbow-coloured pattern can be seen much more easily on a wet road. You should avoid riding over these areas if possible. If you have to go over them do so with extreme caution.

Mark one answer

You leave the choke on for too long. This could make the engine run faster than normal. This will make your motorcycle

Leaving the choke on for longer than necessary will usually make the engine run too fast. This can lead to loss of control, which is especially dangerous when approaching junctions and bends in the road and whenever you need to slow down.

☐ handle much better

☐ corner much safer

☐ stop much more quickly

☐ more difficult to control

8.26   Mark four answers   RES s8

Which FOUR types of road surface increase the risk of skidding for motorcyclists?

☐ White lines

☐ Dry tarmac

☐ Tar banding

☐ Yellow grid lines

☐ Loose chippings

When riding it's important to look out for slippery surfaces. These include, potholes, drain covers (especially in the wet), oily and greasy surfaces, road markings, tram tracks, wet mud and leaves. You will then have more time to brake or change course if you need to.

8.27   Mark one answer   RES s12

You are riding on a wet road. When braking you should

☐ apply the rear brake well before the front

☐ apply the front brake just before the rear

☐ avoid using the front brake at all

☐ avoid using the rear brake at all

On wet roads you will need to be especially careful: brake earlier and more smoothly. Always try to brake when the motorcycle is upright. This is particularly important in wet conditions.

8.28   Mark one answer   RES s8

The road is wet. You are passing a line of queuing traffic and riding on the painted road markings. You should take extra care, particularly when

☐ signalling

☐ braking

☐ carrying a passenger

☐ checking your mirrors

Take extra care when braking or cornering on wet roads and try to avoid slippery objects, such as drain covers and painted road markings.

8.29   Mark one answer   RES s8

You are going ahead and will have to cross tram lines. Why should you be especially careful?

☐ Tram lines are always 'live'

☐ Trams will be stopping here

☐ Pedestrians will be crossing here

☐ The steel rails can be slippery

These rails can affect your steering and be a hazard when braking. The smooth surface of the rails makes them slippery and dangerous for motorcyclists, especially when wet. Try to cross them at right angles.

Mark one answer

You have to brake sharply and your motorcycle starts to skid. You should

☐ continue braking and select a low gear

☐ apply the brakes harder for better grip

☐ select neutral and use the front brake only

☐ release the brakes and reapply

If you skid as a result of braking harshly you need to ease off the brakes to stop the skid. Then reapply them progressively to stop.

Mark one answer

You see a rainbow-coloured pattern across the road. What will this warn you of?

☐ A soft uneven road surface

☐ A polished road surface

☐ Fuel spilt on the road

☐ Water on the road

If fuel, especially diesel, is spilt on the road it will make the surface very slippery. In wet weather this can be seen as a rainbow-coloured pattern on the road.

Mark one answer

Traction Control Systems (TCS) are fitted to some motorcycles. What does this help to prevent?

☐ Wheelspin when accelerating

☐ Skidding when braking too hard

☐ Uneven front tyre wear

☐ Uneven rear tyre wear

Traction Control Systems (TCS) help to prevent the rear wheel from spinning, especially when accelerating on a slippery surface.

Mark one answer

Braking too hard has caused both wheels to skid. What should you do?

☐ Release both brakes together

☐ Release the front then the rear brake

☐ Release the front brake only

☐ Release the rear brake only

Braking too hard will cause a skid. Release the brakes immediately to allow the wheels to turn, then reapply them as firmly as the road surface and conditions will allow.

8.34 — Mark one answer — RES s5

Your motorcycle does NOT have linked brakes. What should you do when braking to a normal stop?

☐ Only apply the front brake

☐ Rely just on the rear brake

☐ Apply both brakes smoothly

☐ Apply either of the brakes gently

In normal riding you should always use both brakes. Braking when the motorcycle is upright and travelling in a straight line helps you to keep control. If your motorcycle has linked brakes refer to the owner's manual.

8.35 — Mark one answer — RES s6

You are sitting on a stationary motorcycle and checking your riding position. You should be able to

☐ just touch the ground with your toes

☐ place both feet on the ground

☐ operate the centre stand

☐ adjust your mirrors by stretching

When sitting astride a stationary motorcycle you should be able to place both feet on the ground to support yourself and your machine.

8.36 — Mark one answer — RES s12, HC r237

It has rained after a long dry spell. You should be very careful because the road surface will be unusually

☐ rough

☐ dry

☐ sticky

☐ slippery

During a long hot, dry spell the road surface will become coated with rubber and dust. When it rains after this the road surface will be unusually slippery. Take extra care, particularly at junctions, bends and roundabouts, and allow double the usual stopping distance.

Riding with the side stand down could cause you to crash. This is most likely to happen when

☐ going uphill

☐ accelerating

☐ braking

☐ cornering

Cornering with the side stand down could lead to a serious crash. Most motorcycles have a device that stops the engine if you try to ride off with the side stand down, but don't rely on this.

You are entering a bend. Your side stand is not fully raised. This could

☐ cause you to crash

☐ improve your balance

☐ alter the motorcycle's centre of gravity

☐ make the motorcycle more stable

If the stand isn't fully up it could dig into the road and cause a serious crash. Always check that it is fully raised before moving off. Most side stands have a safety device or cut-out switch, but do NOT rely on this. CHECK FOR YOURSELF!

In which THREE of these situations may you overtake another vehicle on the left?

☐ When you are in a one-way street

☐ When approaching a motorway slip road where you will be turning off

☐ When the vehicle in front is signalling to turn right

☐ When a slower vehicle is travelling in the right-hand lane of a dual carriageway

☐ In slow-moving traffic queues when traffic in the right-hand lane is moving more slowly

At certain times of the day, traffic might be heavy. If traffic is moving slowly in queues and vehicles in the right-hand lane are moving more slowly, you may overtake on the left. Don't keep changing lanes to try and beat the queue.

8.40 — Mark one answer — RES s12, HC r227

You are travelling in very heavy rain. Your overall stopping distance is likely to be

☐ doubled

☐ halved

☐ up to ten times greater

☐ no different

As well as visibility being reduced, the road will be extremely wet. This will reduce the grip the tyres have on the road and increase the distance it takes to stop. Double your separation distance.

8.41 — Mark two answers — RES s13

Which TWO of the following are correct? When overtaking at night you should

☐ wait until a bend so that you can see the oncoming headlights

☐ sound your horn twice before moving out

☐ be careful because you can see less

☐ beware of bends in the road ahead

☐ put headlights on full beam

Only overtake the vehicle in front if it's really necessary. At night the risks are increased due to the poor visibility. Don't overtake if there's a possibility of

- road junctions
- bends ahead
- the brow of a bridge or hill, except on a dual carriageway
- pedestrian crossings
- double white lines ahead
- vehicles changing direction
- any other potential hazard.

8.42 — Mark one answer — RES s7, HC r174, KYTS p67

When may you wait in a box junction?

☐ When you are stationary in a queue of traffic

☐ When approaching a pelican crossing

☐ When approaching a zebra crossing

☐ When oncoming traffic prevents you turning right

The purpose of a box junction is to keep the junction clear by preventing vehicles from stopping in the path of crossing traffic.

You must not enter a box junction unless your exit is clear. But, you may enter the box and wait if you want to turn right and are only prevented from doing so by oncoming traffic.

Which of these plates normally appear with this road sign?

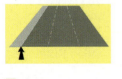

☐ **Humps for ½ mile**

☐ **Hump Bridge**

☐ **Low Bridge**

☐ **Soft Verge**

Road humps are used to slow down the traffic. They are found in places where there are often pedestrians, such as

- in shopping areas
- near schools
- in residential areas.

Watch out for people close to the kerb or crossing the road.

Traffic calming measures are used to

☐ stop road rage

☐ help overtaking

☐ slow traffic down

☐ help parking

Traffic calming measures are used to make the roads safer for vulnerable road users, such as cyclists, pedestrians and children. These can be designed as chicanes, road humps or other obstacles that encourage drivers and riders to slow down.

You are on a motorway in fog. The left-hand edge of the motorway can be identified by reflective studs. What colour are they?

☐ Green

☐ Amber

☐ Red

☐ White

Be especially careful if you're on a motorway in fog. Reflective studs are used to help you in poor visibility. Different colours are used so that you'll know which lane you are in. These are

- red on the left-hand side of the road
- white between lanes
- amber on the right-hand edge of the carriageway
- green between the carriageway and slip roads.

8.46
Mark two answers   **KYTS p75**

A rumble device is designed to

- [ ] give directions
- [ ] prevent cattle escaping
- [ ] alert you to low tyre pressure
- [ ] alert you to a hazard
- [ ] encourage you to reduce speed

A rumble device usually consists of raised markings or strips across the road. It gives an audible, visual and tactile warning of a hazard. These strips are found in places where traffic has constantly ignored warning or restriction signs. They are there for a good reason. Slow down and be ready to deal with a hazard.

8.47
Mark one answer   **RES s12**

You have to make a journey in foggy conditions. You should

- [ ] follow other vehicles' tail lights closely
- [ ] avoid using dipped headlights
- [ ] leave plenty of time for your journey
- [ ] keep two seconds behind other vehicles

If you're planning to make a journey when it's foggy, listen to the weather reports on the radio or television. Don't travel if visibility is very poor or your trip isn't necessary.

If you do travel, leave plenty of time for your journey. If someone is expecting you at the other end, let them know that you'll be taking longer than normal to arrive.

8.48
Mark one answer   **RES s13, HC r114–115**

You are overtaking a car at night. You must be sure that

- [ ] you flash your headlights before overtaking
- [ ] you select a higher gear
- [ ] you have switched your lights to full beam before overtaking
- [ ] you do not dazzle other road users

To prevent your lights from dazzling the driver of the car in front, wait until you've overtaken before switching to full beam.

You are on a road which has speed humps. A driver in front is travelling slower than you. You should

☐ sound your horn

☐ overtake as soon as you can

☐ flash your headlights

☐ slow down and stay behind

Be patient and stay behind the car in front. Normally you should not overtake other vehicles in traffic-calmed areas. If you overtake here your speed may exceed that which is safe along that road, defeating the purpose of the traffic calming measures.

You see these markings on the road. Why are they there?

☐ To show a safe distance between vehicles

☐ To keep the area clear of traffic

☐ To make you aware of your speed

☐ To warn you to change direction

These lines may be painted on the road on the approach to a roundabout, village or a particular hazard. The lines are raised and painted yellow and their purpose is to make you aware of your speed. Reduce your speed in good time so that you avoid having to brake harshly over the last few metres before reaching the junction.

Areas reserved for trams may have

☐ metal studs around them

☐ white line markings

☐ zigzag markings

☐ a different coloured surface

☐ yellow hatch markings

☐ a different surface texture

Trams can run on roads used by other vehicles and pedestrians. The part of the road used by the trams is known as the reserved area and this should be kept clear. It has a coloured surface and is usually edged with white road markings. It might also have different surface texture.

You see a vehicle coming towards you on a single-track road. You should

☐ go back to the main road

☐ do an emergency stop

☐ stop at a passing place

☐ put on your hazard warning lights

You must take extra care when on single track roads. You may not be able to see around bends due to high hedges or fences. Proceed with caution and expect to meet oncoming vehicles around the next bend. If you do, pull into or opposite a passing place.

8.53
Mark one answer
RES s8, HC r213

The road is wet. Why might a motorcyclist steer round drain covers on a bend?

☐ To avoid puncturing the tyres on the edge of the drain covers

☐ To prevent the motorcycle sliding on the metal drain covers

☐ To help judge the bend using the drain covers as marker points

☐ To avoid splashing pedestrians on the pavement

Other drivers or riders may have to change course due to the size or characteristics of their vehicle. Understanding this will help you to anticipate their actions. Motorcyclists and cyclists will be checking the road ahead for uneven or slippery surfaces, especially in wet weather. They may need to move across their lane to avoid surface hazards such as potholes and drain covers.

8.54
Mark one answer
RES s12, HC r121

After this hazard you should test your brakes. Why is this?

A ford is a crossing over a stream that's shallow enough to go through. After you've gone through a ford or deep puddle the water will affect your brakes. To dry them out apply a light brake pressure while moving slowly. Don't travel at normal speeds until you are sure your brakes are working properly again.

☐ You will be on a slippery road

☐ Your brakes will be soaking wet

☐ You will be going down a long hill

☐ You will have just crossed a long bridge

8.55
Mark one answer
RES s12, HC r234

Why should you always reduce your speed when travelling in fog?

☐ The brakes do not work as well

☐ You will be dazzled by other headlights

☐ The engine will take longer to warm up

☐ It is more difficult to see events ahead

You won't be able to see as far ahead in fog as you can on a clear day. You will need to reduce your speed so that, if a hazard looms out of the fog, you have the time and space to take avoiding action.

Travelling in fog is hazardous. If you can, try and delay your journey until it has cleared.

> Case study practice – 8 Road conditions and motorcycle handling

You're carrying a pillion passenger on your motorcycle.

You buy fuel at the service station, then make various checks, including on tyre pressures.

You want to turn left on leaving the forecourt. There are parked cars obscuring your view.

On the main road, you leave a larger gap between you and the vehicle in front.

8.1 How can the passenger affect the way you ride?

Mark **one** answer

- ☐ The extra weight can affect your balance
- ☐ Your stopping distance would be shorter
- ☐ It would be easier for you to accelerate
- ☐ A passenger can help with observation

RES s14

8.2 Other than tyre pressures, what else might need adjusting under these circumstances?

Mark **one** answer

- ☐ Brakes
- ☐ Headlights
- ☐ Handlebars
- ☐ Seating

RES s14

8.3 What should you do about your obstructed view at the junction?

Mark **one** answer

☐ Stop and wait until some of the parked cars move away

☐ Stop and get off, then wheel the motorcycle into the road

☐ Stop and make your passenger signal to oncoming traffic

☐ Stop, then edge forward slowly until you can see clearly

HC r170–171 **RES** s9

8.4 What's one of the things you should instruct your passenger to do before the journey?

Mark **one** answer

☐ Lean to the side in order to see ahead

☐ Lean with you when going round bends

☐ Look behind and then signal for you

☐ Keep upright when going round bends

RES s14

8.5 Why have you chosen to leave a larger gap?

Mark **one** answer

☐ Your passenger will be able to see more clearly

☐ You're trying to keep away from exhaust fumes

☐ Your passenger told you to keep further back

☐ You might need more room in which to stop safely

RES s14

> Section nine
Motorway riding

In this section, you'll learn about

- > how to ride safely on motorways
- > the speed limits that apply on motorways and how they're used to avoid congestion
- > the markings used on motorway lanes
- > what to do if your motorcycle breaks down on the motorway.

Motorway riding

Motorways are designed to help traffic travel at constant, higher speeds than single carriageways. Due to the traffic's speed, situations on motorways can change more quickly than on other roads, so you need to be especially alert at all times.

Check your motorcycle thoroughly before starting a long motorway journey. Riding at high speeds for long periods of time may increase the risk of a breakdown. See section 3, Safety and your motorcycle, for more information about what to check.

RES s11

As a learner you can't drive a car or ride a motorcycle on the motorway but you can drive or ride on dual carriageways.

HC r253

Remember: to ride on a motorway, your motorcycle **MUST** have an engine capacity of 50 cc or more.

Pedestrians and horse riders can't use a motorway. The following vehicles can't be used on a motorway

- bicycles
- motorcycles under 50 cc
- powered wheelchairs/mobility scooters
- agricultural vehicles
- some slow-moving vehicles.

HC r253

> Riding on the motorway

When you join the motorway,

- use the slip road to adjust your speed to match the traffic already on the motorway
- give way to traffic already on the motorway.

HC r259 **RES** s11

All traffic, whatever its speed, should normally use the left-hand lane of the motorway. Use the middle and right-hand lanes only for overtaking other vehicles and return to the left lane when you've finished overtaking.

HC r264, 267 **RES** s11

You should normally only overtake on the right. However, you may overtake on the left if traffic is moving slowly in queues and the queue on your right is moving more slowly than the one you're in.

HC r268 **RES** s11

Where the motorway goes uphill steeply, there may be a separate lane for slow-moving vehicles. This helps the faster-moving traffic to flow more easily.

HC r139 **RES** s11

If you're travelling in the left-hand lane and traffic is joining from a slip road, move to another lane if you're able to do so safely. This helps the flow of traffic joining the motorway, especially at peak times.

RES s11

Take care when filtering through queuing traffic as a driver may change lane into your path.

Countdown markers on the left-hand verge show that you're approaching the next exit. If you want to leave the motorway, try to get into the left-hand lane in good time. If you accidentally go past the exit you wanted, carry on to the next one. Never try to stop and go back.

HC r272 **RES** s11

Improve your motorway riding by watching these videos.

⦿ **highways.gov.uk/ knowledge/15794.aspx**

> Speed limits

The national speed limit for cars and motorcycles on a motorway is 70 mph (112 km/h). The same limit applies to all lanes. Obey any signs showing a lower speed limit.

HC r261, p40 **RES** s11

A vehicle towing a trailer

- is restricted to a lower speed limit of 60 mph (96 km/h)
- isn't allowed to travel in the right-hand lane of a motorway with three or more lanes, unless there are lane closures
- in Northern Ireland shouldn't use the right-hand lane of a three-lane motorway.

TIP

You can use your hazard lights to warn traffic behind you that the traffic ahead is slowing down or stopping suddenly. Switch them off as soon as following traffic has reacted to your signal.

HC r116 **RES** s11

When you're approaching roadworks, watch for lower speed limits, especially if there's a contraflow system. You should

- obey all speed limits
- keep a safe distance from the vehicle ahead.

HC r289–290 **RES** s11

See section 4, Safety margins, for more information about contraflow systems.

> Reducing congestion

Active traffic management (ATM), also known as 'managed motorways', tries to reduce congestion and make journey times more reliable. Where this is in use, **mandatory speed limit** signs will show on the gantries. The speed limit helps to keep the traffic speed constant so that traffic is less likely to bunch up and journey times can be improved.

RES s18

In ATM areas, the hard shoulder is sometimes used as a normal traffic lane. You'll know when you can use this because a speed limit sign will be shown above all lanes, including the hard shoulder. A red cross showing above the hard shoulder means that you shouldn't travel in this lane and it should be used only in an emergency or breakdown.

Emergency refuge areas have been built in these areas for use in cases of emergency or breakdown.

Find out more about ATM here.

> **highways.gov.uk/knowledge/documents/atm_start.swf**

Highways Agency traffic officers operate on most motorways and some 'A' class roads throughout England. They

- can stop and direct anyone on a motorway or an 'A' road
- answer motorway emergency telephones, which are linked to Highways Agency control centres in some areas.

HC r105, 108 **RES** s18

> Lane markings

Reflective studs help you to see where you are on the carriageway, especially at night or in fog. Different colours are used in different places.

HC r132 **RES** s11

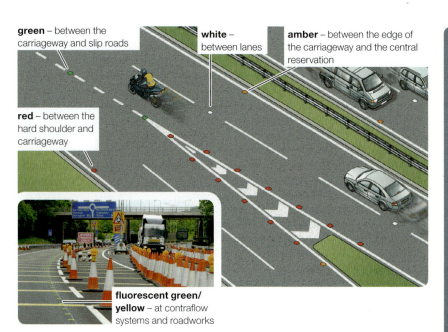

green – between the carriageway and slip roads

white – between lanes

amber – between the edge of the carriageway and the central reservation

red – between the hard shoulder and carriageway

fluorescent green/ yellow – at contraflow systems and roadworks

> Stopping and breakdowns

Motorways are designed to keep traffic moving, so you mustn't stop on the motorway unless you have to.

Only stop on the motorway

- if flashing red lights show above every lane
- when told to do so by the police, Vehicle and Operator Services Agency (VOSA) officers or Highways Agency traffic officers
- in a traffic jam
- in an emergency or breakdown.

Move over if signals on the overhead gantries advise you to do so.

HC r258, 270 RES s11 KYTS p90

Should you need to stop for any other reason, such as to have a rest, make a phone call or look at a map, either leave at the next exit or go to a service area.

HC r270 RES s11

If your motorcycle breaks down or a tyre has a puncture, try to get onto the hard shoulder and call for help. If you can, use one of the emergency telephones. These are

- normally at one-mile intervals. Marker posts at 100-metre intervals point you in the direction of the nearest phone
- connected directly to Highways Agency control. They'll be able to find you easily.

HC r275 **RES** s11, 16

When you're using an emergency phone, stand facing the oncoming traffic so that you can see any hazards approaching – for example, the draught from a large vehicle driving past could take you by surprise.

If you decide to use your mobile phone,

- make a note of your location (the number on the nearest marker post) before you make the call
- give this information to the emergency services.

HC r275 **RES** s11, 16

While your motorcycle is on the hard shoulder,

- switch on the hazard lights, if fitted
- switch on the parking lights at night or if visibility is poor.

RES s11

When you're ready to return to the carriageway, wait for a safe gap in the traffic and then ride along the hard shoulder to gain speed before moving out onto the main carriageway.

HC r276 **RES** s16

Meeting the standards

You must be able to

join a motorway or dual carriageway safely and responsibly from the left or the right

allow for other road users joining or leaving the motorway

change lanes safely and responsibly.

You must know and understand

that you mustn't stop on a motorway except in an emergency

that you mustn't

- pick anybody up on a motorway
- set anybody down on a motorway
- walk on a motorway, except in an emergency

the need to look well ahead for other road users joining or leaving the motorway or for queuing traffic

that some stretches of motorway may have

- local, active traffic management (sometimes called managed motorways)
- control systems installed, which will change speed limits and the direction of flow in particular lanes

You must obey the instructions given by these systems.

> Notes

You can use this page to make your own notes or diagrams about the key points you need to remember.

Think about

- At what speed should you be riding when you join the motorway?
- What should you do if you miss the exit that you want to take off the motorway?
- What information do the marker posts give you?
- What should you do if your motorcycle breaks down on the motorway?

Your notes

Things to discuss and practise with your trainer

These are just a few examples of what you could discuss and practise with your trainer. Read more about motorway rules to come up with your own ideas.

Discuss with your trainer

- how you should join the motorway and what to look out for as you do so
- the different national speed limits for various vehicles on the motorway, and in which lanes they may travel
- what you should do if you break down on the motorway
- what ATM stands for and its purpose on the motorway.

Practise with your trainer

Until you hold a full motorcycle licence, you won't be able to ride on the motorway, so practising your riding there won't be possible. Instead, practise with your trainer

- on a dual carriageway, some of the techniques of riding on the motorway eg joining from a slip road, lane discipline and riding at higher speeds
- identifying motorway signs, signals and road markings from *Know Your Traffic Signs* and *The Official Highway Code*.

9.1 | **Mark one answer** | **RES s11, HC r270**

On a motorway you may ONLY stop on the hard shoulder

☐ in an emergency

☐ If you feel tired and need to rest

☐ if you go past the exit that you wanted to take

☐ to pick up a hitchhiker

You must not stop on the hard shoulder except in an emergency. Never use it to have a rest or a picnic, pick up hitchhikers, answer a mobile phone, or check a road map. You must not travel back along the hard shoulder if you go past your intended exit.

9.2 | **Mark one answer** | **RES s11, HC r272**

You are intending to leave the motorway at the next exit. Before you reach the exit you should normally position your motorcycle

☐ in the middle lane

☐ in the left-hand lane

☐ on the hard shoulder

☐ in any lane

You'll see the first advance warning sign for a junction one mile from the exit. If you're travelling at 60 mph you'll only have about 50 seconds before you reach the countdown markers. Move in to the left-hand lane in good time if you're not there already. Don't cut across traffic at the last moment.

9.3 | **Mark one answer** | **RES s11**

You are joining a motorway from a slip road. You should

☐ adjust your speed to the speed of the traffic on the motorway

☐ accelerate as quickly as you can and ride straight out

☐ ride onto the hard shoulder until a gap appears

☐ expect drivers on the motorway to give way to you

Give way to the traffic already on the motorway and join it where there's a suitable gap in the traffic. Don't expect traffic on the motorway to give way to you, but try to avoid stopping at the end of the slip road.

9.4 | **Mark one answer** | **RES s11, HC r253**

To ride on a motorway your motorcycle must be

☐ 50 cc or more

☐ 100 cc or more

☐ 125 cc or more

☐ 250 cc or more

Traffic on motorways travels at high speeds. Vehicles need to be capable of keeping up with the flow of traffic. For this reason low-powered vehicles are prohibited.

9.5
Mark one answer
RES s11, HC r264

You are riding at 70 mph on a three-lane motorway. There is no traffic ahead. Which lane should you use?

☐ Any lane

☐ Middle lane

☐ Right-hand lane

☐ Left-hand lane

Use the left-hand lane if it's free, regardless of the speed you're travelling.

9.6
NI EXEMPT
Mark one answer
RES s11, HC p40

You are riding on a motorway. Unless signs show otherwise you must NOT exceed

☐ 50 mph

☐ 60 mph

☐ 70 mph

☐ 80 mph

Ride in accordance with the conditions. Bad weather or heavy traffic may mean you have to lower your speed.

9.7
Mark one answer
RES s11

Why is it particularly important to carry out a check of your motorcycle before making a long motorway journey?

☐ You will have to do more harsh braking on motorways

☐ Motorway service stations do not deal with breakdowns

☐ The road surface will wear down the tyres faster

☐ Continuous high speeds may increase the risk of your motorcycle breaking down

Before starting a motorway journey, make sure your motorcycle can cope with the demands of high-speed riding. Things you need to check include oil, water and tyres. When you're travelling a long way it's a good idea to plan rest stops in advance.

9.8
Mark one answer
RES s11, HC r259

When joining a motorway you must always

☐ use the hard shoulder

☐ stop at the end of the acceleration lane

☐ come to a stop before joining the motorway

☐ give way to traffic already on the motorway

You should give way to traffic already on the motorway. Where possible they may move over to let you in but don't force your way into the traffic stream. The traffic may be travelling at high speed so you should match your speed to fit in.

Mark one answer

What is the national speed limit on motorways for cars and motorcycles?

☐ 30 mph

☐ 50 mph

☐ 60 mph

☐ 70 mph

Travelling at the national speed limit doesn't allow you to hog the right-hand lane. Always use the left-hand lane whenever possible. When leaving a motorway get into the left-hand lane well before your exit. Reduce your speed on the slip road and look out for sharp bends or curves and traffic queuing at roundabouts.

Mark one answer

The left-hand lane on a three-lane motorway is for use by

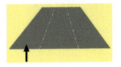

☐ any vehicle

☐ large vehicles only

☐ emergency vehicles only

☐ slow vehicles only

On a motorway all traffic should use the left-hand lane unless overtaking. Use the centre or right-hand lanes if you need to overtake. If you're overtaking a number of slower vehicles move back to the left-hand lane when you're safely past. Check your mirrors frequently and don't stay in the middle or right-hand lane if the left-hand lane is free.

Mark one answer

Which of these IS NOT allowed to travel in the right-hand lane of a three-lane motorway?

☐ A small delivery van

☐ A motorcycle

☐ A vehicle towing a trailer

☐ A motorcycle and sidecar

A vehicle with a trailer is restricted to 60 mph. For this reason it isn't allowed in the right-hand lane as it might hold up the faster-moving traffic that wishes to overtake in that lane.

9.12 Mark one answer RES s11, HC r275

You break down on a motorway. You need to call for help. Why may it be better to use an emergency roadside telephone rather than a mobile phone?

- ☐ It connects you to a local garage
- ☐ Using a mobile phone will distract other drivers
- ☐ It allows easy location by the emergency services
- ☐ Mobile phones do not work on motorways

On a motorway it is best to use a roadside emergency telephone so that the emergency services are able to locate you easily. The nearest telephone is shown by an arrow on marker posts at the edge of the hard shoulder. If you use a mobile, they will need to know your exact location. Before you call, find out the number on the nearest marker post. This number will identify your exact location.

9.13 Mark one answer RES s11, HC r276

After a breakdown you need to rejoin the main carriageway of a motorway from the hard shoulder. You should

- ☐ move out onto the carriageway then build up your speed
- ☐ move out onto the carriageway using your hazard lights
- ☐ gain speed on the hard shoulder before moving out onto the carriageway
- ☐ wait on the hard shoulder until someone flashes their headlights at you

Wait for a safe gap in the traffic before you move out. Indicate your intention and use the hard shoulder to gain speed but don't force your way into the traffic.

9.14 Mark one answer RES s11

A crawler lane on a motorway is found

- ☐ on a steep gradient
- ☐ before a service area
- ☐ before a junction
- ☐ along the hard shoulder

Slow-moving, large vehicles might slow down the progress of other traffic. On a steep gradient this extra lane is provided for these slow-moving vehicles to allow the faster-moving traffic to flow more easily.

What do these motorway signs show?

The exit from a motorway is indicated by countdown markers. These are positioned 90 metres (100 yards) apart, the first being 270 metres (300 yards) from the start of the slip road. Move into the left-hand lane well before you reach the start of the slip road.

☐ They are countdown markers to a bridge

☐ They are distance markers to the next telephone

☐ They are countdown markers to the next exit

☐ They warn of a police control ahead

On a motorway the amber reflective studs can be found between

☐ the hard shoulder and the carriageway

☐ the acceleration lane and the carriageway

☐ the central reservation and the carriageway

☐ each pair of the lanes

On motorways reflective studs are located into the road to help you in the dark and in conditions of poor visibility. Amber-coloured studs are found on the right-hand edge of the main carriageway, next to the central reservation.

What colour are the reflective studs between the lanes on a motorway?

White studs are found between the lanes on motorways. The light from your headlights is reflected back and this is especially useful in bad weather, when visibility is restricted.

☐ Green

☐ Amber

☐ White

☐ Red

9.18
Mark one answer   RES s7, HC r132

What colour are the reflective studs between a motorway and its slip road?

☐ Amber

☐ White

☐ Green

☐ Red

The studs between the carriageway and the hard shoulder are normally red. These change to green where there is a slip road. They will help you identify slip roads when visibility is poor or when it is dark.

9.19
Mark one answer   RES s11, HC r275

You have broken down on a motorway. To find the nearest emergency telephone you should always walk

☐ with the traffic flow

☐ facing oncoming traffic

☐ in the direction shown on the marker posts

☐ in the direction of the nearest exit

Along the hard shoulder there are marker posts at 100-metre intervals. These will direct you to the nearest emergency telephone.

9.20
Mark one answer   RES s11, HC r259

You are joining a motorway. Why is it important to make full use of the slip road?

☐ Because there is space available to turn round if you need to

☐ To allow you direct access to the overtaking lanes

☐ To build up a speed similar to traffic on the motorway

☐ Because you can continue on the hard shoulder

Try to join the motorway without affecting the progress of the traffic already travelling on it. Always give way to traffic already on the motorway. At busy times you may have to slow down to merge into slow-moving traffic.

9.21
Mark one answer   RES s11, HC r275

How should you use the emergency telephone on a motorway?

☐ Stay close to the carriageway

☐ Face the oncoming traffic

☐ Keep your back to the traffic

☐ Stand on the hard shoulder

Traffic is passing you at speed. If the draught from a large lorry catches you by surprise it could blow you off balance and even onto the carriageway. By facing the oncoming traffic you can see approaching lorries and so be prepared for their draught. You are also in a position to see other hazards approaching.

You are on a motorway. What colour are the reflective studs on the left of the carriageway?

☐ Green

☐ Red

☐ White

☐ Amber

Red studs are placed between the edge of the carriageway and the hard shoulder. Where slip roads leave or join the motorway the studs are green.

On a three-lane motorway which lane should you normally use?

☐ Left

☐ Right

☐ Centre

☐ Either the right or centre

On a three-lane motorway you should travel in the left-hand lane unless you're overtaking. This applies regardless of the speed at which you're travelling.

When going through a contraflow system on a motorway you should

There's likely to be a speed restriction in force. Keep to this. Don't

- switch lanes
- get too close to traffic in front of you.

Be aware there will be no permanent barrier between you and the oncoming traffic.

☐ ensure that you do not exceed 30 mph

☐ keep a good distance from the vehicle ahead

☐ switch lanes to keep the traffic flowing

☐ stay close to the vehicle ahead to reduce queues

9.25   Mark one answer   RES s11, HC r132

You are on a three-lane motorway. There are red reflective studs on your left and white ones to your right. Where are you?

- [ ] In the right-hand lane
- [ ] In the middle lane
- [ ] On the hard shoulder
- [ ] In the left-hand lane

The colours of the reflective studs on the motorway and their locations are

- red – between the hard shoulder and the carriageway
- white – lane markings
- amber – between the edge of the carriageway and the central reservation
- green – along slip road exits and entrances
- bright green/yellow – roadworks and contraflow systems.

9.26   Mark one answer   RES s11, HC r288

You are approaching roadworks on a motorway. What should you do?

- [ ] Speed up to clear the area quickly
- [ ] Always use the hard shoulder
- [ ] Obey all speed limits
- [ ] Stay very close to the vehicle in front

Collisions can often happen at roadworks. Be aware of the speed limits, slow down in good time and keep your distance from the vehicle in front.

9.27   Mark four answers   HC r253

Which FOUR of these must NOT use motorways?

- [ ] Learner car drivers
- [ ] Motorcycles over 50cc
- [ ] Double-deck buses
- [ ] Farm tractors
- [ ] Learner motorcyclists
- [ ] Cyclists

Learner car drivers and motorcyclists are not allowed on the motorway until they have passed their practical test.

Motorways have rules that you need to know before you venture out for the first time. When you've passed your practical test it's a good idea to have some lessons on motorways. Check with your instructor about this.

9.28   Mark one answer   RES s11, HC r264

Immediately after joining a motorway you should normally

☐ try to overtake

☐ re-adjust your mirrors

☐ position your vehicle in the centre lane

☐ keep in the left-hand lane

Stay in the left-hand lane long enough to get used to the higher speeds of motorway traffic.

9.29   Mark one answer   RES s11, HC r265

What is the right-hand lane used for on a three-lane motorway?

☐ Emergency vehicles only

☐ Overtaking

☐ Vehicles towing trailers

☐ Coaches only

You should keep to the left and only use the right-hand lane if you're passing slower-moving traffic.

9.30   Mark one answer   RES s11, HC r269, 270

What should you use the hard shoulder of a motorway for?

Don't use the hard shoulder for stopping unless it is an emergency. If you want to stop for any other reason go to the next exit or service station.

☐ Stopping in an emergency

☐ Leaving the motorway

☐ Stopping when you are tired

☐ Joining the motorway

9.31   Mark one answer   HC p102

You are in the right-hand lane on a motorway. You see these overhead signs. This means

- ☐ move to the left and reduce your speed to 50 mph
- ☐ there are roadworks 50 metres (55 yards) ahead
- ☐ use the hard shoulder until you have passed the hazard
- ☐ leave the motorway at the next exit

You MUST obey this sign. There might not be any visible signs of a problem ahead. However, there might be queuing traffic or another hazard which you cannot yet see.

9.32   Mark one answer   RES s11, HC r270

You are allowed to stop on a motorway when you

- ☐ need to walk and get fresh air
- ☐ wish to pick up hitchhikers
- ☐ are told to do so by flashing red lights
- ☐ need to use a mobile telephone

You MUST stop if there are red lights flashing above every lane on the motorway. However, if any of the other lanes do not show flashing red lights or red cross you may move into that lane and continue if it is safe to do so.

9.33   Mark one answer   RES s11

You are travelling along the left-hand lane of a three-lane motorway. Traffic is joining from a slip road. You should

- ☐ race the other vehicles
- ☐ move to another lane
- ☐ maintain a steady speed
- ☐ switch on your hazard flashers

You should move to another lane if it is safe to do so. This can greatly assist the flow of traffic joining the motorway, especially at peak times.

A basic rule when on motorways is

☐ use the lane that has least traffic

☐ keep to the left-hand lane unless overtaking

☐ overtake on the side that is clearest

☐ try to keep above 50 mph to prevent congestion

You should normally travel in the left-hand lane unless you are overtaking a slower-moving vehicle. When you are past that vehicle move back into the left-hand lane as soon as it's safe to do so. Don't cut across in front of the vehicle that you're overtaking.

On motorways you should never overtake on the left unless

☐ you can see well ahead that the hard shoulder is clear

☐ the traffic in the right-hand lane is signalling right

☐ you warn drivers behind by signalling left

☐ there is a queue of slow-moving traffic to your right that is moving more slowly than you are

Only overtake on the left if traffic is moving slowly in queues and the traffic on your right is moving more slowly than the traffic in your lane.

What is an Emergency Refuge Area on a motorway for?

☐ An area to park in when you want to use a mobile phone

☐ To use in cases of emergency or breakdown

☐ For an emergency recovery vehicle to park in a contraflow system

☐ To drive in when there is queuing traffic ahead

In cases of breakdown or emergency try to get your vehicle into an Emergency Refuge Area. This is safer than just stopping on the hard shoulder as it gives you greater distance from the main carriageway. If you are able to re-join the motorway you must take extra care, especially when the hard shoulder is being used as a running lane.

9.37   NI EXEMPT   **Mark one answer**   **RES s18, HC r108**

Highways Agency Traffic Officers

☐ will not be able to assist at a breakdown or emergency

☐ are not able to stop and direct anyone on a motorway

☐ will tow a broken-down vehicle and its passengers home

☐ are able to stop and direct anyone on a motorway

Highways Agency Traffic Officers (HATOs) are able to stop and direct traffic on most motorways and some 'A' class roads. They work in partnership with the police at motorway incidents and provide a highly trained and visible service. Their role is to help keep traffic moving and make your journey as safe and reliable as possible. They are recognised by an orange and yellow jacket and their vehicle has yellow and black markings.

9.38   NI EXEMPT   **Mark one answer**   **RES s18, HC r258, 269**

You are on a motorway. A red cross is displayed above the hard shoulder. What does this mean?

Active Traffic Management schemes are being introduced on motorways. Within these areas at certain times the hard shoulder will be used as a running lane. A red cross above the hard shoulder shows that this lane should NOT be used, except for emergencies and breakdowns.

☐ Pull up in this lane to answer your mobile phone

☐ Use this lane as a running lane

☐ This lane can be used if you need a rest

☐ You should not travel in this lane

You are on a motorway in an Active Traffic Management (ATM) area. A mandatory speed limit is displayed above the hard shoulder. What does this mean?

A mandatory speed limit sign above the hard shoulder shows that it can be used as a running lane between junctions. You must stay within the speed limit. Look out for vehicles that may have broken down and could be blocking the hard shoulder.

☐ You should not travel in this lane

☐ The hard shoulder can be used as a running lane

☐ You can park on the hard shoulder if you feel tired

☐ You can pull up in this lane to answer a mobile phone

The aim of an Active Traffic Management scheme on a motorway is to

☐ prevent overtaking

☐ reduce rest stops

☐ prevent tailgating

☐ reduce congestion

Active Traffic Management schemes are intended to reduce congestion and make journey times more reliable. In these areas the hard shoulder may be used as a running lane to ease congestion at peak times or in the event of an incident. It may appear that you could travel faster for a short distance, but keeping traffic flow at a constant speed may improve your journey time.

You are in an Active Traffic Management area on a motorway. When the Actively Managed mode is operating

☐ speed limits are only advisory

☐ the national speed limit will apply

☐ the speed limit is always 30 mph

☑ all speed limit signals are set

When an Active Traffic Management (ATM) scheme is operating on a motorway you MUST follow the mandatory instructions shown on the gantries above each lane. This includes the hard shoulder.

9.42 | Mark one answer | RES s18, HC r269

Why can it be an advantage for traffic speed to stay constant over a longer distance?

☐ You will do more stop-start driving

☐ You will use far more fuel

☐ You will be able to use more direct routes

☐ Your overall journey time will normally improve

When traffic travels at a constant speed over a longer distance, journey times normally improve. You may feel that you could travel faster for short periods but this won't generally improve your overall journey time. Signs will show the maximum speed at which you should travel.

9.43 | NI EXEMPT | Mark one answer | RES s18, HC r269

You should not normally travel on the hard shoulder of a motorway. When can you use it?

☐ When taking the next exit

☐ When traffic is stopped

☐ When signs direct you to

☐ When traffic is slow moving

Normally you should only use the hard shoulder for emergencies and breakdowns, and at roadworks when signs direct you to do so. Active Traffic Management (ATM) areas are being introduced to ease traffic congestion. In these areas the hard shoulder may be used as a running lane when speed limit signs are shown directly above.

9.44 | Mark one answer | RES s11, HC r267

For what reason may you use the right-hand lane of a motorway?

☐ For keeping out of the way of lorries

☐ For travelling at more than 70 mph

☐ For turning right

☐ For overtaking other vehicles

The right-hand lane of the motorway is for overtaking.

Sometimes you may be directed into a right-hand lane as a result of roadworks or a traffic incident. This will be indicated by signs or officers directing the traffic.

9.45 — Mark one answer — RES s18, HC r261

On a motorway what is used to reduce traffic bunching?

☐ Variable speed limits
☐ Contraflow systems
☐ National speed limits
☐ Lane closures

Congestion can be reduced by keeping traffic at a constant speed. At busy times maximum speed limits are displayed on overhead gantries. These can be varied quickly depending on the amount of traffic. By keeping to a constant speed on busy sections of motorway overall journey times are normally improved.

9.46 — Mark three answers — RES s11, HC r270

When should you stop on a motorway?

☐ If you have to read a map
☐ When you are tired and need a rest
☐ If red lights show above every lane
☐ When told to by the police
☐ If your mobile phone rings
☐ When signalled by a Highways Agency Traffic Officer

There are some occasions when you may have to stop on the carriageway of a motorway. These include when being signalled by the police or a Highways Agency Traffic Officer, when flashing red lights show above every lane and in traffic jams.

9.47 — Mark one answer — RES s11, HC r270

When may you stop on a motorway?

☐ If you have to read a map
☐ When you are tired and need a rest
☐ If your mobile phone rings
☐ In an emergency or breakdown

You should not normally stop on a motorway but there may be occasions when you need to do so. If you are unfortunate enough to break down make every effort to pull up on the hard shoulder.

9.48   NI EXEMPT   Mark one answer   HC r261, p40

You are travelling on a motorway. Unless signs show a lower speed limit you must NOT exceed

☐ 50 mph

☐ 60 mph

☐ 70 mph

☐ 80 mph

The national speed limit for a car or motorcycle on the motorway is 70 mph. Lower speed limits may be in force, for example at roadworks, so look out for the signs. Variable speed limits operate in some areas to control very busy stretches of motorway. The speed limit may change depending on the volume of traffic.

9.49   Mark one answer   HC r275, 280

Motorway emergency telephones are usually linked to the police. In some areas they are now linked to

☐ the local ambulance service

☐ an Highways Agency control centre

☐ the local fire brigade

☐ a breakdown service control centre

The controller will ask you

• the make and colour of your vehicle

• whether you are a member of an emergency breakdown service

• the number shown on the emergency telephone casing

• whether you are travelling alone.

9.50   Mark one answer   RES s11, HC r270

You are on a motorway. There are red flashing lights above every lane. You must

☐ pull onto the hard shoulder

☐ slow down and watch for further signals

☐ leave at the next exit

☐ stop and wait

Red flashing lights above every lane mean you must not go on any further. You'll also see a red cross illuminated. Stop and wait. Don't

• change lanes

• continue

• pull onto the hard shoulder (unless in an emergency).

You are on a three-lane motorway. A red cross is shown above the hard shoulder and mandatory speed limits above all other lanes. This means

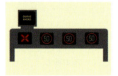

A red cross above the hard shoulder shows it is closed as a running lane and should only be used for emergencies or breakdowns. At busy times within an Active Traffic Management (ATM) area the hard shoulder may be used as a running lane. This will be shown by a mandatory speed limit on the gantry above.

☐ the hard shoulder can be used as a rest area if you feel tired

☐ the hard shoulder is for emergency or breakdown use only

☐ the hard shoulder can be used as a normal running lane

☐ the hard shoulder has a speed limit of 50 mph

You are on a three-lane motorway and see this sign. It means you can use

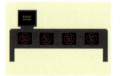

Mandatory speed limit signs above all lanes including the hard shoulder, show that you are in an Active Traffic Management (ATM) area. In this case you can use the hard shoulder as a running lane. You must stay within the speed limit shown. Look out for any vehicles that may have broken down and be blocking the hard shoulder.

☐ any lane except the hard shoulder

☐ the hard shoulder only

☐ the three right hand lanes only

☐ all the lanes including the hard shoulder

You are travelling on a motorway. You decide you need a rest. You should

☐ stop on the hard shoulder

☐ pull in at the nearest service area

☐ pull up on a slip road

☐ park on the central reservation

If you feel tired stop at the nearest service area. If it's too far away leave the motorway at the next exit and find a safe place to stop. You must not stop on the carriageway or hard shoulder of a motorway except in an emergency, in a traffic queue, when signalled to do so by a police or enforcement officer, or by traffic signals. Plan your journey so that you have regular rest stops.

> Case study practice – 9
Motorway riding

Max is riding his motorcycle and newly fitted sidecar. On the motorway, Max rides in the left-hand lane.

He then sees flashing amber lights on the central reservation, with a sign showing '50'.

Later, Max needs to exit at the next junction, so he watches for countdown markers. He then reaches the marker showing three bars.

9.1 What could be affected by the presence of the sidecar?
Mark **one** answer

- ☐ Steering and braking
- ☐ Indicators and fairings
- ☐ Road tax and speed limits
- ☐ Fuel type and exhaust

RES s14

9.2 Why would Max take this position on the motorway?
Mark **one** answer

- ☐ That's the only lane which is completely empty of other traffic
- ☐ He's travelling more slowly and doesn't want to obstruct others
- ☐ All traffic should do so unless they're overtaking other vehicles
- ☐ He's unsure when he'll reach the slip road for the next junction

HC r264 **RES** s11

9.3 How should Max initially ride?

Mark **one** answer

- ☐ The same as normal
- ☐ Slower than normal
- ☐ Faster than normal
- ☐ Only with a passenger

RES s11

9.4 What's meant by the sign and lights?

Mark **one** answer

- ☐ Temporary minimum speed advised
- ☐ Temporary maximum distance advised
- ☐ Temporary maximum speed advised
- ☐ Temporary minimum distance advised

RES s11

9.5 At this marker, how far is Max from the exit he needs?

Mark **one** answer

- ☐ 400 yards
- ☐ 300 yards
- ☐ 200 yards
- ☐ 100 yards

HC p112 **RES** s11

Rules of the road

In this section, you'll learn about

- the speed limits that you need to obey
- how to use junctions and lanes safely
- rules about overtaking
- riding over pedestrian crossings and level crossings
- where you can stop and park safely and legally.

Rules of the road

It's important that everyone knows and follows the rules of the road. Some are legal requirements and some are recommended best practice, but they all help to make the roads safer.

> Speed limits

You **MUST NOT** ride faster than the speed limit for the road you're on or your vehicle type. Where no other limit is shown, the national speed limit for cars and motorcycles is

- 60 mph (96 km/h) on a single carriageway road
- 70 mph (112 km/h) on a dual carriageway or motorway.

There are lower speed limits for these vehicles when towing a trailer or caravan

- 50 mph (80 km/h) on a single carriageway road
- 60 mph (96 km/h) on a dual carriageway or motorway.

HC r124, p40

Where there are street lights, there's normally a 30 mph (48 km/h) speed limit for all vehicles unless signs show otherwise.

HC r124, p40

On some roads you may see a sign showing a minimum speed limit. You should travel above the limit shown on the sign unless it's not safe to do so.

HC p107

Speed limits

Type of vehicle	Built-up areas* mph (km/h)	Single carriage-ways mph (km/h)	Dual carriage-ways mph (km/h)	Motorways mph (km/h)
Cars and motorcycles (including car-derived vans up to 2 tonnes maximum laden weight)	30 (48)	60 (96)	70 (112)	70 (112)
Cars towing caravans or trailers (including car-derived vans and motorcycles)	30 (48)	50 (80)	60 (96)	60 (96)
Buses, coaches and minibuses (not exceeding 12 metres in overall length)	30 (48)	50 (80)	60 (96)	70 (112)
Goods vehicles (not exceeding 7.5 tonnes maximum laden weight)	30 (48)	50 (80)	60 (96)	70† (112)
Goods vehicles (exceeding 7.5 tonnes maximum laden weight)	30 (48)	40 (64)	50 (80)	60 (96)

*The 30 mph limit usually applies to all traffic on all roads with street lighting unless signs show otherwise.
†60 mph (96 km/h) if articulated or towing a trailer.

Be aware that large vehicles may have speed limiters – buses and coaches are restricted to 62 mph and large goods vehicles to 56 mph.

Always ride with care and take account of the road and weather conditions. If you're riding along a street where cars are parked, keep your speed down and beware of

pedestrians (especially children) stepping out from behind parked vehicles

vehicles pulling out

drivers' doors opening.

HC r152 **RES** s10

At roadworks, there may be temporary speed limits to slow traffic down. These are mandatory speed limits and may be enforced by cameras.

HC r288 **KYTS** p90

The Think! road safety website has more advice on speed and speed limits.

http://think.direct.gov.uk/speed.html

> Lanes and junctions

Some roads have lanes reserved for specific vehicles such as cycles, buses or trams. These are marked by signs and road markings, and should only be used by those vehicles during the lanes' hours of operation, unless signs indicate otherwise.

HC r141

Never ride or park in a cycle lane marked by a solid white line during its hours of operation. Don't ride or park in a cycle lane marked by a broken line unless it's unavoidable.

HC r140–141 **KYTS** p32–36

You should only ride over a footpath when it's necessary in order to reach a property.

HC r145

On a dual carriageway, the right-hand lane is only for turning right or overtaking. The same rule applies to three-lane dual carriageways.

> **TIP** If you want to turn right onto a dual carriageway that has a central reservation that's too narrow to fit the length of your vehicle, wait until the road is clear in both directions before you emerge. If you emerge into the central reservation but your vehicle is too long, it could obstruct traffic coming from your right.
>
> **HC** r173 **RES** s9

Always be careful at junctions. As you approach a junction, move into the correct position in plenty of time.

When you're turning left, keep well to the left as you approach the junction. In slow-moving traffic, remember to check for cyclists to your left before you turn.

HC r181–183 **RES** s9

If you're on a busy road and you find you're travelling in the wrong direction, or you're in the wrong lane at a busy junction, keep going until you can find somewhere safe, such as a quiet side road, where you can turn around.

HC r200 **RES** s6, 9

A box junction is marked by yellow hatched lines, and should be kept clear. Only enter it if your exit road is clear – otherwise, wait on your side of the junction. You can, however, wait in the box if you want to turn right and are waiting for a gap in the oncoming traffic before you can turn.

HC r174 **RES** s7, 9

If something is blocking your side of the road, such as a parked car, you should give way to oncoming traffic if there isn't room for you both to continue safely.

RES s8

Crossroads

If you're turning right at a crossroads when an oncoming road user is also turning right, it's normally safer to keep the other vehicle to your right and turn behind it. If you have to pass in front of the other vehicle, take extra care as your view may be blocked.

HC r181

At crossroads where there aren't any signs or markings, no-one has priority. Check very carefully in all directions before you proceed.

HC r146 **RES** s9

Roundabouts

Roundabouts are designed to help traffic flow smoothly. Follow signs and road markings as you approach and ride around them. Normally, if you're going straight ahead,

- don't signal as you approach
- signal left just after you pass the exit before the one you want.

HC r185–186 **RES** s9

Some vehicles may not follow the normal rules.

- Cyclists and horse riders may stay in the left-hand lane even if they're turning right.
- Long vehicles may take up a different position to stop the rear of the vehicle hitting the kerb.

HC r187

> Overtaking

Overtaking can be dangerous. Ask yourself if you really need to do it, and never overtake if you're in any doubt as to whether it's safe.

HC r163 **RES** s8

You should normally overtake other vehicles on the right, but in a one-way street you can pass slower traffic on the left. Take extra care if you're overtaking on a dual carriageway, as the right-hand lane can also be used by traffic turning right.

HC r137–138 **RES** s8

At night, if a vehicle overtakes you, dip your headlights as soon as it passes you otherwise your lights could dazzle the other driver.

HC r115

> Pedestrian crossings

If someone is standing on the pavement waiting to cross at a zebra crossing, stop and let them cross if it's safe to do so.

Pelican crossings are controlled by traffic lights. When the red light changes to flashing amber, wait for any pedestrians to finish crossing before you move off.

On toucan crossings, cyclists are allowed to cycle across at the same time as pedestrians.

HC r195–199 **RES** s8 **KYTS** p124

For more information on pedestrian crossings, see section 6, Vulnerable road users.

> Level crossings

A level crossing is where a railway line crosses the road.

It may have countdown markers to warn you if the crossing is hidden, such as around a bend.

Controlled crossings have traffic light signals with twin flashing red lights, plus a warning alarm for pedestrians.

Crossings may or may not have barriers.

If this happens ...	you should do this
The warning lights come on as you're approaching the crossing.	Stop. You **MUST** obey the red lights, by law.
You're already on the crossing when the warning lights come on or a bell rings.	Keep going and clear the crossing.

You're waiting at a level crossing and a train has passed but the red lights keep flashing.

You **MUST** wait: there may be another train coming.

`HC` r293, p109 `RES` s7 `KYTS` p26–29

Some types of level crossing don't have lights. These include crossings with user-operated gates or barriers, and open crossings. Be careful at all level crossings, and take particular care when crossing rails – they may be slippery, particularly in wet weather.

`HC` r295–299 `RES` s8

See the Network Rail guide to using level crossings safely.

❯ **networkrail.co.uk/level-crossings**

❯ Stopping and parking

Always think carefully about where you stop and park your motorcycle, to make sure it's safe and legal.

At night, the safest place to park your motorcycle is in your garage, if you have one. If you're away from home, try to find a secure car park, or park in a well-lit area.

`HC` r239, p131 `RES` s8

If you have to park on a road at night, you **MUST** leave your parking lights on if the speed limit on that road is over 30 mph (48 km/h). You should normally park on the left-hand side of the road so that other road users can see your reflectors, but in a one-way street you can park on either side.

`HC` r248–250 `RES` s13

You **MUST NOT** stop on a **clearway**. On an urban clearway, you may stop only to drop off and pick up passengers. On a road marked with double white lines (even where one of the lines is broken), you may stop only to drop off and pick up passengers or to load/unload goods.

HC r240 **RES** s7

Definition

clearway
a stretch of road or street where stopping isn't allowed

Don't park where you would cause a danger or get in the way of other road users, such as

- on or near the brow of a hill
- at a bus stop
- opposite a traffic island
- in front of someone else's drive
- near a school entrance
- opposite or within 10 metres (32 feet) of a junction (in Northern Ireland, within 15 metres or 48 feet of a junction), unless there's an authorised parking space.

HC r242–243

You also need to make sure that you don't cause an obstruction by stopping or parking where there are restrictions shown by signs and yellow lines. In a controlled parking zone, you'll have to pay to park. Make sure you park within marked bays on the days and times shown on the zone entry signs.

HC r238, 245 **RES** s7 **KYTS** p39–50

By law, you **MUST** stop
- if you're involved in a road traffic incident
- at a red traffic light
- when signalled to do so by a police officer, traffic warden, Vehicle and Operator Services Agency (VOSA) officer, Highways Agency traffic officer or school crossing patrol.

HC r105, 109, 286

Meeting the standards

You must be able to

apply a safe, systematic procedure to safely and responsibly negotiate

- junctions
- roundabouts
- crossings

turn left and right and go ahead safely and responsibly

emerge safely and responsibly into streams of traffic

cross the path of traffic safely when turning right.

You must know and understand

the rules that apply to particular junctions and roundabouts. For example, priority rules

the rules about

- merging into a stream of traffic
- crossing the path of an approaching stream of traffic
- all types of pedestrian crossing
- train and tram crossings

how to work out the speed limit where you can't see speed-limit signs.

> Notes

You can use this page to make your own notes or diagrams about the key points you need to remember.

Think about

- Where might you see a minimum speed limit sign?
- When can you ride in a bus lane?
- What's a box junction? What mustn't you do at one of these junctions?
- Where could you park your motorcycle when you're away from home?
- What should you do if you've just ridden onto a level crossing and the warning lights start flashing?
- How close to a junction are you allowed to park?

Your notes

Things to discuss and practise with your trainer

These are just a few examples of what you could discuss and practise with your trainer. Read more about rules of the road to come up with your own ideas.

Discuss with your trainer

- what the 'national speed limit applies' sign looks like. What does this mean in mph on different roads and for different vehicles?
- what the speed limit will usually be if there are street lights along the road
- what the different lanes are used for on
  - a two-lane dual carriageway
  - a three-lane dual carriageway
  - a motorway.

Practise with your trainer

- negotiating roundabouts with several lanes on approach
- riding in areas with changing speed limits
- entering, exiting and overtaking on busy dual carriageways.

You are riding slowly in a town centre. Before turning left you should glance over your left shoulder to

☐ check for cyclists

☐ help keep your balance

☐ look for traffic signs

☐ check for potholes

When riding slowly you must remember cyclists. They can travel quickly and fit through surprisingly narrow spaces. Before you turn left in slow-moving traffic it's important to check that a cyclist isn't trying to overtake on your left.

As a motorcycle rider which TWO lanes must you NOT use?

☐ Crawler lane

☐ Overtaking lane

☐ Acceleration lane

☐ Cycle lane

☐ Tram lane

In some towns motorcycles are permitted to use bus lanes. Check the signs carefully.

What does this sign mean?

In some towns and cities there are special areas reserved for parking motorcycles. Look out for these signs.

☐ No parking for solo motorcycles

☐ Parking for solo motorcycles

☐ Passing place for motorcycles

☐ Police motorcycles only

You are riding on a busy dual carriageway. When changing lanes you should

☐ rely totally on mirrors

☐ always increase your speed

☐ signal so others will give way

☐ use mirrors and shoulder checks

Before changing direction, as well as using your mirrors, you need to take a quick sideways glance to check for vehicles in any of your blind spots. These are areas behind and to the side of you which are not covered by the mirrors.

10.5

Mark one answer

RES s8, HC r241

You are looking for somewhere to park your motorcycle. The area is full EXCEPT for spaces marked 'disabled use'. You can

☐ use these spaces when elsewhere is full

☐ park if you stay with your motorcycle

☐ use these spaces, disabled or not

☐ not park there unless permitted

Don't be selfish. These spaces are intended for people with limited mobility. Find somewhere else to park, even if it means that you have to walk further.

10.6

Mark one answer

RES s10, HC r155–156

You are on a road with passing places. It is only wide enough for one vehicle. There is a car coming towards you. What should you do?

☐ Pull into a passing place on your right

☐ Force the other driver to reverse

☐ Turn round and ride back to the main road

☐ Pull into a passing place on your left

If you meet another vehicle in a narrow road and the passing place is on your left, pull into it. If the passing place is on the right, wait opposite it.

10.7

Mark one answer

RES s9, HC r181

You are both turning right at this crossroads. It is safer to keep the car to your right so you can

When turning right at this crossroads you should keep the oncoming car on your right. This will give you a clear view of the road ahead and any oncoming traffic.

☐ see approaching traffic

☐ keep close to the kerb

☐ keep clear of following traffic

☐ make oncoming vehicles stop

When filtering through slow-moving or stationary traffic you should

☐ watch for hidden vehicles emerging from side roads

☐ continually use your horn as a warning

☐ look for vehicles changing course suddenly

☐ always ride with your hazard lights on

☐ stand up on the footrests for a good view ahead

☐ look for pedestrians walking between vehicles

Other road users may not expect or look for motorcycles filtering through slow-moving or stationary traffic. Your view will be reduced by the vehicles around you. Watch out for pedestrians walking between the vehicles, vehicles suddenly changing direction and vehicles pulling out of side roads.

You are riding towards roadworks. The temporary traffic lights are at red. The road ahead is clear. What should you do?

☐ Ride on with extreme caution

☐ Ride on at normal speed

☐ Carry on if approaching cars have stopped

☐ Wait for the green light

You must obey all traffic signs and signals. Just because the lights are temporary it does not mean that you can disregard them.

You intend to go abroad and will be riding on the right-hand side of the road. What should you fit to your motorcycle?

☐ Twin headlights

☐ Headlight deflectors

☐ Tinted yellow brake lights

☐ Tinted red indicator lenses

When abroad and riding on the right, deflectors are usually required to prevent your headlight dazzling approaching drivers.

You want to tow a trailer with your motorcycle. Your engine must be more than

☐ 50 cc

☐ 125 cc

☐ 525 cc

☐ 1000 cc

You must remember that towing a trailer requires special care. You must obey the restrictions which apply to all vehicles towing trailers. Do not forget it is there, especially when negotiating bends and junctions.

10.12
Mark one answer HC r124, p40

What is the national speed limit on a single carriageway?

☐ 40 mph

☐ 50 mph

☐ 60 mph

☐ 70 mph

You don't have to ride at the speed limit. Use your own judgement and ride at a speed that suits the prevailing road, weather and traffic conditions.

10.13
Mark three answers HC r105, 109, 286

On which THREE occasions MUST you stop your motorcycle?

☐ When involved in a collision

☐ At a red traffic light

☐ When signalled to do so by a police officer

☐ At a junction with double broken white lines

☐ At a clear pelican crossing when the amber light is flashing

Don't stop or hold up traffic unnecessarily. However there are occasions when you MUST stop by law. These include, when signalled to do so by a police officer, at a red traffic light and if you have a collision. There are many other instances where you may have to stop.

10.14
Mark one answer HC p106, KYTS p20

What is the meaning of this sign?

☐ Local speed limit applies

☐ No waiting on the carriageway

☐ National speed limit applies

☐ No entry to vehicular traffic

This sign doesn't tell you the speed limit in figures. You should know the speed limit for the type of road that you're on. Study your copy of The Highway Code.

What is the national speed limit for cars and motorcycles on a dual carriageway?

- ☐ 30 mph
- ☐ 50 mph
- ☐ 60 mph
- ☐ 70 mph

Ensure that you know the speed limit for the road that you're on. The speed limit on a dual carriageway or motorway is 70 mph for cars and motorcycles, unless there are signs to indicate otherwise. The speed limits for different types of vehicles are listed in The Highway Code.

There are no speed limit signs on the road. How is a 30 mph limit indicated?

- ☐ By hazard warning lines
- ☐ By street lighting
- ☐ By pedestrian islands
- ☐ By double or single yellow lines

There is usually a 30 mph speed limit where there are street lights unless there are signs showing another limit.

Where you see street lights but no speed limit signs the limit is usually

- ☐ 30 mph
- ☐ 40 mph
- ☐ 50 mph
- ☐ 60 mph

The presence of street lights generally shows that there is a 30 mph speed limit, unless signs tell you otherwise.

What does this sign mean?

- ☐ Minimum speed 30 mph
- ☐ End of maximum speed
- ☐ End of minimum speed
- ☐ Maximum speed 30 mph

A red slash through this sign indicates that the restriction has ended. In this case the restriction was a minimum speed limit of 30 mph.

10.19
Mark one answer RES s8, HC r163

There is a tractor ahead of you. You wish to overtake but you are NOT sure if it is safe to do so. You should

☐ follow another overtaking vehicle through

☐ sound your horn to the slow vehicle to pull over

☐ speed through but flash your lights to oncoming traffic

☐ not overtake if you are in doubt

Never overtake if you're not sure whether it's safe. Can you see far enough down the road to ensure that you can complete the manoeuvre safely? If the answer is no, DON'T GO.

10.20
Mark three answers HC r187

Which three of the following are most likely to take an unusual course at roundabouts?

☐ Horse riders

☐ Milk floats

☐ Delivery vans

☐ Long vehicles

☐ Estate cars

☐ Cyclists

Long vehicles might have to take a slightly different position when approaching the roundabout or going around it. This is to stop the rear of the vehicle cutting in and mounting the kerb.

Horse riders and cyclists might stay in the left-hand lane although they are turning right. Be aware of this and allow them room.

10.21
Mark one answer KYTS p55

On a clearway you must not stop

☐ at any time

☐ when it is busy

☐ in the rush hour

☐ during daylight hours

Clearways are in place so that traffic can flow without the obstruction of parked vehicles. Just one parked vehicle will cause an obstruction for all other traffic. You MUST NOT stop where a clearway is in force, not even to pick up or set down passengers.

What is the meaning of this sign?

This sign indicates that there are waiting restrictions. It is normally accompanied by details of when restrictions are in force.

Details of most signs which are in common use are shown in The Highway Code and a more comprehensive selection is available in Know Your Traffic Signs.

- ☐ No entry
- ☐ Waiting restrictions
- ☐ National speed limit
- ☐ School crossing patrol

You can park on the right-hand side of a road at night

Red rear reflectors show up when headlights shine on them. These are useful when you are parked at night but will only reflect if you park in the same direction as the traffic flow. Normally you should park on the left, but if you're in a one-way street you may also park on the right-hand side.

- ☐ in a one-way street
- ☐ with your sidelights on
- ☐ more than 10 metres (32 feet) from a junction
- ☐ under a lamppost

On a three-lane dual carriageway the right-hand lane can be used for

You should normally use the left-hand lane on any dual carriageway unless you are overtaking or turning right.

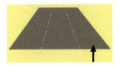

When overtaking on a dual carriageway, look for vehicles ahead that are turning right. They're likely to be slowing or stopped. You need to see them in good time so that you can take appropriate action.

- ☐ overtaking only, never turning right
- ☐ overtaking or turning right
- ☐ fast-moving traffic only
- ☐ turning right only, never overtaking

10.25 Mark one answer RES s8

You are approaching a busy junction. There are several lanes with road markings. At the last moment you realise that you are in the wrong lane. You should

☐ continue in that lane

☐ force your way across

☐ stop until the area has cleared

☐ use clear arm signals to cut across

There are times where road markings can be obscured by queuing traffic, or you might be unsure which lane you need to be in.

If you realise that you're in the wrong lane, don't cut across lanes or bully other drivers to let you in. Follow the lane you're in and find somewhere safe to turn around if you need to.

10.26 Mark one answer RES s8, HC r138

Where may you overtake on a one-way street?

☐ Only on the left-hand side

☐ Overtaking is not allowed

☐ Only on the right-hand side

☐ Either on the right or the left

You can overtake other traffic on either side when travelling in a one-way street. Make full use of your mirrors and ensure that it's clear all around before you attempt to overtake. Look for signs and road markings and use the most suitable lane for your destination.

10.27 Mark one answer RES s9, HC r186

When going straight ahead at a roundabout you should

☐ indicate left before leaving the roundabout

☐ not indicate at any time

☐ indicate right when approaching the roundabout

☐ indicate left when approaching the roundabout

When you want to go straight on at a roundabout, don't signal as you approach it, but indicate left just after you pass the exit before the one you wish to take.

10.28 Mark one answer RES s9, HC r187

Which vehicle might have to use a different course to normal at roundabouts?

☐ Sports car

☐ Van

☐ Estate car

☐ Long vehicle

A long vehicle may have to straddle lanes either on or approaching a roundabout so that the rear wheels don't cut in over the kerb.

If you're following a long vehicle, stay well back and give it plenty of room.

10.29
Mark one answer — RES s7, HC r174

You may only enter a box junction when

Yellow box junctions are marked on the road to prevent the road becoming blocked. Don't enter one unless your exit road is clear. You may only wait in the yellow box if your exit road is clear but oncoming traffic is preventing you from completing the turn.

- ☐ there are less than two vehicles in front of you
- ☐ the traffic lights show green
- ☐ your exit road is clear
- ☐ you need to turn left

10.30
Mark one answer — RES s7, HC r174

You may wait in a yellow box junction when

The purpose of this road marking is to keep the junction clear of queuing traffic. You may only wait in the marked area when you're turning right and your exit lane is clear but you can't complete the turn because of oncoming traffic.

- ☐ oncoming traffic is preventing you from turning right
- ☐ you are in a queue of traffic turning left
- ☐ you are in a queue of traffic to go ahead
- ☐ you are on a roundabout

10.31
Mark three answers — HC r105–109

You MUST stop when signalled to do so by which THREE of these?

Looking well ahead and 'reading' the road will help you to anticipate hazards. This will enable you to stop safely at traffic lights or if ordered to do so by an authorised person.

- ☐ A police officer
- ☐ A pedestrian
- ☐ A school crossing patrol
- ☐ A bus driver
- ☐ A red traffic light

10.32　Mark one answer　RES s8, HC r195

Someone is waiting to cross at a zebra crossing. They are standing on the pavement. You should normally

- ☐ go on quickly before they step onto the crossing
- ☐ stop before you reach the zigzag lines and let them cross
- ☐ stop, let them cross, wait patiently
- ☐ ignore them as they are still on the pavement

By standing on the pavement, the pedestrian is showing an intention to cross. If you are looking well down the road you will give yourself enough time to slow down and stop safely. Don't forget to check your mirrors before slowing down.

10.33　Mark one answer　RES s8, HC r199

At toucan crossings, apart from pedestrians you should be aware of

- ☐ emergency vehicles emerging
- ☐ buses pulling out
- ☐ trams crossing in front
- ☐ cyclists riding across

The use of cycles is being encouraged and more toucan crossings are being installed. These crossings enable pedestrians and cyclists to cross the path of other traffic. Watch out as cyclists will approach the crossing faster than pedestrians.

10.34　Mark two answers　RES s8, HC r199

Who can use a toucan crossing?

- ☐ Trains
- ☐ Cyclists
- ☐ Buses
- ☐ Pedestrians
- ☐ Trams

Toucan crossings are similar to pelican crossings but there is no flashing amber phase. Cyclists share the crossing with pedestrians and are allowed to cycle across when the green cycle symbol is shown.

10.35　Mark one answer　RES s8, HC r196

You are waiting at a pelican crossing. The red light changes to flashing amber. This means you must

- ☐ wait for pedestrians on the crossing to clear
- ☐ move off immediately without any hesitation
- ☐ wait for the green light before moving off
- ☐ get ready and go when the continuous amber light shows

This light allows time for the pedestrians already on the crossing to get to the other side in their own time, without being rushed. Don't rev your engine or start to move off while they are still crossing.

      Mark one answer   HC r240

When can you park on the left opposite these road markings?

You MUST NOT park or stop on a road marked with double white lines (even where one of the lines is broken) except to pick up or set down passengers.

☐ If the line nearest to you is broken

☐ When there are no yellow lines

☐ To pick up or set down passengers

☐ During daylight hours only

10.37   **Mark one answer**   HC r181

You are intending to turn right at a crossroads. An oncoming driver is also turning right. It will normally be safer to

☐ keep the other vehicle to your RIGHT and turn behind it (offside to offside)

☐ keep the other vehicle to your LEFT and turn in front of it (nearside to nearside)

☐ carry on and turn at the next junction instead

☐ hold back and wait for the other driver to turn first

At some junctions the layout may make it difficult to turn offside to offside. If this is the case, be prepared to pass nearside to nearside, but take extra care as your view ahead will be obscured by the vehicle turning in front of you.

10.38   **Mark three answers**   RES s10, HC r152

You are going along a street with parked vehicles on the left-hand side. For which THREE reasons should you keep your speed down?

☐ So that oncoming traffic can see you more clearly

☐ You may set off car alarms

☐ Vehicles may be pulling out

☐ Drivers' doors may open

☐ Children may run out from between the vehicles

Travel slowly and carefully where there are parked vehicles in a built-up area.

Beware of

• vehicles pulling out, especially bicycles and other motorcycles

• pedestrians, especially children, who may run out from between cars

• drivers opening their doors.

10.39   Mark one answer   RES s7

You meet an obstruction on your side of the road. You should

☐ carry on, you have priority

☐ give way to oncoming traffic

☐ wave oncoming vehicles through

☐ accelerate to get past first

Take care if you have to pass a parked vehicle on your side of the road. Give way to oncoming traffic if there isn't enough room for you both to continue safely.

10.40   Mark two answers   HC r137

You are on a two-lane dual carriageway. For which TWO of the following would you use the right-hand lane?

☐ Turning right

☐ Normal progress

☐ Staying at the minimum allowed speed

☐ Constant high speed

☐ Overtaking slower traffic

☐ Mending punctures

Normally you should travel in the left-hand lane and only use the right-hand lane for overtaking or turning right. Move back into the left lane as soon as it's safe but don't cut in across the path of the vehicle you've just passed.

10.41   Mark one answer   RES s9, HC r146

Who has priority at an unmarked crossroads?

☐ The larger vehicle

☐ No one has priority

☐ The faster vehicle

☐ The smaller vehicle

Practise good observation in all directions before you emerge or make a turn. Proceed only when you're sure it's safe to do so.

10.42   NI EXEMPT   Mark one answer   HC r243

What is the nearest you may park to a junction?

☐ 10 metres (32 feet)

☐ 12 metres (39 feet)

☐ 15 metres (49 feet)

☐ 20 metres (66 feet)

Don't park within 10 metres (32 feet) of a junction (unless in an authorised parking place). This is to allow drivers emerging from, or turning into, the junction a clear view of the road they are joining. It also allows them to see hazards such as pedestrians or cyclists at the junction.

In which THREE places must you NOT park?

☐ Near the brow of a hill
☐ At or near a bus stop
☐ Where there is no pavement
☐ Within 10 metres (32 feet) of a junction
☐ On a 40 mph road

Other traffic will have to pull out to pass you. They may have to use the other side of the road, and if you park near the brow of a hill, they may not be able to see oncoming traffic. It's important not to park at or near a bus stop as this could inconvenience passengers, and may put them at risk as they get on or off the bus. Parking near a junction could restrict the view for emerging vehicles.

You are waiting at a level crossing. A train has passed but the lights keep flashing. You must

☐ carry on waiting
☐ phone the signal operator
☐ edge over the stop line and look for trains
☐ park and investigate

If the lights at a level crossing continue to flash after a train has passed, you should still wait as there might be another train coming. Time seems to pass slowly when you're held up in a queue. Be patient and wait until the lights stop flashing.

At a crossroads there are no signs or road markings. Two vehicles approach. Which has priority?

☐ Neither of the vehicles
☐ The vehicle travelling the fastest
☐ Oncoming vehicles turning right
☐ Vehicles approaching from the right

At a crossroads where there are no 'give way' signs or road markings be very careful. No vehicle has priority, even if the sizes of the roads are different.

10.46 — Mark one answer — HC p107

What does this sign tell you?

The blue and red circular sign on its own means that waiting restrictions are in force. This sign shows that you are leaving the controlled zone and waiting restrictions no longer apply.

- ☐ That it is a no-through road
- ☐ End of traffic calming zone
- ☐ Free parking zone ends
- ☐ No waiting zone ends

10.47 — Mark one answer — HC r288, KYTS p139

You are entering an area of roadworks. There is a temporary speed limit displayed. You should

Where there are extra hazards such as roadworks, it's often necessary to slow traffic down by imposing a temporary speed limit. These speed limits aren't advisory, they must be obeyed.

- ☐ not exceed the speed limit
- ☐ obey the limit only during rush hour
- ☐ ignore the displayed limit
- ☐ obey the limit except at night

10.48 — Mark two answers — HC r243

In which TWO places should you NOT park?

It may be tempting to park where you shouldn't while you run a quick errand. Careless parking is a selfish act and could endanger other road users.

- ☐ Near a school entrance
- ☐ Near a police station
- ☐ In a side road
- ☐ At a bus stop
- ☐ In a one-way street

10.49 — Mark one answer — HC r115

You are travelling on a well-lit road at night in a built-up area. By using dipped headlights you will be able to

You may be difficult to see when you're travelling at night, even on a well lit road. If you use dipped headlights rather than sidelights other road users will see you more easily.

- ☐ see further along the road
- ☐ go at a much faster speed
- ☐ switch to main beam quickly
- ☐ be easily seen by others

10.50 — Mark one answer — RES s9, HC r173

The dual carriageway you are turning right onto has a very narrow central reservation. What should you do?

☐ Proceed to the central reservation and wait

☐ Wait until the road is clear in both directions

☐ Stop in the first lane so that other vehicles give way

☐ Emerge slightly to show your intentions

When the central reservation is narrow you should treat a dual carriageway as one road. Wait until the road is clear in both directions before emerging to turn right. If you try to treat it as two separate roads and wait in the middle, you are likely to cause an obstruction and possibly a collision.

10.51 — Mark one answer — HC p40

What is the national speed limit on a single carriageway road for cars and motorcycles?

☐ 30 mph

☐ 50 mph

☐ 60 mph

☐ 70 mph

Exceeding the speed limit is dangerous and can result in you receiving penalty points on your licence. It isn't worth it. You should know the speed limit for the road that you're on by observing the road signs. Different speed limits apply if you are towing a trailer.

10.52 — Mark one answer — RES s13, HC r249

You park at night on a road with a 40 mph speed limit. You should park

☐ facing the traffic

☐ with parking lights on

☐ with dipped headlights on

☐ near a street light

You MUST use parking lights when parking at night on a road or lay-by with a speed limit greater than 30 mph. You MUST also park in the direction of the traffic flow and not close to a junction.

10.53   Mark one answer   KYTS p27

You will see these red and white markers when approaching

- [ ] the end of a motorway
- [ ] a concealed level crossing
- [ ] a concealed speed limit sign
- [ ] the end of a dual carriageway

If there is a bend just before the level crossing you may not be able to see the level crossing barriers or waiting traffic. These signs give you an early warning that you may find these hazards just around the bend.

10.54   NI EXEMPT   Mark one answer   RES s18, HC r108

You are travelling on a motorway. You MUST stop when signalled to do so by which of these?

- [ ] Flashing amber lights above your lane
- [ ] A Highways Agency Traffic Officer
- [ ] Pedestrians on the hard shoulder
- [ ] A driver who has broken down

You will find Highways Agency Traffic Officers on many of Britain's motorways. They work in partnership with the police, helping to keep traffic moving and to make your journey as safe as possible. It is an offence not to comply with the directions given by a Traffic Officer.

10.55   Mark one answer   RES s9, HC r186

You are going straight ahead at a roundabout. How should you signal?

- [ ] Signal right on the approach and then left to leave the roundabout
- [ ] Signal left after you leave the roundabout and enter the new road
- [ ] Signal right on the approach to the roundabout and keep the signal on
- [ ] Signal left just after you pass the exit before the one you will take

To go straight ahead at a roundabout you should normally approach in the left-hand lane. You will not normally need to signal, but look out for the road markings. At some roundabouts the left lane on approach is marked as 'left turn only', so make sure you use the correct lane to go ahead. Signal before you leave as other road users need to know your intentions.

Case study practice – 10 Rules of the road

Ray is riding his motorcycle in the local area.

At a signed mini-roundabout, Ray turns right.

Later he comes to roadworks. There are temporary traffic lights showing red but no oncoming traffic.

Once past, Ray turns right into a road containing road humps and narrowed areas. He sees a sign showing red and black arrows, asking road users to give way to oncoming traffic.

10.1 What colour would this roundabout sign be?
Mark **one** answer

- ☐ Blue and white
- ☐ Red and white
- ☐ Green and white
- ☐ Black and white

HC p107 **KYTS** p19, 69

10.2 How should Ray act at these traffic lights?
Mark **one** answer

- ☐ Go quickly as there's no oncoming traffic
- ☐ Stop and wait until the light turns green
- ☐ Get off and wheel the motorcycle through
- ☐ Ride slowly through while indicating

HC p109

10.3 What should Ray do before making the turn?

Mark **one** answer

☐ Check that his hazard lights are working
☐ Turn and look back over his left shoulder
☐ Remove his helmet so he can see clearly
☐ Take a final look over his right shoulder

 RES s8, 9

10.4 What are these humps for?

Mark **one** answer

☐ To increase reaction time
☐ To monitor tyre pressure
☐ To help slow traffic down
☐ To test the suspension

RES s7

10.5 What shape would the arrowed sign be?

Mark **one** answer

☐ Circular
☐ Triangular
☐ Rectangular
☐ Square

KYTS p18

Road and traffic signs

In this section, you'll learn about

- what the shapes of road sign can tell you
- what road markings mean
- the sequence and meaning of traffic lights
- motorway warning lights
- the signals used by other drivers and by police officers.

Road and traffic signs

Road and traffic signs give important information to keep you safe on the road, so it's essential that you know what they mean and what you need to do when you see them.

> Signs

The shape and colour of a road sign tell you about its meaning.

Circular signs give orders.

Blue circles give an instruction or show which sort of road user can use a route, eg cyclists, pedestrians, trams.

Red rings or circles tell you what you mustn't do.

Triangular signs give warnings.

Rectangular signs give information.

Signs with a brown background give tourist information.

KYTS p9, 84, 100–104

The exception to the shape rule is the 'stop' sign: this is octagonal so that it stands out and can be understood even if it's partly covered, eg by snow.

HC r109 **RES** s7 **KYTS** p9

Maximum speed limits are shown inside red circles: you **MUST NOT** go faster than the speed shown. Where no speed limit is shown, the national speed limits (given on page 294) apply. Speed limit signs may be combined with other signs, such as those indicating a traffic-calmed area.

`HC` p106 `KYTS` p20

It's impossible to mention all the signs here. *Know Your Traffic Signs* shows all the signs you're likely to see and *The Official Highway Code* contains important advice, information on current laws in Great Britain, and best practice in road safety. It's important that you get to know these to make sure that you don't break the law.

Test your knowledge of signs using the activity on the Safe Driving for Life website.

> **safedrivingforlife.info/signsquiz**

> Road markings

Markings on the road give information, orders or warnings. As a general rule, the more paint there is, the more important the message.

`HC` r127–131 `RES` s7 `KYTS` p62–64

There are three types of road markings.

Along the middle of the road
Short broken white lines mark the centre of the road.

Longer broken white lines show that a hazard is ahead: only overtake if the road ahead is clear.

You **MUST NOT** cross or straddle double white lines with a solid white line on your side of the road unless

- you're turning into a junction or an entrance
- you need to pass a stationary vehicle
- you need to overtake a cyclist, horse or road maintenance vehicle if they're moving at 10 mph or less.

White diagonal stripes or chevrons separate lanes of traffic or protect traffic turning right.

Sometimes red tarmac is used within a block of white lines or diagonals. This highlights the area that separates traffic flowing in opposite directions.

HC p114 **RES** s7 **KYTS** p62–64

Along the side of the road

A white line shows the edge of the carriageway.

Yellow lines show waiting and stopping restrictions.

SCHOOL

Zigzag lines (white at pedestrian crossings, yellow outside schools) mean no stopping or parking at any time.

HC p115, 116 **RES** s7 **KYTS** p39–44, 56, 65, 122

Lines on or across the road

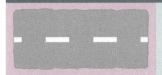 Broken lines across the road mean 'give way'. At a roundabout, give way to traffic from the right.

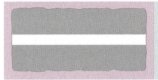 A single solid line means 'stop'.

 Various markings on the road, for example 'give way' triangles, road hump markings and rumble strips, warn of a hazard.

HC p114–116 **KYTS** p62–75

As with signs, you should look at *Know Your Traffic Signs* and *The Official Highway Code* to learn more about road markings.

You may see reflective studs on motorways and other roads. These are especially useful at night and when visibility is poor, as they help to make the lanes and edges of the road easier to see. Different coloured studs are used on motorways to help drivers and riders identify which lane they're using. See section 9, Motorway riding, for more details.

HC r132

Traffic lights and warning lights

Traffic lights work in a sequence.

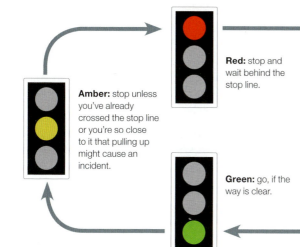

Red: stop and wait behind the stop line.

Red and amber: stop and wait; don't pass or start until the green light shows.

Amber: stop unless you've already crossed the stop line or you're so close to it that pulling up might cause an incident.

Green: go, if the way is clear.

HC p102 **RES** s7 **KYTS** p119–120

On some traffic lights there's a green filter arrow. This means you can go in the direction of the arrow, even if the main light isn't showing green.

If a set of traffic lights is out of order, ride very carefully: nobody has priority. There may be a sign telling you that the lights aren't working.

RES s7

Red flashing lights are used at level crossings and other locations, such as lifting bridges and outside some fire stations. You **MUST** stop when these show.

HC r293, p102 **KYTS** p13, 26–29, 120

At roadworks, traffic can be controlled by

- a police officer
- traffic lights
- a 'stop/go' board.

HC r288 **KYTS** p136

On motorways, signals on the overhead gantries or at the roadside may also have flashing lights.

Amber warns you of a hazard (eg lane closures, to leave at the next exit, fog) or a temporary maximum speed advised for the conditions.

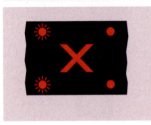

Red above your lane tells you that the lane is closed beyond this point, and you should move into another lane.

Red above all the lanes, on the central reservation or on the roadside tells you to stop. You **MUST NOT** go beyond that point in any lane.

HC r255–258, p102 KYTS p89–91

> Signals given by drivers and the police

Road users normally signal where they're intending to turn by using their indicators. Make sure that you cancel your indicators after you've turned, to avoid confusing other road users. Be aware that another driver may have left their indicator on by mistake.

If you're emerging from a junction and a driver coming along the main road from the right is close to you and indicating left, wait until the vehicle starts to turn before you emerge.

HC r103–104 RES s5

You may need to use an arm signal to strengthen or clarify the message given by your indicators, such as when you're

* signalling to turn right in busy traffic
* slowing down to give way at a zebra crossing.

However, don't keep signalling with your arm while you're turning left or right, because you'll have less control over the steering.

If you're slowing down and stopping just after a junction, wait to signal until you're passing the junction, or just after it.

You can use the horn to warn others that you're there. You **MUST NOT** use it between 11.30 pm and 7.00 am when riding in a built-up area, except when another road user puts you in danger. You **MUST NOT** use your horn when stationary unless another vehicle is likely to cause a danger.

The only reason you should flash your headlights is to warn other road users that you're there.

HC r110–112 **RES** s6

If you're riding on a motorway or unrestricted dual carriageway, you can briefly use your hazard warning lights to warn drivers behind you that there's an obstruction ahead.

HC r116 **RES** s5, 11

Police or traffic officers may signal to you if they're directing traffic. Make sure that you know all the official arm signals in case you need to use or react to them.

HC p103–105

A police or Highways Agency traffic officer following you in a patrol vehicle may flash their headlights, indicate left and point to the left to direct you to stop. Pull up on the left as soon as it's safe to do so.

HC r106

Remember, you **MUST** obey any signals given by police or traffic officers, traffic wardens and signs used by school crossing patrols.

HC r105–108, p104–105

> Road lanes

Contraflow lanes are lanes that flow in the opposite direction to most of the traffic. Bus and cycle contraflow lanes may be found in one-way streets. They'll be signed and marked on the road. Don't try to ride against the flow of traffic in these lanes.

HC r140–141, 143 **RES** s7

You may also see contraflow lanes at roadworks. When you see the signs

- reduce your speed and comply with any temporary speed limits
- choose an appropriate lane in good time
- keep the correct distance from the vehicle in front.

RES s11 **KYTS** p128–133

The centre and right-hand lanes of a three-lane motorway are overtaking lanes. Always move back to a lane on your left after overtaking, to allow other vehicles to overtake. On a free-flowing motorway or dual carriageway, you mustn't overtake other vehicles on their left.

HC r264, 268 **RES** s11

Meeting the standards

You must be able to

respond correctly to all

- permanent traffic signals, signs and road markings
- temporary traffic signals, signs and road markings.

You must know and understand

the meaning of all mandatory traffic signs and how to respond to them

the meaning of all warning signs and how to respond to them

the meaning of all road markings and how to respond to them.

> Notes

You can use this page to make your own notes or diagrams about the key points you need to remember.

Think about

- When are you allowed to cross double white lines along the centre of the road?
- What must you never do on zigzag lines?
- What shape is the 'stop' sign?
- What should you do at an amber traffic light?
- When might you need to use arm signals?

Your notes

Things to discuss and practise with your trainer

These are just a few examples of what you could discuss and practise with your trainer. Read more about road and traffic signs to come up with your own ideas.

Discuss with your trainer

- which is the only octagonal road sign and why it's unique
- what these shapes of sign tell you
  - round
  - triangular
  - rectangular
- what signs are relevant to solo motorcycles and what they mean.

Practise with your trainer

- identifying signs, from *The Official Highway Code* and *Know Your Traffic Signs*
- riding through a busy town centre and identifying all the warning signs that you see. Discuss these after your lesson
- riding to a level crossing and identifying the signs and signals that you find there.

How should you give an arm signal to turn left?

Arm signals can be effective during daylight, especially when you're wearing bright clothing. Practise giving arm signals when you're learning. You need to be able to keep full control of your motorcycle with one hand off the handlebars.

You are giving an arm signal ready to turn left. Why should you NOT continue with the arm signal while you turn?

Consider giving an arm signal if it will help other road users. Situations where you might do this include approaching a pedestrian crossing, in bright sunshine when your indicators may be difficult to see, when your indicators may be obscured in a traffic queue and where your indicators could cause confusion, such as when pulling up close to a side road. Don't maintain an arm signal when turning. Maintain full control by keeping both hands on the handlebars when you turn.

☐ Because you might hit a pedestrian on the corner

☐ Because you will have less steering control

☐ Because you will need to keep the clutch applied

☐ Because other motorists will think that you are stopping on the corner

11.3

Mark one answer

RES s12, HC p109, KYTS p12

This sign is of particular importance to motorcyclists. It means

Strong crosswinds can suddenly blow you off course. Keep your speed down when it's very windy, especially on exposed roads.

☐ side winds

☐ airport

☐ slippery road

☐ service area

11.4

Mark one answer

RES s7, HC p106, KYTS p17

Which one of these signs are you allowed to ride past on a solo motorcycle?

Most regulatory signs are circular, a red circle tells you what you must NOT do.

11.5

Mark one answer

RES s6, HC r103, p103

Which of these signals should you give when slowing or stopping your motorcycle?

Arm signals can be given to reinforce your flashing indicators, especially if the indicator signal could cause confusion, for example if you intend to pull up close to a side road.

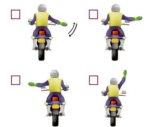

11.6
Mark one answer   RES s6, HC r110

When drivers flash their headlights at you it means

☐ that there is a radar speed trap ahead

☐ that they are giving way to you

☐ that they are warning you of their presence

☐ that there is something wrong with your motorcycle

A driver flashing their headlights has the same meaning as sounding the horn, it's a warning of their presence.

11.7
Mark one answer   RES s6, HC r103–104

Why should you make sure that you cancel your indicators after turning?

☐ To avoid flattening the battery

☐ To avoid misleading other road users

☐ To avoid dazzling other road users

☐ To avoid damage to the indicator relay

Always check that you have cancelled your indicators after turning. Failing to cancel your indicators could lead to a serious or even fatal collision. Other road users may pull out in front of you if they think you are going to turn off before you reach them.

11.8
Mark one answer   RES s6, HC p103

Your indicators are difficult to see due to bright sunshine. When using them you should

☐ also give an arm signal

☐ sound your horn

☐ flash your headlight

☐ keep both hands on the handlebars

Arm signals should be used to confirm your intentions when you aren't sure that your indicators can be seen by other road users. Use the signals shown in The Highway Code and return your hand to the handlebars before you turn.

11.9

Mark one answer

RES s11, HC p113

You are riding on a motorway. There is a slow-moving vehicle ahead. On the back you see this sign. What should you do?

If this vehicle is in your lane you will have to move to the left. Use your mirrors and signal if necessary. When it's safe move into the lane on your left. You should always look well ahead so that you can spot such hazards early, giving yourself time to react safely.

☐ Pass on the right

☐ Pass on the left

☐ Leave at the next exit

☐ Drive no further

11.10

Mark one answer

RES s7, HC p106, KYTS p9, 16

You MUST obey signs giving orders. These signs are mostly in

☐ green rectangles

☐ red triangles

☐ blue rectangles

☐ red circles

There are three basic types of traffic sign, those that warn, inform or give orders. Generally, triangular signs warn, rectangular ones give information or directions, and circular signs usually give orders. An exception is the eight-sided 'STOP' sign.

11.11

Mark one answer

RES s7, HC p106, KYTS p9, 16

Traffic signs giving orders are generally which shape?

Road signs in the shape of a circle give orders. Those with a red circle are mostly prohibitive. The 'stop' sign is octagonal to give it greater prominence. Signs giving orders MUST always be obeyed.

Which type of sign tells you NOT to do something?

☐ ☐

☐ ☐

Signs in the shape of a circle give orders. A sign with a red circle means that you aren't allowed to do something. Study Know Your Traffic Signs to ensure that you understand what the different traffic signs mean.

What does this sign mean?

☐ Maximum speed limit with traffic calming
☐ Minimum speed limit with traffic calming
☐ '20 cars only' parking zone
☐ Only 20 cars allowed at any one time

If you're in places where there are likely to be pedestrians such as outside schools, near parks, residential areas and shopping areas, you should be extra-cautious and keep your speed down.

Many local authorities have taken measures to slow traffic down by creating traffic calming measures such as speed humps. They are there for a reason; slow down.

Which sign means no motor vehicles are allowed?

You would generally see this sign at the approach to a pedestrian-only zone.

11.15   Mark one answer   RES s7, HC p106, KYTS p17

Which of these signs means no motor vehicles?

☐   ☐

☐   ☐

If you are driving a motor vehicle or riding a motorcycle you MUST NOT travel past this sign. This area has been designated for use by pedestrians.

11.16   Mark one answer   RES s7, HC p106, KYTS p20

What does this sign mean?

Where you see this sign the 20 mph restriction ends. Check all around for possible hazards and only increase your speed if it's safe to do so.

☐ New speed limit 20 mph

☐ No vehicles over 30 tonnes

☐ Minimum speed limit 30 mph

☐ End of 20 mph zone

11.17   Mark one answer   RES s7, HC p106, KYTS p17

What does this sign mean?

A sign will indicate which types of vehicles are prohibited from certain roads. Make sure that you know which signs apply to the vehicle you're using.

☐ No overtaking

☐ No motor vehicles

☐ Clearway (no stopping)

☐ Cars and motorcycles only

What does this sign mean?

'No entry' signs are used in places such as one-way streets to prevent vehicles driving against the traffic. To ignore one would be dangerous, both for yourself and other road users, as well as being against the law.

☐ No parking
☐ No road markings
☐ No through road
☐ No entry

What does this sign mean?

The 'no right turn' sign may be used to warn road users that there is a 'no entry' prohibition on a road to the right ahead.

☐ Bend to the right
☐ Road on the right closed
☐ No traffic from the right
☐ No right turn

Which sign means 'no entry'?

Look out for traffic signs. Disobeying or not seeing a sign could be dangerous. It may also be an offence for which you could be prosecuted.

☐
☐
☐
☐

11.21

Mark one answer · RES s7, HC p107, KYTS p30

What does this sign mean?

Avoid blocking tram routes. Trams are fixed on their route and can't manoeuvre around other vehicles and pedestrians. Modern trams travel quickly and are quiet so you might not hear them approaching.

- ☐ Route for trams only
- ☐ Route for buses only
- ☐ Parking for buses only
- ☐ Parking for trams only

11.22

Mark one answer · RES s7, HC p106, KYTS p23

Which type of vehicle does this sign apply to?

The triangular shapes above and below the dimensions indicate a height restriction that applies to the road ahead.

**4.4 m
14'-6"**

- ☐ Wide vehicles
- ☐ Long vehicles
- ☐ High vehicles
- ☐ Heavy vehicles

11.23

Mark one answer · RES s7, HC p106, KYTS p17

Which sign means NO motor vehicles allowed?

This sign is used to enable pedestrians to walk free from traffic. It's often found in shopping areas.

- ☐
- ☐
- ☐
- ☐

What does this sign mean?

Road signs that prohibit overtaking are placed in locations where passing the vehicle in front is dangerous. If you see this sign don't attempt to overtake. The sign is there for a reason and you must obey it.

☐ You have priority
☐ No motor vehicles
☐ Two-way traffic
☐ No overtaking

What does this sign mean?

If you're behind a slow-moving vehicle be patient. Wait until the restriction no longer applies and you can overtake safely.

☐ Keep in one lane
☐ Give way to oncoming traffic
☐ Do not overtake
☐ Form two lanes

Which sign means no overtaking?

This sign indicates that overtaking here is not allowed and you could face prosecution if you ignore this prohibition.

☐ ☐
☐ ☐

What does this sign mean?

There will be a plate or additional sign to tell you when the restrictions apply.

☐ Waiting restrictions apply
☐ Waiting permitted
☐ National speed limit applies
☐ Clearway (no stopping)

What does this sign mean?

Even though you have left the restricted area, make sure that you park where you won't endanger other road users or cause an obstruction.

☐ End of restricted speed area
☐ End of restricted parking area
☐ End of clearway
☐ End of cycle route

Which sign means 'no stopping'?

Stopping where this clearway restriction applies is likely to cause congestion. Allow the traffic to flow by obeying the signs.

☐
☐
☐
☐

Section eleven Questions

You see this sign ahead. It means

☐ national speed limit applies

☐ waiting restrictions apply

☐ no stopping

☐ no entry

Clearways are stretches of road where you aren't allowed to stop unless in an emergency. You'll see this sign. Stopping where these restrictions apply may be dangerous and likely to cause an obstruction. Restrictions might apply for several miles and this may be indicated on the sign.

What does this sign mean?

P
1 mile

☐ Distance to parking place ahead

☐ Distance to public telephone ahead

☐ Distance to public house ahead

☐ Distance to passing place ahead

If you intend to stop and rest, this sign allows you time to reduce speed and pull over safely.

11.32

Mark one answer

RES s7, KYTS p50

What does this sign mean?

In order to keep roads free from parked cars, there are some areas where you're allowed to park on the verge. Only do this where you see the sign. Parking on verges or footways anywhere else could lead to a fine.

☐ Vehicles may not park on the verge or footway

☐ Vehicles may park on the left-hand side of the road only

☐ Vehicles may park fully on the verge or footway

☐ Vehicles may park on the right-hand side of the road only

11.33

Mark one answer

RES s7, HC p106, KYTS p18

What does this traffic sign mean?

Priority signs are normally shown where the road is narrow and there isn't enough room for two vehicles to pass. These can be at narrow bridges, road works and where there's a width restriction.

Make sure that you know who has priority, don't force your way through. Show courtesy and consideration to other road users.

☐ No overtaking allowed

☐ Give priority to oncoming traffic

☐ Two way traffic

☐ One-way traffic only

Mark one answer RES s7, HC p113, KYTS p73

What does this sign mean?

Don't force your way through if oncoming vehicles fail to give way. If necessary, slow down and give way to avoid confrontation or a collision.

☐ No overtaking

☐ You are entering a one-way street

☐ Two-way traffic ahead

☐ You have priority over vehicles from the opposite direction

---

11.35 **Mark one answer** RES s7, HC p106, KYTS p16

What shape is a STOP sign at a junction?

To make it easy to recognise, the 'stop' sign is the only sign of this shape. You must stop and take effective observation before proceeding.

☐ ○

☐ △

☐ ▭

☐ ⬛

11.36 **Mark one answer** RES s7, HC p106, KYTS p16

At a junction you see this sign partly covered by snow. What does it mean?

The STOP sign is the only road sign that is octagonal. This is so that it can be recognised and obeyed even if it is obscured, for example by snow.

☐ Cross roads

☐ Give way

☐ Stop

☐ Turn right

11.37

Mark one answer   RES s7, HC p107, KYTS p21

What does this sign mean?

This sign is shown where slow-moving vehicles would impede the flow of traffic, for example in tunnels. However, if you need to slow down or even stop to avoid an incident or potential collision, you should do so.

☐ Service area 30 miles ahead
☐ Maximum speed 30 mph
☐ Minimum speed 30 mph
☐ Lay-by 30 miles ahead

11.38

Mark one answer   RES s7, HC p107, KYTS p19

What does this sign mean?

These signs are often seen in one-way streets that have more than one lane. When you see this sign, use the route that's the most convenient and doesn't require a late change of direction.

☐ Give way to oncoming vehicles
☐ Approaching traffic passes you on both sides
☐ Turn off at the next available junction
☐ Pass either side to get to the same destination

11.39

Mark one answer   RES s7, HC p107, KYTS p30

What does this sign mean?

Take extra care when you encounter trams. Look out for road markings and signs that alert you to them. Modern trams are very quiet and you may not hear them approaching.

☐ Route for trams
☐ Give way to trams
☐ Route for buses
☐ Give way to buses

11.40

What does a circular traffic sign with a blue background do?

Signs with blue circles give a positive instruction. These are often found in urban areas and include signs for mini-roundabouts and directional arrows.

☐ Give warning of a motorway ahead

☐ Give directions to a car park

☐ Give motorway information

☐ Give an instruction

11.41

Where would you see a contraflow bus and cycle lane?

In a contraflow lane the traffic permitted to use it travels in the opposite direction to traffic in the other lanes on the road.

☐ On a dual carriageway

☐ On a roundabout

☐ On an urban motorway

☐ On a one-way street

11.42

What does this sign mean?

There will also be markings on the road surface to indicate the bus lane. You must not use this lane for parking or overtaking.

☐ Bus station on the right

☐ Contraflow bus lane

☐ With-flow bus lane

☐ Give way to buses

11.43   Mark one answer   RES s7, KYTS p84

What does a sign with a brown background show?

Signs with a brown background give directions to places of interest. They will often be seen on a motorway directing you along the easiest route to the attraction.

☐ Tourist directions
☐ Primary roads
☐ Motorway routes
☐ Minor routes

11.44   Mark one answer   RES s7, KYTS p100

This sign means

These signs indicate places of interest and are designed to guide you by the easiest route. They are particularly useful if you are unfamiliar with the area.

☐ tourist attraction
☐ beware of trains
☐ level crossing
☐ beware of trams

11.45   Mark one answer   RES s7, HC p108, KYTS p10

What are triangular signs for?

This type of sign will warn you of hazards ahead.

Make sure you look at each sign that you pass on the road, so that you do not miss any vital instructions or information.

☐ To give warnings
☐ To give information
☐ To give orders
☐ To give directions

What does this sign mean?

This type of sign will warn you of hazards ahead. Make sure you look at each sign and road markings that you pass, so that you do not miss any vital instructions or information. This particular sign shows there is a T-junction with priority over vehicles from the right.

- ☐ Turn left ahead
- ☐ T-junction
- ☐ No through road
- ☐ Give way

What does this sign mean?

It will take up to ten times longer to stop when it's icy. Where there is a risk of icy conditions you need to be aware of this and take extra care. If you think the road may be icy, don't brake or steer harshly as your tyres could lose their grip on the road.

- ☐ Multi-exit roundabout
- ☐ Risk of ice
- ☐ Six roads converge
- ☐ Place of historical interest

What does this sign mean?

The priority through the junction is shown by the broader line. You need to be aware of the hazard posed by traffic crossing or pulling out onto a major road.

- ☐ Crossroads
- ☐ Level crossing with gate
- ☐ Level crossing without gate
- ☐ Ahead only

11.49 | **Mark one answer** | RES s7, HC p108, KYTS p10

What does this sign mean?

As you approach a roundabout look well ahead and check all signs. Decide which exit you wish to take and move into the correct position as you approach the roundabout, signalling as required.

☐ Ring road
☐ Mini-roundabout
☐ No vehicles
☐ Roundabout

11.50 | **Mark four answers** | RES s7, HC p108–109, KYTS p10–14

Which FOUR of these would be indicated by a triangular road sign?

Warning signs are there to make you aware of potential hazards on the road ahead. Act on the signs so you are prepared and can take whatever action is necessary.

☐ Road narrows
☐ Ahead only
☐ Low bridge
☐ Minimum speed
☐ Children crossing
☐ T-junction

Mark one answer

What does this sign mean?

Where there's a cycle route ahead, a sign will show a bicycle in a red warning triangle. Watch out for children on bicycles and cyclists rejoining the main road.

☐ Cyclists must dismount
☐ Cycles are not allowed
☐ Cycle route ahead
☐ Cycle in single file

Mark one answer

Which sign means that pedestrians may be walking along the road?

☐ ☐

☐ ☐

When you pass pedestrians in the road, leave plenty of room. You might have to use the right-hand side of the road, so look well ahead, as well as in your mirrors, before pulling out. Take great care if there is a bend in the road obscuring your view ahead.

Mark one answer

Which of these signs means there is a double bend ahead?

☐ ☐

☐ ☐

Triangular signs give you a warning of hazards ahead. They are there to give you time to prepare for the hazard, for example by adjusting your speed.

11.54

Mark one answer

RES s7, KYTS p30

What does this sign mean?

Obey the 'give way' signs. Trams are unable to steer around you if you misjudge when it is safe to enter the junction.

☐ Wait at the barriers
☐ Wait at the crossroads
☐ Give way to trams
☐ Give way to farm vehicles

11.55

Mark one answer

RES s7, HC p108, KYTS p11

Which of these signs means the end of a dual carriageway?

☐   ☐

☐   ☐

If you're overtaking make sure you move back safely into the left-hand lane before you reach the end of the dual carriageway.

11.56

Mark one answer

RES s7, HC p108, KYTS p11

What does this sign mean?

Don't leave moving into the left-hand lane until the last moment. Plan ahead and don't rely on other traffic letting you in.

☐ End of dual carriageway
☐ Tall bridge
☐ Road narrows
☐ End of narrow bridge

What does this traffic sign mean?

This sign is there to alert you to the likelihood of danger ahead. It may be accompanied by a plate indicating the type of hazard. Be ready to reduce your speed and take avoiding action.

☐ Slippery road ahead

☐ Tyres liable to punctures ahead

☐ Danger ahead

☐ Service area ahead

You are about to overtake when you see this sign. You should

Hidden dip

You won't be able to see any hazards that might be hidden in the dip. As well as oncoming traffic the dip may conceal

• cyclists
• horse riders
• parked vehicles
• pedestrians

in the road.

☐ overtake the other driver as quickly as possible

☐ move to the right to get a better view

☐ switch your headlights on before overtaking

☐ hold back until you can see clearly ahead

11.59

Mark one answer

RES s7, HC p108, KYTS p26

What does this sign mean?

Some crossings have gates but no attendant or signals. You should stop, look both ways, listen and make sure that there is no train approaching. If there is a telephone, contact the signal operator to make sure that it's safe to cross.

- ☐ Level crossing with gate or barrier
- ☐ Gated road ahead
- ☐ Level crossing without gate or barrier
- ☐ Cattle grid ahead

11.60

Mark one answer

RES s7, HC p108, KYTS p30

What does this sign mean?

This sign warns you to beware of trams. If you don't usually drive in a town where there are trams, remember to look out for them at junctions and look for tram rails, signs and signals.

- ☐ No trams ahead
- ☐ Oncoming trams
- ☐ Trams crossing ahead
- ☐ Trams only

11.61

Mark one answer

RES s7, HC p108, KYTS p12

What does this sign mean?

This sign will give you an early warning that the road ahead will slope downhill. Prepare to alter your speed and gear. Looking at the sign from left to right will show you whether the road slopes uphill or downhill.

- ☐ Adverse camber
- ☐ Steep hill downwards
- ☐ Uneven road
- ☐ Steep hill upwards

What does this sign mean?

This sign is found where a shallow stream crosses the road. Heavy rainfall could increase the flow of water. If the water looks too deep or the stream has spread over a large distance, stop and find another route.

☐ Uneven road surface

☐ Bridge over the road

☐ Road ahead ends

☐ Water across the road

What does this sign mean?

If you intend to take a left turn, this sign shows you that you can't get through to another route using the left-turn junction ahead.

☐ Turn left for parking area

☐ No through road on the left

☐ No entry for traffic turning left

☐ Turn left for ferry terminal

What does this sign mean?

You will not be able to find a through route to another road. Use this road only for access.

☐ T-junction

☐ No through road

☐ Telephone box ahead

☐ Toilet ahead

11.65 | Mark one answer | RES s7, HC p113, KYTS p114

Which sign means 'no through road'?

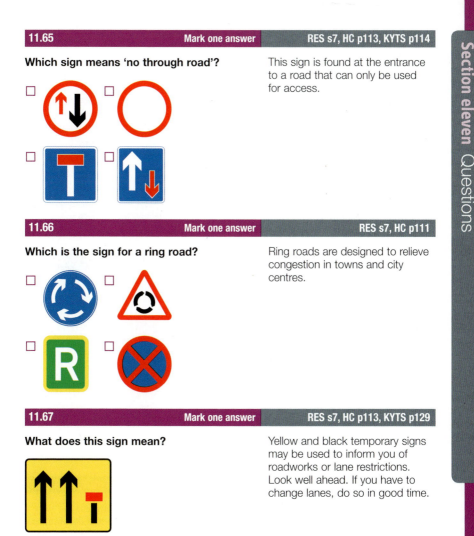

This sign is found at the entrance to a road that can only be used for access.

11.66 | Mark one answer | RES s7, HC p111

Which is the sign for a ring road?

Ring roads are designed to relieve congestion in towns and city centres.

11.67 | Mark one answer | RES s7, HC p113, KYTS p129

What does this sign mean?

Yellow and black temporary signs may be used to inform you of roadworks or lane restrictions. Look well ahead. If you have to change lanes, do so in good time.

- ☐ The right-hand lane ahead is narrow
- ☐ Right-hand lane for buses only
- ☐ Right-hand lane for turning right
- ☐ The right-hand lane is closed

What does this sign mean?

If you use the right-hand lane in a contraflow system, you'll be travelling with no permanent barrier between you and the oncoming traffic. Observe speed limits and keep a good distance from the vehicle ahead.

- ☐ Change to the left lane
- ☐ Leave at the next exit
- ☐ Contraflow system
- ☐ One-way street

What does this sign mean?

Where there's a long, steep, uphill gradient on a motorway, a crawler lane may be provided. This helps the traffic to flow by diverting the slower heavy vehicles into a dedicated lane on the left.

- ☐ Leave motorway at next exit
- ☐ Lane for heavy and slow vehicles
- ☐ All lorries use the hard shoulder
- ☐ Rest area for lorries

A red traffic light means

Make sure you learn and understand the sequence of traffic lights. Whatever light appears you will then know what light is going to appear next and be able to take the appropriate action. For example if amber is showing on its own you'll know that red will appear next, giving you ample time to slow and stop safely.

- ☐ you should stop unless turning left
- ☐ stop, if you are able to brake safely
- ☐ you must stop and wait behind the stop line
- ☐ proceed with caution

11.71

Mark one answer

RES s7, HC p102, KYTS p119

At traffic lights, amber on its own means

When amber is showing on its own red will appear next. The amber light means STOP, unless you have already crossed the stop line or you are so close to it that pulling up might cause a collision.

☐ prepare to go

☐ go if the way is clear

☐ go if no pedestrians are crossing

☐ stop at the stop line

11.72

Mark one answer

RES s7, HC p102, KYTS p119

You are at a junction controlled by traffic lights. When should you NOT proceed at green?

As you approach the lights look into the road you wish to take. Only proceed if your exit road is clear. If the road is blocked hold back, even if you have to wait for the next green signal.

☐ When pedestrians are waiting to cross

☐ When your exit from the junction is blocked

☐ When you think the lights may be about to change

☐ When you intend to turn right

You are in the left-hand lane at traffic lights. You are waiting to turn left. At which of these traffic lights must you NOT move on?

At some junctions there may be a separate signal for different lanes. These are called 'filter' lights. They're designed to help traffic flow at major junctions. Make sure that you're in the correct lane and proceed if the way is clear and the green light shows for your lane.

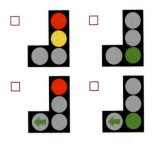

What does this sign mean?

Where traffic lights are out of order you might see this sign. Proceed with caution as nobody has priority at the junction.

- ☐ Traffic lights out of order
- ☐ Amber signal out of order
- ☐ Temporary traffic lights ahead
- ☐ New traffic lights ahead

When traffic lights are out of order, who has priority?

- ☐ Traffic going straight on
- ☐ Traffic turning right
- ☐ Nobody
- ☐ Traffic turning left

When traffic lights are out of order you should treat the junction as an unmarked crossroads. Be cautious as you may need to give way or stop. Keep a look out for traffic attempting to cross the junction at speed.

11.76   Mark three answers   RES s7, HC p102, KYTS p13, 26, 120

These flashing red lights mean STOP. In which THREE of the following places could you find them?

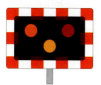

You must always stop when the red lights are flashing, whether or not the way seems to be clear.

- ☐ Pelican crossings
- ☐ Lifting bridges
- ☐ Zebra crossings
- ☐ Level crossings
- ☐ Motorway exits
- ☐ Fire stations

11.77   Mark one answer   RES s8, HC r191, KYTS p122

What do these zigzag lines at pedestrian crossings mean?

The approach to, and exit from, a pedestrian crossing is marked with zigzag lines. You must not park on them or overtake the leading vehicle when approaching the crossing. Parking here would block the view for pedestrians and the approaching traffic.

- ☐ No parking at any time
- ☐ Parking allowed only for a short time
- ☐ Slow down to 20 mph
- ☐ Sounding horns is not allowed

When may you cross a double solid white line in the middle of the road?

You may cross the solid white line to pass a stationary vehicle, pedal cycle, horse or road maintenance vehicle if they are travelling at 10 mph or less. You may also cross the solid line to enter into a side road or access a property.

- ☐ To pass traffic that is queuing back at a junction
- ☐ To pass a car signalling to turn left ahead
- ☐ To pass a road maintenance vehicle travelling at 10 mph or less
- ☐ To pass a vehicle that is towing a trailer

What does this road marking mean?

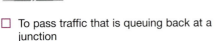

Road markings will warn you of a hazard ahead. A single, broken line along the centre of the road, with long markings and short gaps, is a hazard warning line. Don't cross it unless you can see that the road is clear well ahead.

- ☐ Do not cross the line
- ☐ No stopping allowed
- ☐ You are approaching a hazard
- ☐ No overtaking allowed

11.80

Mark one answer

RES s7, KYTS p73

Where would you see this road marking?

Due to the dark colour of the road, changes in level aren't easily seen. White triangles painted on the road surface give you an indication of where there are road humps.

☐ At traffic lights

☐ On road humps

☐ Near a level crossing

☐ At a box junction

11.81

Mark one answer

RES s7, HC r127, p114, KYTS p62

Which is a hazard warning line?

You need to know the difference between the normal centre line and a hazard warning line. If there is a hazard ahead, the markings are longer and the gaps shorter. This gives you advanced warning of an unspecified hazard ahead.

☐ ☐ ☐ ☐

11.82

Mark one answer

RES s7, HC p114, KYTS p9, 67

At this junction there is a stop sign with a solid white line on the road surface. Why is there a stop sign here?

If your view is restricted at a road junction you must stop. There may also be a 'stop' sign. Don't emerge until you're sure there's no traffic approaching.

IF YOU DON'T KNOW, DON'T GO.

☐ Speed on the major road is de-restricted

☐ It is a busy junction

☐ Visibility along the major road is restricted

☐ There are hazard warning lines in the centre of the road

You see this line across the road at the entrance to a roundabout. What does it mean?

Slow down as you approach the roundabout and check for traffic from the right. If you need to stop and give way, stay behind the broken line until it is safe to emerge onto the roundabout.

☐ Give way to traffic from the right

☐ Traffic from the left has right of way

☐ You have right of way

☐ Stop at the line

How will a police officer in a patrol vehicle normally get you to stop?

☐ Flash the headlights, indicate left and point to the left

☐ Wait until you stop, then approach you

☐ Use the siren, overtake, cut in front and stop

☐ Pull alongside you, use the siren and wave you to stop

You must obey signals given by the police. If a police officer in a patrol vehicle wants you to pull over they will indicate this without causing danger to you or other traffic.

You approach a junction. The traffic lights are not working. A police officer gives this signal. You should

If a police officer or traffic warden is directing traffic you must obey them. They will use the arm signals shown in The Highway Code. Learn what these mean and act accordingly.

☐ turn left only

☐ turn right only

☐ stop level with the officer's arm

☐ stop at the stop line

The driver of the car in front is giving this arm signal. What does it mean?

There might be an occasion where another driver uses an arm signal. This may be because the vehicle's indicators are obscured by other traffic. In order for such signals to be effective all drivers should know the meaning of them. Be aware that the 'left turn' signal might look similar to the 'slowing down' signal.

- ☐ The driver is slowing down
- ☐ The driver intends to turn right
- ☐ The driver wishes to overtake
- ☐ The driver intends to turn left

Where would you see these road markings?

When driving on a motorway or slip road, you must not enter into an area marked with chevrons and bordered by a solid white line for any reason, except in an emergency.

- ☐ At a level crossing
- ☐ On a motorway slip road
- ☐ At a pedestrian crossing
- ☐ On a single-track road

What does this motorway sign mean?

Look out for signs above your lane or on the central reservation. These will give you important information or warnings about the road ahead. Due to the high speed of motorway traffic these signs may light up some distance from any hazard. Don't ignore the signs just because the road looks clear to you.

- ☐ Temporary minimum speed 50 mph
- ☐ No services for 50 miles
- ☐ Obstruction 50 metres (164 feet) ahead
- ☐ Temporary maximum speed 50 mph

What does this sign mean?

☐ Through traffic to use left lane

☐ Right-hand lane T-junction only

☐ Right-hand lane closed ahead

☐ 11 tonne weight limit

You should move into the lanes as directed by the sign. Here the right-hand lane is closed and the left-hand and centre lanes are available. Merging in turn is recommended when it's safe and traffic is going slowly, for example at road works or a road traffic incident. When vehicles are travelling at speed this is not advisable and you should move into the appropriate lane in good time.

On a motorway this sign means

☐ move over onto the hard shoulder

☐ overtaking on the left only

☐ leave the motorway at the next exit

☐ move to the lane on your left

It is important to know and obey temporary signs on the motorway: they are there for a reason. You may not be able to see the hazard straight away, as the signs give warnings well in advance, due to the speed of traffic on the motorway.

What does '25' mean on this motorway sign?

☐ The distance to the nearest town

☐ The route number of the road

☐ The number of the next junction

☐ The speed limit on the slip road

Before you set out on your journey use a road map to plan your route. When you see advance warning of your junction, make sure you get into the correct lane in plenty of time. Last-minute harsh braking and cutting across lanes at speed is extremely hazardous.

11.92
Mark one answer RES s11

The right-hand lane of a three-lane motorway is

☐ for lorries only

☐ an overtaking lane

☐ the right-turn lane

☐ an acceleration lane

You should stay in the left-hand lane of a motorway unless overtaking. The right-hand lane of a motorway is an overtaking lane and not a 'fast lane'.

After overtaking, move back to the left when it is safe to do so.

11.93
Mark one answer RES s11, HC r132, KYTS p71

Where can you find reflective amber studs on a motorway?

☐ Separating the slip road from the motorway

☐ On the left-hand edge of the road

☐ On the right-hand edge of the road

☐ Separating the lanes

At night or in poor visibility reflective studs on the road help you to judge your position on the carriageway.

11.94
Mark one answer RES s11, HC r132, KYTS p71

Where on a motorway would you find green reflective studs?

☐ Separating driving lanes

☐ Between the hard shoulder and the carriageway

☐ At slip road entrances and exits

☐ Between the carriageway and the central reservation

Knowing the colours of the reflective studs on the road will help you judge your position, especially at night, in foggy conditions or when visibility is poor.

11.95
Mark one answer RES s11, HC p102, KYTS p90

You are travelling along a motorway. You see this sign. You should

You'll see this sign if the motorway is closed ahead. Pull into the nearside lane as soon as it is safe to do so. Don't leave it to the last moment.

☐ leave the motorway at the next exit

☐ turn left immediately

☐ change lane

☐ move onto the hard shoulder

What does this sign mean?

When you leave the motorway make sure that you check your speedometer. You may be going faster than you realise. Slow down and look out for speed limit signs.

☐ No motor vehicles
☐ End of motorway
☐ No through road
☐ End of bus lane

Which of these signs means that the national speed limit applies?

You should know the speed limit for the road on which you are travelling, and the vehicle that you are driving. The different speed limits are shown in The Highway Code.

☐ ☐

☐ ☐

What is the maximum speed on a single carriageway road?

If you're travelling on a dual carriageway that becomes a single carriageway road, reduce your speed gradually so that you aren't exceeding the limit as you enter. There might not be a sign to remind you of the limit, so make sure you know what the speed limits are for different types of roads and vehicles.

☐ 50 mph
☐ 60 mph
☐ 40 mph
☐ 70 mph

11.99   Mark one answer   RES s7, HC p102, KYTS p91

What does this sign mean?

Temporary restrictions on motorways are shown on signs which have flashing amber lights. At the end of the restriction you will see this sign without any flashing lights.

☐ End of motorway

☐ End of restriction

☐ Lane ends ahead

☐ Free recovery ends

11.100   Mark one answer   RES s7, HC p111, KYTS p107

This sign is advising you to

When a diversion route has been put in place, drivers are advised to follow a symbol which may be a triangle, square, circle or diamond shape on a yellow background.

☐ follow the route diversion

☐ follow the signs to the picnic area

☐ give way to pedestrians

☐ give way to cyclists

11.101   Mark one answer   RES s7, HC p113, KYTS p138

Why would this temporary speed limit sign be shown?

In the interests of road safety, temporary speed limits are imposed at all major road works. Signs like this, giving advanced warning of the speed limit, are normally placed about three quarters of a mile ahead of where the speed limit comes into force.

☐ To warn of the end of the motorway

☐ To warn you of a low bridge

☐ To warn you of a junction ahead

☐ To warn of road works ahead

This traffic sign means there is

The sign gives you an early warning of a speed restriction. If you are travelling at a higher speed, slow down in good time. You could come across queuing traffic due to roadworks or a temporary obstruction.

- ☐ a compulsory maximum speed limit
- ☐ an advisory maximum speed limit
- ☐ a compulsory minimum speed limit
- ☐ an advised separation distance

You are signalling to turn right in busy traffic. How would you confirm your intention safely?

- ☐ Sound the horn
- ☐ Give an arm signal
- ☐ Flash your headlights
- ☐ Position over the centre line

In some situations you may feel your indicators cannot be seen by other road users. If you think you need to make your intention more clearly seen, give the arm signal shown in The Highway Code.

What does this sign mean?

You must comply with all traffic signs and be especially aware of those signs which apply specifically to the type of vehicle you are using.

- ☐ Motorcycles only
- ☐ No cars
- ☐ Cars only
- ☐ No motorcycles

11.105
Mark one answer   RES s7, HC p113, KYTS p135

You are on a motorway. You see this sign on a lorry that has stopped in the right-hand lane. You should

Sometimes work is carried out on the motorway without closing the lanes. When this happens, signs are mounted on the back of lorries to warn other road users of roadworks ahead.

- ☐ move into the right-hand lane
- ☐ stop behind the flashing lights
- ☐ pass the lorry on the left
- ☐ leave the motorway at the next exit

11.106
Mark one answer   RES s7, HC p102, KYTS p91

You are on a motorway. Red flashing lights appear above your lane only. What should you do?

- ☐ Continue in that lane and look for further information
- ☐ Move into another lane in good time
- ☐ Pull onto the hard shoulder
- ☐ Stop and wait for an instruction to proceed

Flashing red lights above your lane show that your lane is closed. You should move into another lane as soon as you can do so safely.

11.107
Mark one answer   RES s6, HC r103, p103

The driver of this car is giving an arm signal. What are they about to do?

In some situations drivers may need to give arm signals, in addition to indicators, to make their intentions clear. For arm signals to be effective, all road users should know their meaning.

- ☐ Turn to the right
- ☐ Turn to the left
- ☐ Go straight ahead
- ☐ Let pedestrians cross

11.108

Mark one answer

RES s6, HC r112

When may you sound the horn?

- ☐ To give you right of way
- ☐ To attract a friend's attention
- ☐ To warn others of your presence
- ☐ To make slower drivers move over

Never sound the horn aggressively. You MUST NOT sound it when driving in a built-up area between 11.30 pm and 7.00 am or when you are stationary, an exception to this is when another road user poses a danger. Do not scare animals by sounding your horn.

11.109

Mark one answer

RES s6, HC r112

You must not use your horn when you are stationary

- ☐ unless a moving vehicle may cause you danger
- ☐ at any time whatsoever
- ☐ unless it is used only briefly
- ☐ except for signalling that you have just arrived

When stationary only sound your horn if you think there is a risk of danger from another road user. Don't use it just to attract someone's attention. This causes unnecessary noise and could be misleading.

11.110

Mark one answer

RES s7, HC p107, KYTS p55

What does this sign mean?

- ☐ You can park on the days and times shown
- ☐ No parking on the days and times shown
- ☐ No parking at all from Monday to Friday
- ☐ End of the urban clearway restrictions

Urban clearways are provided to keep traffic flowing at busy times. You may stop only briefly to set down or pick up passengers. Times of operation will vary from place to place so always check the signs.

11.111 | Mark one answer | RES s7, HC p109, KYTS p12

What does this sign mean?

You should be careful in these locations as the road surface is likely to be wet and slippery. There may be a steep drop to the water, and there may not be a barrier along the edge of the road.

☐ Quayside or river bank
☐ Steep hill downwards
☐ Uneven road surface
☐ Road liable to flooding

11.112 | Mark one answer | RES s7, HC p113, KYTS p73

Which sign means you have priority over oncoming vehicles?

☐ [sign] ☐ [sign]

☐ [sign] ☐ [sign]

Even though you have priority, be prepared to give way if other drivers don't. This will help to avoid congestion, confrontation or even a collision.

11.113 | Mark one answer | RES s7, HC r127, p114, KYTS p62

A white line like this along the centre of the road is a

The centre of the road is usually marked by a broken white line, with lines that are shorter than the gaps. When the lines become longer than the gaps this is a hazard warning line. Look well ahead for these, especially when you are planning to overtake or turn off.

☐ bus lane marking
☐ hazard warning
☐ give way marking
☐ lane marking

What is the reason for the yellow criss-cross lines painted on the road here?

Yellow 'box junctions' like this are often used where it's busy. Their purpose is to keep the junction clear for crossing traffic. Don't enter the painted area unless your exit is clear. The exception to this is when you are turning right and are only prevented from doing so by oncoming traffic or by other vehicles waiting to turn right.

- ☐ To mark out an area for trams only
- ☐ To prevent queuing traffic from blocking the junction on the left
- ☐ To mark the entrance lane to a car park
- ☐ To warn you of the tram lines crossing the road

What is the reason for the area marked in red and white along the centre of this road?

Areas of 'hatched markings' such as these are to separate traffic streams which could be a danger to each other. They are often seen on bends or where the road becomes narrow. If the area is bordered by a solid white line, you must not enter it except in an emergency.

- ☐ It is to separate traffic flowing in opposite directions
- ☐ It marks an area to be used by overtaking motorcyclists
- ☐ It is a temporary marking to warn of the roadworks
- ☐ It is separating the two sides of the dual carriageway

11.116 Mark one answer RES s6, HC r110

Other drivers may sometimes flash their headlights at you. In which situation are they allowed to do this?

☐ To warn of a radar speed trap ahead

☐ To show that they are giving way to you

☐ To warn you of their presence

☐ To let you know there is a fault with your vehicle

If other drivers flash their headlights this isn't a signal to show priority. The flashing of headlights has the same meaning as sounding the horn, it's a warning of their presence.

11.117 Mark one answer RES s7, HC r152

In some narrow residential streets you may find a speed limit of

☐ 20 mph

☐ 25 mph

☐ 35 mph

☐ 40 mph

In some built-up areas, you may find the speed limit reduced to 20 mph. Driving at a slower speed will help give you the time and space to see and deal safely with hazards such as pedestrians and parked cars.

11.118 Mark one answer RES s7, HC p102, KYTS p31

At a junction you see this signal. It means

The white light shows that trams must stop, but the green light shows that other vehicles may go if the way is clear. You may not live in an area where there are trams but you should still learn the signs. You never know when you may go to a town with trams.

☐ cars must stop

☐ trams must stop

☐ both trams and cars must stop

☐ both trams and cars can continue

Where would you find these road markings?

These markings show the direction in which the traffic should go at a mini-roundabout.

- ☐ At a railway crossing
- ☐ At a junction
- ☐ On a motorway
- ☐ On a pedestrian crossing

There is a police car following you. The police officer flashes the headlights and points to the left. What should you do?

You must pull up on the left as soon as it's safe to do so and switch off your engine.

- ☐ Turn left at the next junction
- ☐ Pull up on the left
- ☐ Stop immediately
- ☐ Move over to the left

You see this amber traffic light ahead. Which light or lights, will come on next?

At junctions controlled by traffic lights you must stop behind the white line until the lights change to green. Red and amber lights showing together also mean stop.

You may proceed when the light is green unless your exit road is blocked or pedestrians are crossing in front of you.

If you're approaching traffic lights that are visible from a distance and the light has been green for some time they are likely to change. Be ready to slow down and stop.

- ☐ Red alone
- ☐ Red and amber together
- ☐ Green and amber together
- ☐ Green alone

11.122

Mark one answer

RES s7, HC r127, p114, KYTS p62

This broken white line painted in the centre of the road means

A long white line with short gaps means that you are approaching a hazard. If you do need to cross it, make sure that the road is clear well ahead.

- ☐ oncoming vehicles have priority over you
- ☐ you should give priority to oncoming vehicles
- ☐ there is a hazard ahead of you
- ☐ the area is a national speed limit zone

11.123

Mark one answer

RES s11, HC p102, KYTS p90

You see this signal overhead on the motorway. What does it mean?

You will see this sign if there has been an incident ahead and the motorway is closed. You MUST obey the sign. Make sure that you prepare to leave as soon as you see the warning sign.

Don't pull over at the last moment or cut across other traffic.

- ☐ Leave the motorway at the next exit
- ☐ All vehicles use the hard shoulder
- ☐ Sharp bend to the left ahead
- ☐ Stop, all lanes ahead closed

What is the purpose of these yellow criss-cross lines on the road?

You MUST NOT enter a box junction until your exit road or lane is clear. The exception to this is if you want to turn right and are only prevented from doing so by oncoming traffic or by other vehicles waiting to turn right.

- ☐ To make you more aware of the traffic lights
- ☐ To guide you into position as you turn
- ☐ To prevent the junction becoming blocked
- ☐ To show you where to stop when the lights change

What MUST you do when you see this sign?

STOP

STOP signs are situated at junctions where visibility is restricted or there is heavy traffic. They MUST be obeyed. You MUST stop.

Take good all-round observation before moving off.

- ☐ Stop, only if traffic is approaching
- ☐ Stop, even if the road is clear
- ☐ Stop, only if children are waiting to cross
- ☐ Stop, only if a red light is showing

Which shape is used for a 'give way' sign?

Other warning signs are the same shape and colour, but the 'give way' sign triangle points downwards. When you see this sign you MUST give way to traffic on the road which you are about to enter.

- ☐ △
- ☐ ◯
- ☐ ⬟
- ☐ ▽

11.127

Mark one answer

RES s7, HC p107, KYTS p19

What does this sign mean?

When you see this sign, look out for any direction signs and judge whether you need to signal your intentions. Do this in good time so that other road users approaching the roundabout know what you're planning to do.

☐ Buses turning
☐ Ring road
☐ Mini-roundabout
☐ Keep right

11.128

Mark one answer

RES s7, HC p108, KYTS p11

What does this sign mean?

Be prepared for traffic approaching from junctions on either side of you. Try to avoid unnecessary changing of lanes just before the junction.

☐ Two-way traffic straight ahead
☐ Two-way traffic crosses a one-way road
☐ Two-way traffic over a bridge
☐ Two-way traffic crosses a two-way road

11.129

Mark one answer

RES s7, HC p108, KYTS p11

What does this sign mean?

This sign may be at the end of a dual carriageway or a one-way street. It is there to warn you of oncoming traffic.

☐ Two-way traffic ahead across a one-way road
☐ Traffic approaching you has priority
☐ Two-way traffic straight ahead
☐ Motorway contraflow system ahead

What does this sign mean?

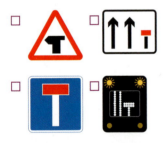

- ☐ Hump bridge
- ☐ Traffic calming hump
- ☐ Low bridge
- ☐ Uneven road

You will need to slow down. At hump bridges your view ahead will be restricted and the road will often be narrow on the bridge. If the bridge is very steep or your view is restricted sound your horn to warn others of your approach. Going too fast over the bridge is highly dangerous to other road users and could even cause your wheels to leave the road, with a resulting loss of control.

Which of the following signs informs you that you are coming to a 'no through road'?

☐   ☐

☐   ☐

This sign is found at the entrance to a road that can only be used for access.

What does this sign mean?

- ☐ Direction to park-and-ride car park
- ☐ No parking for buses or coaches
- ☐ Directions to bus and coach park
- ☐ Parking area for cars and coaches

To ease the congestion in town centres, some cities and towns provide park-and-ride schemes. These allow you to park in a designated area and ride by bus into the centre.

Park-and-ride schemes are usually cheaper and easier than car parking in the town centre.

11.133 | Mark one answer | RES s7, HC p102, KYTS p119

You are approaching traffic lights. Red and amber are showing. This means

Be aware that other traffic might still be clearing the junction. Make sure the way is clear before continuing.

- [ ] pass the lights if the road is clear
- [ ] there is a fault with the lights – take care
- [ ] wait for the green light before you cross the stop line
- [ ] the lights are about to change to red

11.134 | Mark one answer | RES s7, HC p116, KYTS p69

This marking appears on the road just before a

Where you see this road marking you should give way to traffic on the main road. It might not be used at junctions where there is relatively little traffic. However, if there is a double broken line across the junction the 'give way' rules still apply.

- [ ] 'no entry' sign
- [ ] 'give way' sign
- [ ] 'stop' sign
- [ ] 'no through road' sign

11.135 | Mark one answer | RES s7, HC r293, p102

At a railway level crossing the red light signal continues to flash after a train has gone by. What should you do?

- [ ] Phone the signal operator
- [ ] Alert drivers behind you
- [ ] Wait
- [ ] Proceed with caution

You MUST always obey red flashing stop lights. If a train passes but the lights continue to flash, another train will be passing soon. Cross only when the lights go off and the barriers open.

You are in a tunnel and you see this sign. What does it mean?

If you have to leave your vehicle in a tunnel and leave by an emergency exit, do so as quickly as you can. Follow the signs directing you to the nearest exit point. If there are several people using the exit, don't panic but try to leave in a calm and orderly manner.

☐ Direction to emergency pedestrian exit

☐ Beware of pedestrians, no footpath ahead

☐ No access for pedestrians

☐ Beware of pedestrians crossing ahead

Which of these signs shows that you are entering a one-way system?

If the road has two lanes you can use either lane and overtake on either side. Use the lane that's more convenient for your destination unless signs or road markings indicate otherwise.

☐   ☐

☐   ☐

What does this sign mean?

Buses and cycles can travel in this lane. In this case they will flow in the same direction as other traffic. If it's busy they may be passing you on the left, so watch out for them. Times on the sign will show its hours of operation. No times shown, or no sign at all, means it's 24 hours. In some areas other vehicles, such as taxis and motorcycles, are allowed to use bus lanes. The sign will show these.

☐ With-flow bus and cycle lane

☐ Contraflow bus and cycle lane

☐ No buses and cycles allowed

☐ No waiting for buses and cycles

11.139   Mark one answer   RES s7, HC p109, KYTS p13

Which of these signs warns you of a zebra crossing?

Look well ahead and check the pavements and surrounding areas for pedestrians. Look for anyone walking towards the crossing. Check your mirrors for traffic behind, in case you have to slow down or stop.

11.140   Mark one answer   RES s7, HC p109, KYTS p13

What does this sign mean?

You need to be aware of the various signs that relate to pedestrians. Some of the signs look similar but have very different meanings. Make sure you know what they all mean and be ready for any potential hazard.

- ☐ No footpath
- ☐ No pedestrians
- ☐ Zebra crossing
- ☐ School crossing

11.141   Mark one answer   RES s7, HC p108, KYTS p11

Which sign means there will be two-way traffic crossing your route ahead?

This sign is found in or at the end of a one-way system. It warns you that traffic will be crossing your path from both directions.

Which arm signal tells you that the car you are following is going to pull up?

There may be occasions when drivers need to give an arm signal to confirm an indicator. This could include in bright sunshine, at a complex road layout, when stopping at a pedestrian crossing or when turning right just after passing a parked vehicle. You should understand what each arm signal means. If you give arm signals, make them clear, correct and decisive.

Which of these signs means turn left ahead?

Blue circles tell you what you must do and this sign gives a clear instruction to turn left ahead. You should be looking out for signs at all times and know what they mean.

Which sign shows that traffic can only travel in one direction on the road you're on?

This sign means that traffic can only travel in one direction. The others show different priorities on a two-way road.

11.145

Mark one answer

RES s7, HC p107, KYTS p19

You have just driven past this sign. You should be aware that

In a one-way system traffic may be passing you on either side. Always be aware of all traffic signs and understand their meaning. Look well ahead and react to them in good time.

☐ it is a single-track road

☐ you cannot stop on this road

☐ there is only one lane in use

☐ all traffic is going one way

11.146

Mark one answer

RES s7, HC p102, KYTS p119

You are approaching a red traffic light. What will the signal show next?

If you know which light is going to show next you can plan your approach accordingly. This can help prevent excessive braking or hesitation at the junction.

☐ Red and amber

☐ Green alone

☐ Amber alone

☐ Green and amber

11.147

Mark one answer

RES s7, HC p108, KYTS p12

What does this sign mean?

When approaching a tunnel switch on your dipped headlights. Be aware that your eyes might need to adjust to the sudden darkness. You may need to reduce your speed.

☐ Low bridge ahead

☐ Tunnel ahead

☐ Ancient monument ahead

☐ Traffic danger spot ahead

> Case study practice – 11 Road and traffic signs

You're riding in the town centre. There are different types of road layouts and staggered junctions with various types of sign. Some roads have 'no entry' signs, others are one-way only.

At a large junction with traffic lights, there are filter arrows for traffic going left.

Beyond the junction, there are bus lanes on either side of the road. There are no signs showing times of operation.

11.1 What type of sign is the one for 'no entry'?

Mark **one** answer

- ☐ Advisory
- ☐ Warning
- ☐ Regulatory
- ☐ Information

HC p106 **KYTS** p16

11.2 What's meant by 'staggered'?

Mark **one** answer

- ☐ The joining side roads are both narrow one-way streets
- ☐ The joining side roads are exactly opposite each other
- ☐ The joining side roads are reserved for pedestrians only
- ☐ The joining side roads are slightly offset from each other

RES s9

11.3 What colours are used on the 'one way only' sign?

Mark **one** answer

- ☐ White with red arrow
- ☐ Blue with white arrow
- ☐ Red with green arrow
- ☐ White with black arrow

HC p107 **KYTS** p19

11.4 What colour is the filter arrow?

Mark **one** answer

- ☐ White
- ☐ Amber
- ☐ Green
- ☐ Blue

HC p102 **RES** s7

11.5 What's meant by the lack of bus lane signs?

Mark **one** answer

- ☐ The lane is in operation at all times for buses
- ☐ The lane isn't yet finished and still needs signs
- ☐ The lane is available for use by any vehicle
- ☐ The lane is being discontinued or removed

HC r141

Essential documents

In this section, you'll learn about

- ▸ the documents you need when owning and keeping a motorcycle
- ▸ the driving licence
- ▸ buying insurance
- ▸ the MOT test.

Essential documents

Before you can ride as a learner on a public road, you **MUST** have

- successfully completed a compulsory basic training (CBT) course, given by a DSA-approved training body
- a valid tax disc displayed on the motorcycle you're riding
- a valid provisional driving licence
- valid insurance cover
- L plates (D plates in Wales) correctly displayed at the front and rear of the motorcycle
- a valid MOT certificate, if it's required for the motorcycle you're using.

You won't be able to tax your motorcycle unless you have

- a valid MOT certificate if your motorcycle is more than three years old (four in Northern Ireland)
- appropriate, current insurance cover.

HC p122 **RES** s2

As a learner, you **MUST NOT** carry a **pillion passenger**, pull a trailer or ride your motorcycle on a motorway. You can do these things once you've passed your practical tests, provided your motorcycle has an engine capacity

- over 125 cc if you wish to tow a trailer
- of at least 50 cc if you wish to ride on the motorway.

HC r85, p122 **RES** s2

Definition

pillion passenger
a passenger who sits on the rear seat of a motorcycle, behind the rider

> Registering and owning a motorcycle

The vehicle registration certificate (V5C) contains details of

- the vehicle, including make, model, engine size and year of registration
- the registered keeper.

If you're the registered keeper, you **MUST** tell the Driver and Vehicle Licensing Agency (DVLA), or the Driver and Vehicle Agency (DVA) in Northern Ireland, when you change

- your motorcycle
- your name
- your permanent address.

If you buy a second-hand motorcycle, tell DVLA/DVA immediately that the keeper of the motorcycle has changed.

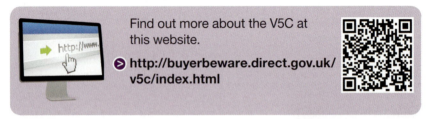

Find out more about the V5C at this website.

❯ **http://buyerbeware.direct.gov.uk/v5c/index.html**

Vehicles used on public roads **MUST** have a valid tax disc clearly displayed. This shows that the vehicle excise duty (road tax) has been paid.

`HC` `p122` `RES` `s2`

If you're not going to use your motorcycle on public roads, you won't have to pay road tax as long as you tell DVLA/DVA in advance. This is called a Statutory Off-Road Notification (SORN) declaration and lasts for 12 months.

`RES` `s2`

❯ Your motorcycle licence

Before riding on a public road, a learner **MUST** have a valid provisional driving licence and a CBT completion certificate. The CBT certificate is valid for two years. If you don't pass a practical test within that time, you'll have to retake the CBT.

`HC` `p122` `RES` `s2`

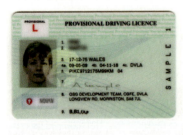

You **MUST** tell the licensing authority if

- your health is likely to affect your riding
- your eyesight doesn't meet the required standard.

HC r90 **RES** s1

> **Eyesight:** to be able to ride you **MUST** be able to read in good daylight, with glasses or contact lenses if you wear them, a vehicle number plate from 20 metres (about 66 feet) – which is about five car lengths.

For two years after you pass your first practical test (car or motorcycle), there's a probation period. This means that if you get six or more penalty points within this two-year probation period, you'll lose your licence. You'll then have to

- reapply for a provisional licence
- take your theory and practical tests, and your CBT, again.

Any points on your provisional licence will be transferred to your new licence when you pass your test.

HC p127, 134

> Insurance

You **MUST** have at least third-party insurance cover before riding on public roads. This covers

- injury to another person
- damage to someone else's property
- damage to other vehicles.

Riding without insurance is a criminal offence. It can lead to a maximum fine of £5000, and possibly disqualification.

HC p121–122 **RES** s2

You'll need to show your insurance certificate when you're taxing your motorcycle or if a police officer asks you for it. Your insurer may give you a temporary cover note until you receive your insurance certificate.

Remember, if your vehicle is unused or off the road it **MUST** have either a SORN declaration or valid insurance. If you have neither, and ignore any subsequent reminders sent to you as the registered keeper, you risk

- a fixed-penalty fine of £100
- court prosecution and a fine of up to £1000
- having the vehicle clamped, seized and destroyed.

RES s2

If a police officer asks to see your documents and you don't have them with you, you can produce them at a police station within seven days.
HC p122 **RES** s16

The cost of your insurance is generally lower if you're over 25 years old. Your insurance policy may have an excess of, for example, £100. This means you'll have to pay the first £100 of any claim.

Before you ride anyone else's motorcycle, make sure that it's insured for your use.
HC p121–122 **RES** s2

> MOT test

The MOT test makes sure your motorcycle meets road safety and environmental standards. Motorcycles **MUST** first have an MOT test when they're three years old (four in Northern Ireland). MOT certificates are valid for one year.
HC p121 **RES** s2

If your motorcycle has a sidecar, the MOT costs slightly more. Motorcycle trailers don't need an MOT, but they do need to be kept in good order.

The only time when you can ride your motorcycle without an MOT certificate is when you're riding to or from an appointment at an MOT centre or to have MOT repairs carried out.

If your motorcycle needs an MOT certificate and you don't have one

- you won't be able to renew your road tax
- you could be prosecuted
- your insurance may be invalid.

HC p121 **RES** s2

For more information about MOT tests, see this website.

> **direct.gov.uk/en/Motoring/ OwningAVehicle/Mot/ DG_10020539**

Meeting the standards

You must be able to

make sure that your driving licence is valid for the category of machine that you're riding

make sure that the machine is registered and a valid tax disc is correctly displayed

make sure that you have valid insurance for your use of the machine

make sure that the machine has a current MOT certificate (if necessary).

You must know and understand

that you must have a valid driving licence for the machine you ride. You must also comply with any restrictions on your licence

that the machine must be registered with DVLA/DVA

that you must tell DVLA/DVA if you

- change your name
- change your address
- have or develop a medical condition that will affect your ability to ride

that the vehicle you ride must have a valid MOT certificate if it's more than three years old.

> Notes

You can use this page to make your own notes or diagrams about the key points you need to remember.

Think about

- What documents do you need when taxing your motorcycle?
- You must tell DVLA/DVA when certain details change: what are they?
- What's a SORN?
- What's the minimum level of insurance you must have before riding on public roads?
- What does an MOT test cover?

Your notes

Things to discuss and practise with your trainer

These are just a few examples of what you could discuss and practise with your trainer. Read more about documents to come up with your own ideas.

Discuss with your trainer

- what the New Drivers Act means to someone whose first full licence is a motorcycle licence
- what the letters 'SORN' stand for and what this means to the keeper of a vehicle
- different types of insurance for your motorcycle and what they cover, eg third party, pillion passenger, etc.

Practise with your trainer

It's difficult to practise your knowledge and understanding of documents. Just remember that the safer and more responsibly you ride, the less likely you are to

- cause high wear and tear to your motorcycle
- accumulate penalty points
- be involved in an incident and damage your motorcycle.

This means that

- your motorcycle will be more likely to be roadworthy and pass its MOT test
- you'll be able to find cheaper insurance
- you won't lose your licence under the New Drivers Act and beyond.

Which of the following information is found on your motorcycle registration document?

☐ Make and model

☐ Service history record

☐ Ignition key security number

☐ Engine size and number

☐ Purchase price

☐ Year of first registration

Each motorcycle has a registration document which describes the vehicle's make, model and other details; it also gives details of the registered keeper. If you buy a new motorcycle the dealer will register your motorcycle with the licensing authority, who will send the registration document to you.

Compulsory Basic Training (CBT) can only be carried out by

☐ any ADI (Approved Driving Instructor)

☐ any road safety officer

☐ any DSA (Driving Standards Agency) approved training body

☐ any motorcycle main dealer

CBT courses can only be given by training bodies that are approved by DSA. The standard of training is monitored by DSA examiners. The course is designed to give you basic skills before going on the road.

Before riding anyone else's motorcycle you should make sure that

☐ the owner has third-party insurance cover

☐ your own motorcycle has insurance cover

☐ the motorcycle is insured for your use

☐ the owner has the insurance documents with them

If you borrow a motorcycle you must make sure that you are insured. Find out yourself. Don't take anyone else's word for it.

Vehicle excise duty is often called 'Road Tax' or 'The Tax Disc'. You must

☐ keep it with your registration document

☐ display it clearly on your motorcycle

☐ keep it concealed safely in your motorcycle

☐ carry it on you at all times

You must display a current, valid tax disc on your vehicle. It can't be transferred from one vehicle to another. A vehicle that is exempt from duty must display a valid nil licence instead.

12.5 · NI EXEMPT · Mark one answer · RES s2, HC p121

Motorcycles must FIRST have an MOT test certificate when they are

☐ one year old

☐ three years old

☐ five years old

☐ seven years old

Any motorcycle you ride must be in good condition and roadworthy. If it's over three years old it must have a valid MOT test certificate.

12.6 · Mark three answers · RES s2, HC p122

Which THREE pieces of information are found on a registration document?

☐ Registered keeper

☐ Make of the motorcycle

☐ Service history details

☐ Date of the MOT

☐ Type of insurance cover

☐ Engine size

Every motorcycle used on the road has a registration document issued by the Driver and Vehicle Licensing Agency (DVLA) or Driver and Vehicle Agency (DVA) in Northern Ireland. It is used to record any change of ownership and gives date of first registration, registration number, previous keeper, registered keeper, make of motorcycle, engine size and frame number, year of manufacture and colour.

12.7 · Mark three answers · RES s2, HC p120, 122

You have a duty to contact the licensing authority when

☐ you go abroad on holiday

☐ you change your motorcycle

☐ you change your name

☐ your job status is changed

☐ your permanent address changes

☐ your job involves travelling abroad

The licensing authority will need to keep their records up to date. They send out a reminder when your road tax is due and need your current address for this purpose. Every motorcycle in the country is registered, so it is possible to trace its history.

Your motorcycle is insured third-party only. This covers

☐ damage to your motorcycle

☐ damage to other vehicles

☐ injury to yourself

☐ injury to others

☐ all damage and injury

Third-party insurance cover is usually cheaper than fully comprehensive. However, it does not cover any damage to your own motorcycle or property and it does not provide cover if your motorcycle is stolen.

What is the legal minimum insurance cover you must have to ride on public roads?

☐ Third party, fire and theft

☐ Fully comprehensive

☐ Third party only

☐ Personal injury cover

The minimum insurance cover required by law is third party only. This covers other people and vehicles involved in a collision, but not you or your vehicle. Also basic third party insurance won't cover you for theft or fire damage. Make sure you carefully read and understand your policy.

A Vehicle Registration Document will show

☐ the service history

☐ the year of first registration

☐ the purchase price

☐ the tyre sizes

A Vehicle Registration Document contains a number of details that are unique to a particular vehicle. You must notify DVLA (or DVA in Northern Ireland) of any changes to, for example, the registered keeper, registration number or any modifications to the vehicle.

What is the purpose of having a vehicle test certificate (MOT)?

☐ To make sure your motorcycle is roadworthy

☐ To certify how many miles per gallon it does

☐ To prove you own the motorcycle

☐ To allow you to park in restricted areas

It is your responsibility to make sure that any motorcycle you ride is in a roadworthy condition. Any faults that develop should be promptly corrected. If your motorcycle fails an MOT test, it should not be used on the road unless you're taking it to have the faults repaired or for a previously arranged retest.

12.12 NI EXEMPT Mark one answer RES s2, HC p118

Before taking a practical motorcycle test you need

☐ a full moped licence

☐ a full car licence

☐ a CBT (Compulsory Basic Training) certificate

☐ 12 months' riding experience

The purpose of a CBT (Compulsory Basic Training) course is to teach you basic theory and practical skills before riding on the road, on your own, for the first time. They can only be given by Approved Training Bodies (ATBs).

12.13 Mark three answers RES s2, HC r90, 92, p122

You must notify the licensing authority when

☐ your health affects your riding

☐ your eyesight does not meet a set standard

☐ you intend lending your motorcycle

☐ your motorcycle requires an MOT certificate

☐ you change your motorcycle

The Driver and Vehicle Licensing Agency (DVLA) hold the records of all vehicles, drivers and riders in Great Britain (DVA in Northern Ireland). They need to know of any change in circumstances so they can keep their records up to date. Your health might affect your ability to ride safely. Don't put yourself or other road users at risk.

12.14 Mark two answers RES s2, HC p127, 134

You have just passed your practical motorcycle test. This is your first full licence. Within two years you get six penalty points. You will have to

☐ retake only your theory test

☐ retake your theory and practical tests

☐ retake only your practical test

☐ reapply for your full licence immediately

☐ reapply for your provisional licence

If, during your first two years of holding a full licence, the number of points on your licence reaches six or more, your licence will be revoked. This includes offences you committed before you passed your test. You may ride only as a learner until you pass both the theory and practical tests again.

You hold a provisional motorcycle licence. This means you must NOT

☐ exceed 30 mph

☐ ride on a motorway

☐ ride after dark

☐ carry a pillion passenger

☐ ride without L plates displayed

Provisional entitlement means that restrictions apply to your use of motorcycles. The requirements are there to protect you and other road users. Make sure you are aware of all the restrictions that apply before you ride your motorcycle on the road.

A full category A1 licence will allow you to ride a motorcycle up to

☐ 125 cc

☐ 250 cc

☐ 350 cc

☐ 425 cc

When you pass your test on a motorcycle between 75 cc and 125 cc you will be issued with a full light motorcycle licence of category A1. You will then be allowed to ride any motorcycle up to 125 cc and with a power output of 11 kW (14.6 bhp).

You want a licence to ride a large motorcycle via Direct Access. You will

☐ not require L plates if you have passed a car test

☐ require L plates only when learning on your own machine

☐ require L plates while learning with a qualified instructor

☐ not require L plates if you have passed a moped test

While training through the Direct Access scheme you must be accompanied by an instructor on another motorcycle and be in radio contact. You must display L plates on your motorcycle and follow all normal learner restrictions.

12.18   NI EXEMPT   Mark three answers   RES s14, HC r85

A motorcyclist may only carry a pillion passenger when

☐ the rider has successfully completed CBT (Compulsory Basic Training)

☐ the rider holds a full licence for the category of motorcycle

☐ the motorcycle is fitted with rear footrests

☐ the rider has a full car licence and is over 21

☐ there is a proper passenger seat fitted

☐ there is no sidecar fitted to the machine

Before carrying a passenger on a motorcycle the rider must hold a full licence for the category being ridden. They must also ensure that a proper passenger seat and footrests are fitted.

12.19   NI EXEMPT   Mark one answer   RES s2, HC p118

You have a CBT (Compulsory Basic Training) certificate. How long is it valid?

☐ one year

☐ two years

☐ three years

☐ four years

All new learner motorcycle and moped riders must complete a Compulsory Basic Training (CBT) course before riding on the road. This can only be given by an Approved Training Body (ATB). If you don't pass your practical test within two years you will need to retake and pass CBT to continue riding.

12.20   Mark one answer   RES s2

Your road tax disc is due to expire. To renew it you may need a renewal form, the fee, and valid MOT (if required). What else will you need?

☐ Proof of purchase receipt

☐ Compulsory Basic Training certificate

☐ A valid certificate of insurance

☐ A complete service record

You will normally be sent a reminder automatically by the DVLA (DVA in Northern Ireland) close to the time of renewal. Make sure that all your documentation is correct, up to date and valid. You can renew, by post, in person, by phone or online.

You want to carry a pillion passenger on your motorcycle. To do this

☐ your motorcycle must be larger than 125 cc

☐ they must be a full motorcycle licence-holder

☐ you must have passed your test for a full motorcycle licence

☐ you must have three years' motorcycle riding experience

As a learner motorcyclist you are not allowed to carry a pillion passenger, even if they hold a full motorcycle licence. You MUST NOT carry a pillion, or tow a trailer, until you have passed your test.

A friend asks you to give them a lift on your motorcycle. What conditions apply?

☐ Your motorcycle must be larger than 125 cc

☐ You must have three years' motorcycle riding experience

☐ The pillion must be a full motorcycle licence-holder

☐ You must have passed your test for a full motorcycle licence

By law, you can only carry a pillion passenger after you have gained a full motorcycle licence. Even if they hold a full licence it makes no difference. As a learner you are also restricted from towing a trailer.

Your motorcycle insurance policy has an excess of £100. What does this mean?

☐ The insurance company will pay the first £100 of any claim

☐ You will be paid £100 if you do not have a crash

☐ Your motorcycle is insured for a value of £100 if it is stolen

☐ You will have to pay the first £100 of any claim

This is a method used by insurance companies to keep annual premiums down. Generally, the higher the excess you choose to pay, the lower the annual premium you will be charged.

12.24 — Mark one answer — RES s2, HC p121

An MOT certificate is normally valid for

☐ three years after the date it was issued

☐ 10,000 miles

☐ one year after the date it was issued

☐ 30,000 miles

Make a note of the date that your MOT certificate expires. Some garages remind you that your vehicle is due an MOT but not all do. You may take your vehicle for MOT up to one month in advance and have the certificate post dated.

12.25 — Mark one answer — RES s2, HC p122

A cover note is a document issued before you receive your

☐ driving licence

☐ insurance certificate

☐ registration document

☐ MOT certificate

Sometimes an insurance company will issue a temporary insurance certificate called a cover note. It gives you the same insurance cover as your certificate, but lasts for a limited period, usually one month.

12.26 — Mark two answers — HC p127, 134

You have just passed your practical test. You do not hold a full licence in another category. Within two years you get six penalty points on your licence. What will you have to do?

☐ Retake only your theory test

☐ Retake your theory and practical tests

☐ Retake only your practical test

☐ Reapply for your full licence immediately

☐ Reapply for your provisional licence

If you accumulate six or more penalty points within two years of gaining your first full licence it will be revoked. The six or more points include any gained due to offences you committed before passing your test. If this happens you may only drive as a learner until you pass both the theory and practical tests again.

12.27 — Mark one answer — RES s2, HC p122

How long will a Statutory Off Road Notification (SORN) last for?

☐ 12 months

☐ 24 months

☐ 3 years

☐ 10 years

A SORN declaration allows you to keep a vehicle off road and untaxed for 12 months. If you want to keep your vehicle off road beyond that you must send a further SORN form to DVLA, or DVA in Northern Ireland. If the vehicle is sold SORN will end and the new owner becomes responsible immediately.

What is a Statutory Off Road Notification (SORN) declaration?

☐ A notification to tell VOSA that a vehicle does not have a current MOT

☐ Information kept by the police about the owner of the vehicle

☐ A notification to tell DVLA that a vehicle is not being used on the road

☐ Information held by insurance companies to check the vehicle is insured

If you want to keep a vehicle off the public road you must declare SORN. It is an offence not to do so. You then won't have to pay road tax. If you don't renew the SORN declaration or re-license the vehicle, you will incur a penalty.

A Statutory Off Road Notification (SORN) declaration is

☐ to tell DVLA that your vehicle is being used on the road but the MOT has expired

☐ to tell DVLA that you no longer own the vehicle

☐ to tell DVLA that your vehicle is not being used on the road

☐ to tell DVLA that you are buying a personal number plate

This will enable you to keep a vehicle off the public road for 12 months without having to pay road tax. You must send a further SORN declaration after 12 months.

What is the maximum specified fine for driving without insurance?

☐ £50

☐ £500

☐ £1,000

☐ £5,000

It is a serious offence to drive without insurance. As well as a heavy fine you may be disqualified or incur penalty points.

12.31
Mark one answer
RES s2, HC p122

Who is legally responsible for ensuring that a Vehicle Registration Certificate (V5C) is updated?

☐ The registered vehicle keeper

☐ The vehicle manufacturer

☐ Your insurance company

☐ The licensing authority

It is your legal responsibility to keep the details of your Vehicle Registration Certificate (V5C) up to date. You should tell the licensing authority of any changes. These include your name, address, or vehicle details. If you don't do this you may have problems when you sell your vehicle.

12.32
Mark one answer
RES s2, HC p122

For which of these MUST you show your insurance certificate?

☐ When making a SORN declaration

☐ When buying or selling a vehicle

☐ When a police officer asks you for it

☐ When having an MOT inspection

You MUST be able to produce your valid insurance certificate when requested by a police officer. If you can't do this immediately you may be asked to take it to a police station. Other documents you may be asked to produce are your driving licence and MOT certificate.

12.33
Mark one answer
RES s2

You must have valid insurance before you can

☐ make a SORN declaration

☐ buy or sell a vehicle

☐ apply for a driving licence

☐ obtain a tax disc

You MUST have valid insurance before you can apply for a tax disc. Your vehicle will also need to have a valid MOT certificate, if applicable. You can apply online, at certain post offices or by post. It is illegal and can be dangerous to drive without valid insurance or an MOT.

12.34
Mark one answer
RES s2

Your vehicle needs a current MOT certificate. Until you have one you will NOT be able to

☐ renew your driving licence

☐ change your insurance company

☐ renew your road tax disc

☐ notify a change of address

If your vehicle is required to have an MOT certificate you will need to make sure this is current before you are able to renew your tax disc (also known as vehicle excise duty). You can renew online, by phone or by post.

12.35 — Mark three answers — RES s2, HC p120

Which THREE of these do you need before you can use a vehicle on the road legally?

☐ A valid driving licence
☐ A valid tax disc clearly displayed
☐ Proof of your identity
☐ Proper insurance cover
☐ Breakdown cover
☐ A vehicle handbook

Using a vehicle on the road illegally carries a heavy fine and can lead to penalty points on your licence. Things you MUST have include a valid driving licence, a current valid tax disc, and proper insurance cover.

12.36 — Mark one answer — RES s2

When you apply to renew your Vehicle Excise Duty (tax disc) you must have

☐ valid insurance
☐ the old tax disc
☐ the handbook
☐ a valid driving licence

Tax discs can be renewed at post offices, vehicle registration offices, online, or by post. When applying make sure you have all the relevant valid documents, including MOT where applicable.

12.37 — Mark one answer — RES s2, HC p122

A police officer asks to see your documents. You do not have them with you. You may be asked to take them to a police station within

☐ 5 days
☐ 7 days
☐ 14 days
☐ 21 days

You don't have to carry the documents for your vehicle around with you. If a police officer asks to see them and you don't have them with you, you may be asked to produce them at a police station within seven days.

12.38 — Mark one answer — RES s2

When you apply to renew your vehicle excise licence (tax disc) what must you have?

☐ Valid insurance
☐ The old tax disc
☐ The vehicle handbook
☐ A valid driving licence

Tax discs can be renewed online, at most post offices, your nearest vehicle registration office or by post to the licensing authority. Make sure you have or take all the relevant documents with your application.

When should you update your Vehicle Registration Certificate?

☐ When you pass your driving test

☐ When you move house

☐ When your vehicle needs an MOT

☐ When you have a collision

As the registered keeper of a vehicle it is up to you to inform DVLA (DVA in Northern Ireland) of any changes in your vehicle or personal details, for example, change of name or address. You do this by completing the relevant section of the Registration Certificate and sending it to them.

Casey's old motorcycle has just failed an MOT and needs some repair work.

Casey rides the failed motorcycle to a local repairer a few miles away from the MOT centre. The parts can be ordered and the repairer can do the work. The repair takes five days.

A week later, Casey has the motorcycle retested. It successfully passes the second MOT.

Casey has the cheapest type of insurance cover available.

12.1 For how long does an MOT certificate last?
Mark **one** answer

☐ Six months
☐ Twelve months
☐ Two years
☐ Three years

`HC` p121 `RES` s2

12.2 Why could Casey ride to the repairer?
Mark **one** answer

☐ It's allowed during daylight hours but not at night
☐ It's allowed but only until vehicle excise duty expires
☐ It's allowed in order to get the machine to a repairer
☐ It's allowed for a period of seven days after failure

`HC` p121

12.3 Which of these MUST be displayed on the vehicle?

Mark **one** answer

- ☐ Vehicle Excise Duty
- ☐ Name and address details
- ☐ MOT certificate
- ☐ Registration document

HC p120–122 **RES** s2

12.4 What does the law say about insurance?

Mark **one** answer

- ☐ It's a provisional requirement
- ☐ It's a security requirement
- ☐ It's a voluntary requirement
- ☐ It's a legal requirement

HC p121 **RES** s2

12.5 What's the cheapest insurance cover called?

Mark **one** answer

- ☐ Third policy
- ☐ Third practice
- ☐ Third party
- ☐ Third procedure

HC p121–122 **RES** s2

Incidents, accidents and emergencies

In this section, you'll learn about

- what to do if your motorcycle breaks down
- how to ride safely in a tunnel, and what to do if you have an emergency
- what to do if you're the first to arrive at an incident
- first aid and how to help casualties at an incident
- reporting an incident to the police.

Incidents, accidents and emergencies

If you're involved in an incident on the road, such as your motorcycle breaking down or arriving first at the scene of a crash, knowing what to do can prevent a more serious situation from developing.

TIP

It's useful to carry a first aid kit, a warning triangle and a fire extinguisher for use in an emergency. This equipment could help to prevent or lessen an injury. You may be able to tackle a small fire if you have a fire extinguisher, but don't take any risks.

Breakdowns

Knowing what to do if your motorcycle breaks down will help keep you safe, and avoid creating problems for other road users, such as traffic jams.

If a warning light shows on the instrument panel of your motorcycle, you may have a problem that affects the safety of the vehicle. If necessary, stop as soon as you can do so safely and check the problem.

HC p128

If a tyre bursts or you get a puncture while you're riding,

- hold the handlebars firmly
- gently roll to a stop at the side of the road.

TIP

If you smell petrol while you're riding, stop and investigate as soon as you can do so safely. Don't ignore it.

If an emergency happens while you're on a motorway, try to get onto the hard shoulder and call for help from an emergency telephone. Marker posts show you the way to the nearest phone. The police or Highways Agency will answer and ask you

- the number on the phone, which will tell the services where you are
- details of yourself and your motorcycle
- whether you belong to a motoring organisation.

HC r270, 275 **RES** s16

Driver location signs can help you give the emergency services precise information about where you are. See this link for more details.

❯ **direct.gov.uk/prod_consum_dg/ groups/dg_digitalassets/@dg/@ en/documents/digitalasset/ dg_185820.pdf**

If you break down on a level crossing, get yourself, any passenger and your motorcycle off the crossing area immediately. If you can't move your motorcycle, phone the signal operator and follow any instructions given to you.

If you're waiting at a level crossing and the red light signal continues to flash after a train has gone by, you **MUST** wait, as another train may be coming.

HC r293, 299 **RES** s7 **KYTS** p27

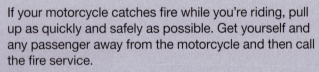

If your motorcycle catches fire while you're riding, pull up as quickly and safely as possible. Get yourself and any passenger away from the motorcycle and then call the fire service.

HC p130 **RES** s11

Watch the Think! 'Van of Elvises' video to find out what to do if you break down on a motorway.

❯ **youtube.com/thinkuk**

> Warning others of a breakdown or incident

Use your hazard warning lights

- if you need to suddenly slow down or stop on a motorway or high-speed road because of an incident or hazard ahead; as soon as the traffic behind you has reacted to your hazard lights, you should turn them off
- when your vehicle has broken down and is temporarily obstructing traffic.

HC r116, 274

If you have a warning triangle, place it at least 45 metres (147 feet) behind your motorcycle. This will warn other road users that you've broken down. Never place a warning triangle on a motorway: there's too much danger from passing traffic.

HC r274 **RES** s16

If you're riding on a motorway and you see something fall from another vehicle, or if anything falls from your motorcycle, stop at the next emergency telephone and report the hazard to the police. Don't try to retrieve it yourself.

RES s16

> Safety in tunnels

You need to take extra care when riding in a tunnel because

- when you enter the tunnel, visibility is suddenly reduced
- the confined space can make incidents difficult to deal with.

Before riding through a tunnel, remove your sunglasses or sun visor if you're using them and make sure your dipped headlights are on. It's particularly important to keep a safe distance from the vehicle in front when riding in a tunnel, even if it's congested.

Look out for signs that warn of incidents or congestion.

If your motorcycle is involved in an incident or breaks down in a tunnel,

- switch off the engine
- put your hazard warning lights on
- go and call for help immediately from the nearest emergency telephone point.

RES s8

> Stopping at an incident

If you're the first to arrive at the scene of an incident or crash, stop and warn other traffic. Switch on your hazard warning lights. Don't put yourself at risk.

- Make sure that the emergency services are called as soon as possible.
- Ensure that the engines of any vehicles at the scene are switched off.
- Move uninjured people away from the scene.

HC r283 RES s16

A vehicle carrying dangerous goods will display an orange label or a hazard warning plate on the back. If a vehicle carrying something hazardous is involved in an incident, report what the label says when you call the emergency services. The different plates are shown in *The Official Highway Code*.

HC p117 RES s16

> Helping others and giving first aid

Even if you don't know any first aid, you can help any injured people by

- keeping them warm and comfortable
- keeping them calm by talking to them reassuringly
- making sure they're not left alone.

HC p131 RES s16

Don't move an injured person if the area is safe. Only move them if they're in obvious danger, and then with extreme care. If a motorcyclist is involved, never remove their helmet unless it's essential in order to keep them alive, because removing the helmet could cause more serious injury. Always get medical help and never offer a casualty any food or drink, or a cigarette to calm them down.

HC p131–133 **RES** s16

There are three vital priorities

1. ensure a clear airway
2. check for breathing
3. try to stop any heavy bleeding.

If someone is unconscious, follow the **DR ABC** code.

Danger 	Check for danger, such as approaching traffic, before you move towards the casualty.	
Response 	Ask the casualty questions and gently shake the shoulders to check for a response.	
Airway 	Check the airway is clear.	
Breathing 	Check for breathing for up to 10 seconds.	

Compressions

Using two hands in the centre of the chest, press down 4–5 cm at a rate of 100 per minute. Use one hand, gently for a small child (two fingers for an infant).

If the casualty isn't breathing, consider giving mouth-to-mouth resuscitation.

Check and, if necessary, clear their mouth and airway.

Gently tilt their head back as far as possible.

Pinch their nostrils together.

Place your mouth over theirs. Give two breaths, each lasting one second.

Continue with cycles of 30 chest compressions and two breaths until medical help arrives.

Only stop when they can breathe without help. If the casualty is a small child, breathe very gently. Once the casualty is breathing normally, place them in the recovery position and check the airway to make sure it's clear. Keep checking, and don't leave them alone.

If they're bleeding, apply firm pressure to the wound. If the casualty is bleeding from a limb, raise it as long as it isn't broken. This will help reduce the bleeding.

People at the scene may be suffering from shock: signs include a rapid pulse, sweating and pale grey skin.

To help someone suffering from shock,

- reassure them constantly
- keep them warm
- make them as comfortable as you can
- avoid moving them unless it's necessary
- make sure they're not left alone.

If someone is suffering from burns,

- douse the burns thoroughly with cool non-toxic liquid for at least 10 minutes
- don't remove anything sticking to the burn.

❯ Reporting an incident

You **MUST** stop if you're involved in an incident. It's an offence not to stop and call the police if any other person is injured. If there's damage to another vehicle, property or animal, report it to the owner. If you don't do this at the time, you **MUST** report the incident to the police within 24 hours (immediately in Northern Ireland).

HC r286 **RES** s16

If another vehicle is involved, find out

- who owns the vehicle
- the make and registration number of the vehicle
- the other driver's name, address and telephone number and details of their insurance.

Following an incident (or at any other time), the police may ask you for

- your insurance certificate
- the MOT certificate for the motorcycle you're riding
- your driving licence.

HC r286, p122

Meeting the standards

You must be able to

stop and park your machine in a safe place, if necessary

make sure that warning is given to other road users

give help to others at the scene if you can

where possible, record information about what you saw or the scene that you found. It may be helpful to take photographs and draw sketch plans.

You must know and understand

how to keep control of the machine, where possible, if it breaks down

how and when to use hazard warning lights

what the law says about stopping if you're involved in an incident that causes damage or injury to

- any other person
- another vehicle
- an animal
- someone's property

This includes what to do about

- stopping
- providing your details
- giving statements
- producing documents

how to contact the emergency services and how important it is to give them accurate information.

> Notes

You can use this page to make your own notes or diagrams about the key points you need to remember.

Think about

- What should you do if your motorcycle breaks down on the motorway?
- How can you warn other road users if you've broken down on the road?
- If you're the first person to arrive at the scene of a crash, what should you do?
- If a motorcyclist is involved in the crash, should you remove their helmet?
- What does DR ABC stand for?
- If you're involved in an incident with another vehicle, what must you do?

Your notes

Things to discuss and practise with your trainer

These are just a few examples of what you could discuss and practise with your trainer. Read more about incidents, accidents and emergencies to come up with your own ideas.

Discuss with your trainer

- what it means if you see a driver displaying a 'help' pennant
- when you may and may not use your hazard warning lights
- what you should do if you arrive at the scene of a crash and find
  - an injured motorcyclist wearing a helmet
  - someone bleeding badly with nothing embedded in their wound
  - someone with a burn
  - someone who isn't breathing normally.

Practise with your trainer

Hopefully, you won't have the opportunity to practise what to do in the event of an incident or emergency during your lesson. Instead, practise with your trainer

- learning the rules relating to
  - breakdowns on all roads, including motorways
  - obstructions
  - incidents, eg warning signs and flashing lights
  - passing and being involved in a crash
  - incidents involving dangerous goods
  - which documents you'll need to produce if you're involved in a crash
  - incidents in tunnels.

    Mark one answer   **RES s11, HC r275**

Your motorcycle has broken down on a motorway. How will you know the direction of the nearest emergency telephone?

☐ By walking with the flow of traffic

☐ By following an arrow on a marker post

☐ By walking against the flow of traffic

☐ By remembering where the last phone was

If you break down on a motorway pull onto the hard shoulder and stop as far over to the left as you can. Switch on hazard lights (if fitted) and go to the nearest emergency telephone. Marker posts spaced every 100 metres will show you where the nearest telephone is.

    Mark one answer   **RES s5**

You should use the engine cut-out switch to

☐ stop the engine in an emergency

☐ stop the engine on short journeys

☐ save wear on the ignition switch

☐ start the engine if you lose the key

Most motorcycles are fitted with an engine cut-out switch. This is designed to stop the engine in an emergency and so reduce the risk of fire.

    Mark one answer   **HC r116**

You are riding on a motorway. The car in front switches on its hazard warning lights whilst moving. This means

☐ they are going to take the next exit

☐ there is a danger ahead

☐ there is a police car in the left lane

☐ they are trying to change lanes

When riding on a motorway, or a dual carriageway subject to a national speed limit, vehicles may switch on their hazard warning lights to warn following traffic of an obstruction ahead.

    Mark three answers   **RES s11, HC r275**

You have broken down on a motorway. When you use the emergency telephone you will be asked

☐ for the number on the telephone that you are using

☐ for your driving licence details

☐ for the name of your vehicle insurance company

☐ for details of yourself and your motorcycle

☐ whether you belong to a motoring organisation

Have these details ready before you phone and be sure to give the correct information. For your own safety face the traffic when you speak on the telephone.

13.5

Mark one answer

RES s11, HC r116

You are on a motorway. When can you use hazard warning lights?

☐ When a vehicle is following too closely

☐ When you slow down quickly because of danger ahead

☐ When you are being towed by another vehicle

☐ When riding on the hard shoulder

Hazard lights will warn the traffic behind you that there is a potential hazard ahead. Don't forget to turn them off again when your signal has been seen.

13.6

Mark one answer

RES s16, HC r116, 274

You are riding through a tunnel. Your motorcycle breaks down. What should you do?

☐ Switch on hazard warning lights

☐ Remain on your motorcycle

☐ Wait for the police to find you

☐ Rely on CCTV cameras seeing you

If your motorcycle breaks down in a tunnel it could present a danger to other traffic. First switch on your hazard warning lights and then call for help from an emergency telephone point. Don't rely on being found by the police or being seen by a CCTV camera.

13.7

Mark one answer

RES s11, HC r280

You are on a motorway. Luggage falls from your motorcycle. What should you do?

☐ Stop at the next emergency telephone and report the hazard

☐ Stop on the motorway and put on hazard lights while you pick it up

☐ Walk back up the motorway to pick it up

☐ Pull up on the hard shoulder and wave traffic down

If any of your luggage falls onto the road, pull onto the hard shoulder near an emergency telephone and phone for assistance. Don't stop on the carriageway or attempt to retrieve anything.

13.8 Mark four answers RES s16, HC r286–287

You are in collision with another vehicle. Someone is injured. Your motorcycle is damaged. Which FOUR of the following should you find out?

☐ Whether the driver owns the other vehicle involved

☐ The other driver's name, address and telephone number

☐ The make and registration number of the other vehicle

☐ The occupation of the other driver

☐ The details of the other driver's vehicle insurance

☐ Whether the other driver is licensed to drive

If you are involved in a collision where someone is injured, your first priority is to warn other traffic and call the emergency services.

When exchanging details, make sure you have all the information you need before you leave the scene. Don't ride your motorcycle if it is unroadworthy.

13.9 Mark one answer HC r278

You see a car on the hard shoulder of a motorway with a HELP pennant displayed. This means the driver is most likely to be

☐ a disabled person

☐ first aid trained

☐ a foreign visitor

☐ a rescue patrol person

If a disabled driver's vehicle breaks down and they are unable to walk to an emergency phone, they are advised to stay in their car and switch on the hazard warning lights. They may also display a 'Help' pennant in their vehicle.

13.10 Mark one answer RES s16, HC r116

When are you allowed to use hazard warning lights?

☐ When stopped and temporarily obstructing traffic

☐ When travelling during darkness without headlights

☐ When parked for shopping on double yellow lines

☐ When travelling slowly because you are lost

You must not use hazard warning lights when moving, except when slowing suddenly on a motorway or unrestricted dual carriageway to warn the traffic behind.

Never use hazard warning lights to excuse dangerous or illegal parking.

13.11
Mark one answer
RES s8, HC r126

You are going through a congested tunnel and have to stop. What should you do?

☐ Pull up very close to the vehicle in front to save space

☐ Ignore any message signs as they are never up to date

☐ Keep a safe distance from the vehicle in front

☐ Make a U-turn and find another route

It's important to keep a safe distance from the vehicle in front at all times. This still applies in congested tunnels even if you are moving very slowly or have stopped. If the vehicle in front breaks down you may need room to manoeuvre past it.

13.12
Mark one answer
RES s11, HC r275

On the motorway, the hard shoulder should be used

☐ to answer a mobile phone

☐ when an emergency arises

☐ for a short rest when tired

☐ to check a road atlas

Pull onto the hard shoulder and use the emergency telephone to report your problem. This lets the emergency services know your exact location so they can send help. Never cross the carriageway to use the telephone on the other side.

13.13
Mark one answer
RES s16, HC p132

You arrive at the scene of a crash. Someone is bleeding badly from an arm wound. There is nothing embedded in it. What should you do?

☐ Apply pressure over the wound and keep the arm down

☐ Dab the wound

☐ Get them a drink

☐ Apply pressure over the wound and raise the arm

If possible, lay the casualty down. Check for anything that may be in the wound. Apply firm pressure to the wound using clean material, without pressing on anything which might be in it. Raising the arm above the level of the heart will also help to stem the flow of blood.

13.14
Mark one answer
RES s16, HC p132

You are at an incident where a casualty is unconscious. Their breathing should be checked. This should be done for at least

☐ 2 seconds

☐ 10 seconds

☐ 1 minute

☐ 2 minutes

Once the airway is open, check breathing. Listen and feel for breath. Do this by placing your cheek over their mouth and nose, and look to see if the chest rises. This should be done for up to 10 seconds.

Following a collision someone has suffered a burn. The burn needs to be cooled. What is the shortest time it should be cooled for?

☐ 5 minutes

☐ 10 minutes

☐ 15 minutes

☐ 20 minutes

Check the casualty for shock and if possible try to cool the burn for at least ten minutes. Use a clean, cold non-toxic liquid preferably water.

After a collision someone has suffered a burn. The burn needs to be cooled. What is the shortest time it should be cooled for?

☐ 30 seconds

☐ 60 seconds

☐ 5 minutes

☐ 10 minutes

It's important to cool a burn for at least ten minutes. Use a clean, cold non-toxic liquid preferably water. Bear in mind the person may also be in shock.

A casualty is not breathing normally. Chest compressions should be given. At what rate?

☐ 50 per minute

☐ 100 per minute

☐ 200 per minute

☐ 250 per minute

If a casualty is not breathing normally chest compressions may be needed to maintain circulation. Place two hands on the centre of the chest and press down about 4–5 centimetres, at the rate of 100 per minute.

A person has been injured. They may be suffering from shock. What are the warning signs to look for?

☐ Flushed complexion

☐ Warm dry skin

☐ Slow pulse

☐ Pale grey skin

The effects of shock may not be immediately obvious. Warning signs are rapid pulse, sweating, pale grey skin and rapid shallow breathing.

13.19
Mark one answer
RES s16, HC p132

An injured person has been placed in the recovery position. They are unconscious but breathing normally. What else should be done?

☐ Press firmly between the shoulders

☐ Place their arms by their side

☐ Give them a hot sweet drink

☐ Check the airway is clear

After a casualty has been placed in the recovery position, their airway should be checked to make sure it's clear. Don't leave them alone until medical help arrives. Where possible do NOT move a casualty unless there's further danger.

13.20
Mark one answer
RES s16

An injured motorcyclist is lying unconscious in the road. You should always

☐ remove the safety helmet

☐ seek medical assistance

☐ move the person off the road

☐ remove the leather jacket

If someone has been injured, the sooner proper medical attention is given the better. Send someone to phone for help or go yourself. An injured person should only be moved if they're in further danger. An injured motorcyclist's helmet should NOT be removed unless it is essential.

13.21
Mark one answer
RES s11, HC r280

You are on a motorway. A large box falls onto the road from a lorry. The lorry does not stop. You should

☐ go to the next emergency telephone and report the hazard

☐ catch up with the lorry and try to get the driver's attention

☐ stop close to the box until the police arrive

☐ pull over to the hard shoulder, then remove the box

Lorry drivers can be unaware of objects falling from their vehicles. If you see something fall onto a motorway look to see if the driver pulls over. If they don't stop, do not attempt to retrieve it yourself. Pull on to the hard shoulder near an emergency telephone and report the hazard. You will be connected to the police or a Highways Agency control centre.

13.22
Mark one answer
RES s8

You are going through a long tunnel. What will warn you of congestion or an incident ahead?

☐ Hazard warning lines

☐ Other drivers flashing their lights

☐ Variable message signs

☐ Areas marked with hatch markings

Follow the instructions given by the signs or by tunnel officials.

In congested tunnels a minor incident can soon turn into a major one with serious or even fatal results.

An adult casualty is not breathing. To maintain circulation, compressions should be given. What is the correct depth to press?

☐ 1 to 2 centimetres

☐ 4 to 5 centimetres

☐ 10 to 15 centimetres

☐ 15 to 20 centimetres

An adult casualty is not breathing normally. To maintain circulation place two hands on the centre of the chest. Then press down 4 to 5 centimetres at a rate of 100 times per minute.

You are the first to arrive at the scene of a crash. Which TWO of these should you do?

☐ Leave as soon as another motorist arrives

☐ Make sure engines are switched off

☐ Drag all casualties away from the vehicles

☐ Call the emergency services promptly

At a crash scene you can help in practical ways, even if you aren't trained in first aid. Make sure you do not put yourself or anyone else in danger. The safest way to warn other traffic is by switching on your hazard warning lights.

At the scene of a traffic incident you should

☐ not put yourself at risk

☐ go to those casualties who are screaming

☐ pull everybody out of their vehicles

☐ leave vehicle engines switched on

It's important that people at the scene of a collision do not create further risk to themselves or others. If the incident is on a motorway or major road, traffic will be approaching at speed. Do not put yourself at risk when trying to help casualties or warning other road users.

13.26 Mark three answers RES s16, HC p131

You are the first person to arrive at an incident where people are badly injured. Which THREE should you do?

☐ Switch on your own hazard warning lights

☐ Make sure that someone telephones for an ambulance

☐ Try and get people who are injured to drink something

☐ Move the people who are injured clear of their vehicles

☐ Get people who are not injured clear of the scene

If you're the first to arrive at a crash scene the first concerns are the risk of further collision and fire. Ensuring that vehicle engines are switched off will reduce the risk of fire. Use hazard warning lights so that other traffic knows there's a need for caution. Make sure the emergency services are contacted, don't assume this has already been done.

13.27 Mark one answer RES s16, HC p131

You arrive at the scene of a motorcycle crash. The rider is injured. When should the helmet be removed?

☐ Only when it is essential

☐ Always straight away

☐ Only when the motorcyclist asks

☐ Always, unless they are in shock

DO NOT remove a motorcyclist's helmet unless it is essential. Remember they may be suffering from shock. Don't give them anything to eat or drink but do reassure them confidently.

13.28 Mark three answers RES s16, HC p132

You arrive at a serious motorcycle crash. The motorcyclist is unconscious and bleeding. Your THREE main priorities should be to

☐ try to stop the bleeding

☐ make a list of witnesses

☐ check their breathing

☐ take the numbers of other vehicles

☐ sweep up any loose debris

☐ check their airways

Further collisions and fire are the main dangers immediately after a crash. If possible get others to assist you and make the area safe. Help those involved and remember DR ABC, Danger, Response, Airway, Breathing, Compressions. This will help when dealing with any injuries.

Mark one answer

You arrive at an incident. A motorcyclist is unconscious. Your FIRST priority is the casualty's

☐ breathing

☐ bleeding

☐ broken bones

☐ bruising

At the scene of an incident always be aware of danger from further collisions or fire. The first priority when dealing with an unconscious person is to ensure they can breathe. This may involve clearing their airway if you can see an obstruction, or if they're having difficulty breathing.

Mark three answers

At an incident a casualty is unconscious. Which THREE of these should you check urgently?

☐ Circulation

☐ Airway

☐ Shock

☐ Breathing

☐ Broken bones

Remember DR ABC. An unconscious casualty may have difficulty breathing. Check that their airway is clear by tilting the head back gently and unblock it if necessary. Then make sure they are breathing. If there is bleeding, stem the flow by placing clean material over any wounds but without pressing on any objects in the wound. Compressions may need to be given to maintain circulation.

Mark three answers

You arrive at the scene of an incident. It has just happened and someone is unconscious. Which THREE of these should be given urgent priority to help them?

☐ Clear the airway and keep it open

☐ Try to get them to drink water

☐ Check that they are breathing

☐ Look for any witnesses

☐ Stop any heavy bleeding

☐ Take the numbers of vehicles involved

Make sure that the emergency services are called immediately. Once first aid has been given, stay with the casualty.

13.32 — Mark three answers — RES s16, HC p131

You have stopped at an incident to give help. Which THREE things should you do?

- ☐ Keep injured people warm and comfortable
- ☐ Keep injured people calm by talking to them reassuringly
- ☐ Keep injured people on the move by walking them around
- ☐ Give injured people a warm drink
- ☐ Make sure that injured people are not left alone

There are a number of things you can do to help, even without expert training. Be aware of further danger and fire, make sure the area is safe. People may be in shock. Don't give them anything to eat or drink. Keep them warm and comfortable and reassure them. Don't move injured people unless there is a risk of further danger.

13.33 — Mark three answers — RES s16, HC p132

You arrive at an incident. It has just happened and someone is injured. Which THREE should be given urgent priority?

- ☐ Stop any severe bleeding
- ☐ Give them a warm drink
- ☐ Check they are breathing
- ☐ Take numbers of vehicles involved
- ☐ Look for witnesses
- ☐ Clear their airway and keep it open

The first priority with a casualty is to make sure their airway is clear and they are breathing. Any wounds should be checked for objects and then bleeding stemmed using clean material. Ensure the emergency services are called, they are the experts. If you're not first aid trained consider getting training. It might save a life.

13.34 — Mark one answer — RES s16, HC p131

Which of the following should you NOT do at the scene of a collision?

- ☐ Warn other traffic by switching on your hazard warning lights
- ☐ Call the emergency services immediately
- ☐ Offer someone a cigarette to calm them down
- ☐ Ask drivers to switch off their engines

Keeping casualties or witnesses calm is important, but never offer a cigarette because of the risk of fire. Bear in mind they may be in shock. Don't offer an injured person anything to eat or drink. They may have internal injuries or need surgery.

13.35   Mark two answers   RES s16, HC p131

There has been a collision. A driver is suffering from shock. What TWO of these should you do?

☐ Give them a drink

☐ Reassure them

☐ Not leave them alone

☐ Offer them a cigarette

☐ Ask who caused the incident

Be aware they could have an injury that is not immediately obvious. Ensure the emergency services are called. Reassure and stay with them until the experts arrive.

13.36   Mark one answer   RES s16, HC p131

You have to treat someone for shock at the scene of an incident. You should

☐ reassure them constantly

☐ walk them around to calm them down

☐ give them something cold to drink

☐ cool them down as soon as possible

Stay with the casualty and talk to them quietly and firmly to calm and reassure them. Avoid moving them unnecessarily in case they are injured. Keep them warm, but don't give them anything to eat or drink.

13.37   Mark one answer   RES s16, HC p131

You arrive at the scene of a motorcycle crash. No other vehicle is involved. The rider is unconscious and lying in the middle of the road. The FIRST thing you should do is

☐ move the rider out of the road

☐ warn other traffic

☐ clear the road of debris

☐ give the rider reassurance

The motorcyclist is in an extremely vulnerable position, exposed to further danger from traffic. Approaching vehicles need advance warning in order to slow down and safely take avoiding action or stop. Don't put yourself or anyone else at risk. Use the hazard warning lights on your vehicle to alert other road users to the danger.

13.38   Mark one answer   RES s16, HC p132

At an incident a small child is not breathing. To restore normal breathing you should breathe into their mouth

☐ sharply

☐ gently

☐ heavily

☐ rapidly

If a young child has stopped breathing, first check that the airway is clear. Then give compressions to the chest using one hand (two fingers for an infant) and begin mouth-to-mouth resuscitation. Breathe very gently and continue the procedure until they can breathe without help.

13.39 — Mark one answer — RES s16, HC p133

You arrive at an incident. There has been an engine fire and someone's hands and arms have been burnt. You should NOT

☐ douse the burn thoroughly with clean cool non-toxic liquid

☐ lay the casualty down on the ground

☐ remove anything sticking to the burn

☐ reassure them confidently and repeatedly

This could cause further damage and infection to the wound. Your first priority is to cool the burn with a clean, cool, non-toxic liquid, preferably water. Don't forget the casualty may be in shock.

13.40 — Mark one answer — RES s16, HC p133

You arrive at an incident where someone is suffering from severe burns. You should

☐ apply lotions to the injury

☐ burst any blisters

☐ remove anything stuck to the burns

☐ douse the burns with clean cool non-toxic liquid

Use a liquid that is clean, cold and non-toxic, preferably water. Its coolness will help take the heat out of the burn and relieve the pain. Keep the wound doused for at least ten minutes. If blisters appear don't attempt to burst them as this could lead to infection.

13.41 — Mark two answers — RES s16, HC p132

You arrive at an incident. A pedestrian has a severe bleeding leg wound. It is not broken and there is nothing in the wound. What TWO of these should you do?

☐ Dab the wound to stop bleeding

☐ Keep both legs flat on the ground

☐ Apply firm pressure to the wound

☐ Raise the leg to lessen bleeding

☐ Fetch them a warm drink

First check for anything that may be in the wound such as glass. If there's nothing in it apply a pad of clean cloth or bandage. Raising the leg will lessen the flow of blood. Don't tie anything tightly round the leg. This will restrict circulation and can result in long-term injury.

13.42 — Mark one answer — RES s16, HC p131

At an incident a casualty is unconscious but still breathing. You should only move them if

☐ an ambulance is on its way

☐ bystanders advise you to

☐ there is further danger

☐ bystanders will help you to

Do not move a casualty unless there is further danger, for example, from other traffic or fire. They may have unseen or internal injuries. Moving them unnecessarily could cause further injury. Do NOT remove a motorcyclist's helmet unless it's essential.

At a collision you suspect a casualty has back injuries. The area is safe. You should

☐ offer them a drink

☐ not move them

☐ raise their legs

☐ not call an ambulance

Talk to the casualty and keep them calm. Do not attempt to move them as this could cause further injury. Call an ambulance at the first opportunity.

At an incident it is important to look after any casualties. When the area is safe, you should

☐ get them out of the vehicle

☐ give them a drink

☐ give them something to eat

☐ keep them in the vehicle

When the area is safe and there's no danger from other traffic or fire it's better not to move casualties. Moving them may cause further injury.

A tanker is involved in a collision. Which sign shows that it is carrying dangerous goods?

☐ LONG VEHICLE ☐ 2YE 1089

There will be an orange label on the side and rear of the tanker. Look at this carefully and report what it says when you phone the emergency services. Details of hazard warning plates are given in The Highway Code.

13.46 — Mark three answers — HC r286, p122

You are involved in a collision. Because of this which THREE of these documents may the police ask you to produce?

☐ Vehicle registration document
☐ Driving licence
☐ Theory test certificate
☐ Insurance certificate
☐ MOT test certificate
☐ Vehicle service record

You MUST stop if you have been involved in a collision which results in injury or damage. The police may ask to see your documents at the time or later at a police station.

13.47 — Mark one answer — RES s16, HC p131

After a collision someone is unconscious in their vehicle. When should you call the emergency services?

☐ Only as a last resort
☐ As soon as possible
☐ After you have woken them up
☐ After checking for broken bones

It is important to make sure that emergency services arrive on the scene as soon as possible. When a person is unconscious, they could have serious injuries that are not immediately obvious.

13.48 — Mark one answer — RES s16, HC p132

A casualty has an injured arm. They can move it freely but it is bleeding. Why should you get them to keep it in a raised position?

☐ Because it will ease the pain
☐ It will help them to be seen more easily
☐ To stop them touching other people
☐ It will help to reduce the blood flow

If a casualty is bleeding heavily, raise the limb to a higher position. This will help to reduce the blood flow. Before raising the limb you should make sure that it is not broken.

13.49 — Mark one answer — RES s8

You are going through a tunnel. What systems are provided to warn of any incidents, collisions or congestion?

☐ Double white centre lines
☐ Variable message signs
☐ Chevron 'distance markers'
☐ Rumble strips

Take notice of any instructions given on variable message signs or by tunnel officials. They will warn you of any incidents or congestion ahead and advise you what to do.

A collision has just happened. An injured person is lying in a busy road. What is the FIRST thing you should do to help?

☐ Treat the person for shock

☐ Warn other traffic

☐ Place them in the recovery position

☐ Make sure the injured person is kept warm

The most immediate danger is further collisions and fire. You could warn other traffic by displaying an advance warning triangle or sign (but not on a motorway), switching on hazard warning lights or by any other means that does not put you or others at risk.

At an incident a casualty has stopped breathing. You should

☐ remove anything that is blocking the mouth

☐ keep the head tilted forwards as far as possible

☐ raise the legs to help with circulation

☐ try to give the casualty something to drink

☐ tilt the head back gently to clear the airway

Unblocking the airway and gently tilting the head back will help the casualty to breathe. They will then be in the correct position if mouth-to-mouth resuscitation is required. Don't move a casualty unless there's further danger.

You are at the scene of an incident. Someone is suffering from shock. You should

☐ reassure them constantly

☐ offer them a cigarette

☐ keep them warm

☐ avoid moving them if possible

☐ avoid leaving them alone

☐ give them a warm drink

The signs of shock may not be immediately obvious. Prompt treatment can help to minimise the effects. Lay the casualty down, loosen tight clothing, call an ambulance and check their breathing and pulse.

There has been a collision. A motorcyclist is lying injured and unconscious. Unless it's essential, why should you usually NOT attempt to remove their helmet?

☐ Because they may not want you to

☐ This could result in more serious injury

☐ They will get too cold if you do this

☐ Because you could scratch the helmet

When someone is injured, any movement which is not absolutely necessary should be avoided since it could make injuries worse. Unless it is essential, it's generally safer to leave a motorcyclist's helmet in place.

Case study practice – 13 Incidents, accidents and emergencies

John witnesses an incident involving a car and a motorcycle. The car driver is unhurt.

The motorcyclist is lying against the kerb with his helmet still on. He's conscious but very dazed, bruised and shocked.

John leaves his own motorcycle standing on the road with the hazard warning lights on. He calls the emergency services and stays with both victims until the services arrive.

He then gives his contact details to a police officer.

13.1 What condition could still affect the car driver?

Mark **one** answer

☐ Head injury
☐ Stomach pain
☐ Broken bones
☐ Shock symptoms

HC p131

13.2 Why should the helmet stay on for the time being?

Mark **one** answer

☐ Someone might steal the helmet if he takes it off
☐ The helmet may get lost on the way to hospital
☐ Because removing it could cause further injuries
☐ The helmet will keep his head from getting cold

HC p131

13.3 Why did John leave his motorcycle positioned in this way?

Mark **one** answer

☐ To warn following traffic of the incident hazard
☐ To ensure that the battery stays fully charged
☐ To highlight the incident for the emergency services
☐ To help him locate the motorcycle again later

HC r283 **RES** s16

13.4 How should you deal with people suffering from shock?

Mark **one** answer

☐ Offer them a cigarette
☐ Give them a drink
☐ Keep them warm
☐ Leave them alone

HC p131 **RES** s16

13.5 Why did John provide his details?

Mark **one** answer

☐ He was in a hurry to leave
☐ He witnessed the incident
☐ He wanted to be involved
☐ He left his licence at home

RES s16

Motorcycle loading

In this section, you'll learn about

- › how to carry loads safely on your motorcycle
- › using a sidecar
- › carrying a pillion passenger safely
- › towing a trailer.

Motorcycle loading

Loading your motorcycle carefully will help to ensure that you can travel safely, whether your load is a passenger, a trailer or simply an overnight bag.

> Keeping your motorcycle stable

As a rider, you need to make sure that your motorcycle isn't overloaded. Overloading can seriously affect the motorcycle's handling, especially the steering and braking.

HC r98 **RES** s14

You **MUST** securely fasten any load you're carrying before you start riding: it's an offence to travel with an insecure load.

A heavy or bulky load can make your motorcycle less stable.

When carrying a passenger or a heavy load on a motorcycle, you may need to adjust

- the tyre pressures
- the headlight aim
- the suspension.

RES s14

 You should inflate your tyres to a higher pressure than normal

- when you're carrying a heavy load or pillion passenger
- if you're riding for a long distance on a dual carriageway or motorway at the speed limit for these roads.

Your motorcycle handbook should tell you the correct pressure for different circumstances.

RES s14, 15

Find out about motorcycle luggage systems at this website.

> **geton.co.uk/motorcycle-kit**

> Sidecars

Before fitting a sidecar, you need to make sure that your motorcycle is suitable for use with a sidecar. The sidecar must be aligned correctly otherwise your motorcycle will be difficult to control and is likely to be dangerous to ride.

When you ride for the first time with a sidecar fitted, keep your speed down and be careful when riding round bends and corners and at junctions. A motorcycle with a sidecar handles very differently to a solo motorcycle.

Remember that your stopping distance may also increase due to the extra weight of the sidecar.

RES s14

> Pillion passengers

A pillion passenger **MUST** wear a helmet that's correctly fastened. They **MUST** sit astride the machine, facing forwards, on a proper passenger seat. Your motorcycle should have passenger footrests too.

You **MUST NOT** carry a pillion passenger unless

- you've passed a practical motorcycle test
- you have a full motorcycle licence for the category of motorcycle being ridden.

HC r83, 85 **RES** s14

Your pillion passenger needs to understand that they should lean with you when you lean the motorcycle over to steer around bends. If it's the first time the passenger has ridden, explain what to do and how to hold onto either your waist or the passenger grab rail.

Children should only be carried as pillion passengers when they can reach the handholds and footrests. They **MUST** also wear a helmet that's the right size and securely fastened, and sit properly on the pillion seat, facing forwards.

The extra weight of a passenger may change the way the motorcycle handles, so give yourself time to get used to it. The additional weight may also increase your stopping distance, so keep well back when following other traffic.

When you're riding with a passenger, think about their comfort and try to ride smoothly, avoiding harsh acceleration or braking.

Your passenger's clothing should be

- warm
- waterproof
- bright or reflective.

Passengers who wear protective motorcyclist clothing will gain protection from

- the weather
- the road surface, if they fall off the motorcycle.

Don't let your passenger wear a trailing scarf or belt as this could become tangled in the rear wheel or drive chain and cause a serious incident.

RES s14

❯ Towing a trailer

To tow a trailer, you must have a full motorcycle licence and your motorcycle must have an engine capacity of more than 125 cc. A motorcycle trailer must be no wider than 1 metre (3 feet 3 inches). Remember that your stopping distance may increase due to the extra weight of the trailer.

If the trailer starts to swerve or snake as you're riding along,

- ease off the throttle
- reduce your speed gradually to regain control.

There's a lower national speed limit for all vehicles towing trailers.

On a dual carriageway or motorway	Maximum speed 60 mph (96 km/h)
	A vehicle towing a trailer on a motorway that has more than two lanes **MUST NOT** be driven in the right-hand lane.
On a single carriageway	Maximum speed 50 mph (80 km/h)

HC r98, p40 **RES** s14

Find out more about towing a trailer at this website.

▶ **direct.gov.uk/en/ Motoring/DriverLicensing/ CaravansTrailersCommercial Vehicles/DG_192285**

Meeting the standards

You must be able to

make sure that a pillion passenger is seated legally, correctly and securely

make sure that loads are secure and distributed correctly, depending on the machine

allow for the effect that any extra load may have on how the machine handles.

You must know and understand

what to tell a passenger about how to behave when being carried on the machine

how to adjust the machine to allow for extra weight. For example, you may need to put more air in the tyres

how to change your riding to allow for extra weight. For example

- earlier braking
- use of lower gears.

> Notes

You can use this page to make your own notes or diagrams about the key points you need to remember.

Think about

- What sorts of load might you carry on your motorcycle that could affect its stability?
- When might you need to increase the tyre pressures?
- What would you need to tell a first-time pillion passenger about before you began riding?
- If you wanted to tow a trailer, what speed limits would you have to observe?

Your notes

Things to discuss and practise with your trainer

These are just a few examples of what you could discuss and practise with your trainer. Read more about motorcycle loading to come up with your own ideas.

Discuss with your trainer

- the effects that carrying a heavy load, such as panniers or a top box, might have on your riding
- the rules and advice for carrying a pillion passenger
  - your licence requirement
  - how a passenger should sit and behave on your motorcycle
  - what they should wear
  - the riding technique that you should use when carrying a passenger
- the techniques that you'll need to use and rules to follow when
  - riding with a sidecar
  - pulling a trailer.

Practise with your trainer

- the checks that you'll need to make when carrying a load
  - your tyre pressure
  - the preload on your shock absorbers
  - the angle of your headlights.

If a trailer swerves or snakes when you are towing it you should

☐ ease off the throttle and reduce your speed

☐ let go of the handlebars and let it correct itself

☐ brake hard and hold the brake on

☐ increase your speed as quickly as possible

Don't be tempted to use harsh braking to stop swerving or snaking as this won't help the situation. You should reduce your speed by easing off the throttle.

When riding with a sidecar attached for the first time you should

☐ keep your speed down

☐ be able to stop more quickly

☐ accelerate quickly round bends

☐ approach corners more carefully

A motorcycle with a sidecar will feel very different to ride than a solo motorcycle. Keep your speed down until you get used to the outfit, especially when negotiating bends and junctions.

When carrying extra weight on a motorcycle, you may need to make adjustments to the

☐ headlight

☐ gears

☐ suspension

☐ tyres

☐ footrests

Carrying extra weight such as luggage or a pillion passenger, will probably affect the aim of the headlight. Adjust this so that it does not dazzle other road users. The feel and balance will also be affected so you may need to adjust the suspension and tyre pressures to help overcome this.

To obtain the full category 'A' licence through the accelerated or direct access scheme, your motorcycle must be

☐ solo with maximum power 25 kW (33 bhp)

☐ solo with maximum power of 11 kW (14.6 bhp)

☐ fitted with a sidecar and have minimum power of 35 kW (46.6 bhp)

☐ solo with minimum power of 35 kW (46.6 bhp)

From the age of 21 you may take a category A test via the Direct or Accelerated Access schemes. The motorcycle you use for your practical test under the Direct or Accelerated Access scheme is one that has an engine with a minimum power output of 35 kW (46.6 bhp).

14.5
Mark one answer   RES s14

Any load that is carried on a luggage rack MUST be

☐ securely fastened when riding

☐ carried only when strictly necessary

☐ visible when you are riding

☐ covered with plastic sheeting

Don't risk losing any luggage while riding: it could fall into the path of following vehicles and cause danger. It is an offence to travel with an insecure load.

14.6
Mark one answer   RES s14, HC r83

Pillion passengers should

☐ have a provisional motorcycle licence

☐ be lighter than the rider

☐ always wear a helmet

☐ signal for the rider

Pillion passengers must sit astride the machine on a proper passenger seat and rear footrests should be fitted. They must wear a safety helmet which is correctly fastened.

14.7
Mark one answer   RES s14

When you are going around a corner your pillion passenger should

☐ give arm signals for you

☐ check behind for other vehicles

☐ lean with you on bends

☐ lean to one side to see ahead

A pillion passenger should not give signals or look round for you.

If your passenger has never been on a motorcycle before, make sure they know that they need to lean with you while going around bends.

14.8
Mark one answer   RES s14

Which of these may need to be adjusted when carrying a pillion passenger?

☐ Indicators

☐ Exhaust

☐ Fairing

☐ Headlight

Your headlight must be properly adjusted to avoid dazzling other road users. You will probably need to do this when carrying a heavy load or the extra weight of a pillion passenger. You may also need to adjust suspension and tyre pressures.

You are towing a trailer with your motorcycle. You should remember that your

☐ stopping distance may increase

☐ fuel consumption will improve

☐ tyre grip will increase

☐ stability will improve

When you tow a trailer remember that you must obey the relevant speed limits. Ensure that the trailer is hitched correctly and that any load in the trailer is secure. You should also bear in mind that your stopping distance may increase.

Heavy loads in a motorcycle top box may

Carrying heavy loads in your top box could make your motorcycle unstable because the weight is high up and at the very back of the machine. Take extra care.

☐ improve stability

☐ cause low-speed wobble

☐ cause a puncture

☐ improve braking

Who is responsible for making sure that a motorcycle is not overloaded?

☐ The rider of the motorcycle

☐ The owner of the items being carried

☐ The licensing authority

☐ The owner of the motorcycle

Correct loading is the responsibility of the rider. Overloading a motorcycle can seriously affect the control and handling. It could result in a crash with serious or even fatal consequences.

Before fitting a sidecar to a motorcycle you should

☐ have the wheels balanced

☐ have the engine tuned

☐ pass the extended bike test

☐ check that the motorcycle is suitable

Make sure that the sidecar is fixed securely and properly aligned. If your motorcycle is registered on or after 1 August 1981 the sidecar must be fitted on the left-hand side of the motorcycle.

14.13
Mark one answer   RES s14

You are using throwover saddlebags. Why is it important to make sure they are evenly loaded?

☐ They will be uncomfortable for you to sit on

☐ They will slow your motorcycle down

☐ They could make your motorcycle unstable

☐ They will be uncomfortable for a pillion passenger to sit on

Panniers or saddlebags should be loaded so that you carry about the same weight in each bag. Uneven loading could affect your balance, especially when cornering.

14.14
Mark one answer   RES s14

You are carrying a bulky tank bag. What could this affect?

☐ Your ability to steer

☐ Your ability to accelerate

☐ Your view ahead

☐ Your insurance premium

If your tank bag is too bulky it could get in the way of your arms or restrict the movement of the handlebars.

14.15
NI EXEMPT   Mark one answer   RES s14, HC r85, p119

To carry a pillion passenger you must

☐ hold a full car licence

☐ hold a full motorcycle licence

☐ be over the age of 21

☐ be over the age of 25

The law requires you to have a full licence for the category of motorcycle you are riding before you can carry a pillion passenger.

14.16
Mark one answer   RES s14

When carrying a heavy load on your luggage rack, you may need to adjust your

☐ carburettor

☐ fuel tap

☐ seating position

☐ tyre pressures

The load will increase the overall weight that your motorcycle is carrying. You may need to adjust your tyre pressures according to the manufacturer's instructions to allow for this. You may also need to adjust your headlight beam alignment.

You are carrying a pillion passenger. When following other traffic, which of the following should you do?

- ☐ Keep to your normal following distance
- ☐ Get your passenger to keep checking behind
- ☐ Keep further back than you normally would
- ☐ Get your passenger to signal for you

The extra weight of a passenger may increase your stopping distance. Allow for this when following another vehicle by increasing the separation distance.

You should only carry a child as a pillion passenger when

- ☐ they are over 14 years old
- ☐ they are over 16 years old
- ☐ they can reach the floor from the seat
- ☐ they can reach the handholds and footrests

Any passenger you carry must be able to reach footrests and handholds properly to remain safe on your machine. Ensure they are wearing protective weatherproof kit and a properly fitting helmet.

You have fitted a sidecar to your motorcycle. You should make sure that the sidecar

- ☐ has a registration plate
- ☐ is correctly aligned
- ☐ has a waterproof cover
- ☐ has a solid cover

If the sidecar is not correctly aligned to the mounting points it will result in the outfit being difficult to control and even dangerous.

Riding with a sidecar attached requires a different technique to riding a solo motorcycle and you should keep your speed down while learning this skill.

You are riding a motorcycle and sidecar. The extra weight

- ☐ will allow you to corner more quickly
- ☐ will allow you to brake later for hazards
- ☐ may increase your stopping distance
- ☐ will improve your fuel consumption

You will need to adapt your riding technique when riding a motorcycle fitted with a sidecar. The extra weight will affect the handling and may increase your overall stopping distance.

14.21

You are carrying a pillion passenger. To allow for the extra weight which of the following is most likely to need adjustment?

☐ Preload on the front forks

☐ Preload on the rear shock absorber(s)

☐ The balance of the rear wheel

☐ The front and rear wheel alignment

When carrying a passenger or other extra weight, you may need to make adjustments, particularly to the rear shock absorber(s), tyre pressures and headlight alignment. Check your owner's handbook for details.

14.22

A trailer on a motorcycle must be no wider than

☐ 0.5 metres (1 foot 8 inches)

☐ 1 metre (3 feet 3 inches)

☐ 1.5 metres (4 feet 11inches)

☐ 2 metres (6 feet 6 inches)

When you're towing a trailer you must remember that you may not be able to filter through traffic. Don't forget that the trailer is there, especially when riding round bends and negotiating junctions.

14.23

You want to tow a trailer with your motorcycle. Which one applies?

☐ The motorcycle should be attached to a sidecar

☐ The trailer should weigh more than the motorcycle

☐ The trailer should be fitted with brakes

☐ The trailer should NOT be more than 1 metre (3 feet 3 inches) wide

To tow a trailer behind a motorcycle you must have, a full motorcycle licence and a motorcycle with an engine larger than 125 cc. Motorcycle trailers must not exceed 1 metre (3 feet 3 inches) in width.

14.24

You have a sidecar fitted to your motorcycle. What effect will it have?

☐ Reduce stability

☐ Make steering lighter

☐ Increase stopping distance

☐ Increase fuel economy

If you want to fit a sidecar to your motorcycle make sure that your motorcycle is suitable to cope with the extra load. Make sure that the sidecar is fixed correctly and properly aligned. A sidecar will alter the handling considerably. Give yourself time to adjust to the different characteristics.

14.25   Mark three answers   RES s2, 14

Which THREE must a learner motorcyclist under 21 NOT do?

- ☐ Ride a motorcycle with an engine capacity greater than 125 cc
- ☐ Pull a trailer
- ☐ Carry a pillion passenger
- ☐ Ride faster than 30 mph
- ☐ Use the right-hand lane on dual carriageways

Learner motorcyclists are not allowed to pull a trailer or carry a pillion passenger. In addition, if you are a learner motorcyclist under 21, you may not ride a motorcycle on the road with an engine capacity of more than 125 cc.

14.26   Mark two answers   RES s14, HC p119

You want to tow a trailer behind your motorcycle. You should

- ☐ display a 'long vehicle' sign
- ☐ fit a larger battery
- ☐ have a full motorcycle licence
- ☐ ensure that your engine is more than 125 cc
- ☐ ensure that your motorcycle has shaft drive

When you tow a trailer your stopping distance will be increased. Any load on the trailer must be secure and the trailer must be fitted to the motorcycle correctly. You must obey the lower speed limit restrictions that apply to vehicles with trailers. Any trailer towed by a motorcycle must be no wider than 1 metre. The laden weight should be no greater than 150 kg or two-thirds of the kerbside weight of the motorcycle, whichever is less.

14.27   Mark two answers   RES s14, HC r85

To carry a pillion passenger your motorcycle should be fitted with

- ☐ rear footrests
- ☐ an engine of 250 cc or over
- ☐ a top box
- ☐ a grab handle
- ☐ a proper pillion seat

When carrying a pillion there are certain things they should NOT do. Before carrying a pillion tell them NOT to give hand signals, lean away from the rider when cornering, fidget or move around, put their feet down to try and support the machine when you stop, or wear long, loose items that might get caught in the rear wheel or drive chain.

14.28 — Mark three answers — RES s14

Your motorcycle is fitted with a top box. It is unwise to carry a heavy load in the top box because it may

☐ reduce stability

☐ improve stability

☐ make turning easier

☐ cause high-speed weave

☐ cause low-speed wobble

☐ increase fuel economy

Carrying a heavy weight high up and at the very back of the motorcycle can cause problems in maintaining control.

14.29 — Mark one answer — RES s2, HC r85

You hold a provisional motorcycle licence. Are you allowed to carry a pillion passenger?

☐ Only if the passenger holds a full licence

☐ Not at any time

☐ Not unless you are undergoing training

☐ Only if the passenger is under 21

You are not allowed to carry a pillion passenger until you hold a full motorcycle licence. This allows you to gain riding experience. Even when you've passed, don't carry a passenger if you are not confident of being able to do so safely. You are responsible for their safety.

14.30 — Mark one answer — RES s14

Overloading your motorcycle can seriously affect the

☐ gearbox

☐ weather protection

☐ handling

☐ battery life

Any load will affect the handling of your motorcycle by changing its centre of gravity. Try to keep any load as low as possible. When using panniers spread the weight evenly. Avoid carrying heavy items in a top box, as this could make your steering dangerously light.

14.31 — Mark two answers — HC r98, p40

You are towing a small trailer on a busy three-lane motorway. All the lanes are open. You must

☐ not exceed 60 mph

☐ not overtake

☐ have a stabiliser fitted

☐ use only the left and centre lanes

You should be aware of the motorway regulations for vehicles towing trailers. These state that a vehicle towing a trailer must not

- use the right-hand lane of a three-lane motorway unless directed to do so, for example, at roadworks or due to a lane closure

- exceed 60 mph.

Case study practice – 14 Motorcycle loading

Sandy and Chris are taking a road trip on their motorcycle. Sandy carefully connects up and checks their loaded trailer while Chris carefully packs the rigid panniers evenly.

They go to the service station to buy fuel and make final checks.

Once on the motorway, they travel at the speed limit when it's safe to do so and leave a good separation distance from the vehicle in front. They don't use the right-hand lane.

14.1 Why does Sandy check the trailer?

Mark **one** answer

☐ To ensure it's securely shut and locked

☐ To ensure the paintwork isn't scratched

☐ To ensure it's correctly connected up

☐ To ensure the colour matches the motorcycle

RES s14

14.2 Why would Chris pack the panniers in this manner?

Mark **one** answer

☐ So that nothing rattles while they're riding

☐ Uneven load distribution can affect balance

☐ So that they haven't forgotten anything

☐ Even loads on each side look much better

HC r98, 160, 265 **RES** s14

14.3 What's the speed limit for their machine?

Mark **one** answer

- [ ] 40 mph
- [ ] 50 mph
- [ ] 60 mph
- [ ] 70 mph

RES s14

14.4 Why would Sandy leave more distance?

Mark **one** answer

- [ ] The trailer might become detached from the motorcycle
- [ ] Chris doesn't like Sandy riding too close to other vehicles
- [ ] The motorway isn't very busy so there's plenty of room
- [ ] Stopping distance is increased on a fully loaded vehicle

RES s14

14.5 Why would they not use this lane?

Mark **one** answer

- [ ] Their trailer might cause buffeting and wind resistance
- [ ] That lane mustn't be used by vehicles with trailers
- [ ] Only cars towing trailers can use the right-hand lane
- [ ] They don't want to travel at a very high speed

HC r265

Case study practice

Case study practice

Some of the questions within the test will be presented as a case study.

You'll be presented with a scenario – the case study – which will appear on the left-hand side of the screen. The scenario will be presented in a text format and may be accompanied by a supporting picture or diagram. As you move within the case study, the questions will appear, one by one, on the right-hand side of the screen, and you'll be asked to respond. You can re-read the scenario throughout the case study should you wish to do so.

A case study example is shown below and on the following pages.

In this section, you'll also find five mixed-topic, practice case studies similar to the ones in the actual test. Use these to help you prepare for the real thing.

Answers to all the case studies in this book are in section 16, Answers.

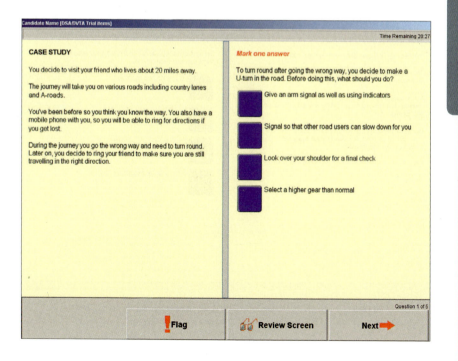

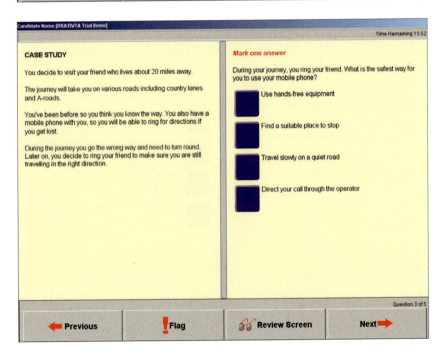

CASE STUDY

You decide to visit your friend who lives about 20 miles away.

The journey will take you on various roads including country lanes and A-roads.

You've been before so you think you know the way. You also have a mobile phone with you, so you will be able to ring for directions if you get lost.

During the journey you go the wrong way and need to turn round. Later on, you decide to ring your friend to make sure you are still travelling in the right direction.

Mark three answers
What should you do as you approach this bridge on your journey?

☐ Move into the middle of the road to get a better view

☐ Slow down

☐ Consider using the horn

☐ Find another route

☐ Beware of pedestrians

Question 2 of 5

◀ **Previous**   ❗**Flag**   **Review Screen**   **Next**▶

CASE STUDY

You decide to visit your friend who lives about 20 miles away.

The journey will take you on various roads including country lanes and A-roads.

You've been before so you think you know the way. You also have a mobile phone with you, so you will be able to ring for directions if you get lost.

During the journey you go the wrong way and need to turn round. Later on, you decide to ring your friend to make sure you are still travelling in the right direction.

Mark one answer
During your journey, you ring your friend. What is the safest way for you to use your mobile phone?

☐ Use hands-free equipment

☐ Find a suitable place to stop

☐ Travel slowly on a quiet road

☐ Direct your call through the operator

Question 3 of 5

◀ **Previous**   ❗**Flag**   **Review Screen**   **Next**▶

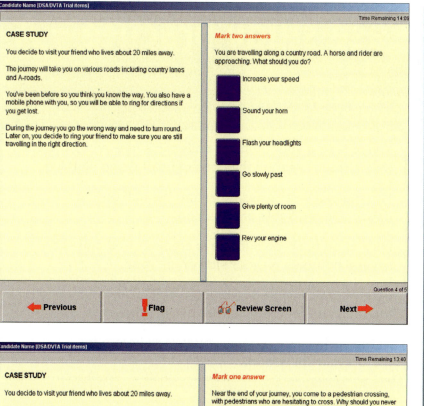

CASE STUDY

You decide to visit your friend who lives about 20 miles away.

The journey will take you on various roads including country lanes and A-roads.

You've been before so you think you know the way. You also have a mobile phone with you, so you will be able to ring for directions if you get lost.

During the journey you go the wrong way and need to turn round. Later on, you decide to ring your friend to make sure you are still travelling in the right direction.

Mark two answers

You are travelling along a country road. A horse and rider are approaching. What should you do?

- Increase your speed
- Sound your horn
- Flash your headlights
- Go slowly past
- Give plenty of room
- Rev your engine

Previous | Flag | Review Screen | Next

CASE STUDY

You decide to visit your friend who lives about 20 miles away.

The journey will take you on various roads including country lanes and A-roads.

You've been before so you think you know the way. You also have a mobile phone with you, so you will be able to ring for directions if you get lost.

During the journey you go the wrong way and need to turn round. Later on, you decide to ring your friend to make sure you are still travelling in the right direction.

Mark one answer

Near the end of your journey, you come to a pedestrian crossing, with pedestrians who are hesitating to cross. Why should you never wave people across at pedestrian crossings?

- There may be another vehicle coming
- They may not be looking
- It is safer for you to carry on
- They may not be ready to cross

Previous | Flag | Review Screen | Next

You're taking your friend to collect his new motorcycle. He's already wearing the correct helmet and clothing.

You reach a level crossing where the half barriers are down. The red lights are flashing.

Further on the road surface is cracked. You can see several potholes on your side of the road.

Later there's a high-occupancy vehicle lane marked on the road and motorcycles are allowed to use it.

At the end of your journey you turn right into the motorcycle showroom.

1   What might your friend be wearing?

Mark **one** answer

☐ Leather clothing, hi-vis waistcoat and white helmet

☐ Jeans, anorak, trainers and a light-coloured helmet

☐ Thick trousers, boots, hi-vis jacket and black helmet

☐ Tracksuit bottoms, hi-vis jacket and a dark helmet

RES s4

2 What should you do at the level crossing?

Mark **one** answer

☐ Ride on quickly as the lights may be faulty

☐ Wait as another train may be coming

☐ Turn round and find an alternative route

☐ Proceed slowly and check before crossing

HC r293 **RES** s7

3 What might you need to do on this road surface?

Mark **one** answer

☐ Ride in the gutter until you're past the affected area

☐ Dismount and quickly wheel the motorcycle past

☐ Ride along on the other side of the road for a while

☐ Slow down to go round the potholes and cracks

RES s8

4 How can you tell that you're allowed to ride in this lane?

Mark **one** answer

☐ The yellow sign will show a motorcycle

☐ The brown sign will show a motorcycle

☐ The blue sign will show a motorcycle

☐ The green sign will show a motorcycle

HC r142 **RES** s7 **KYTS** p140

5 What's the last thing you should do before turning into the showroom?

Mark **one** answer

☐ Take a look over your right shoulder

☐ Take a look in the left-hand mirror

☐ Take a look over your left shoulder

☐ Take a look at the road ahead

RES s8

> Case study practice – B

You're going away for the weekend with a friend as pillion passenger. You're using your motorcycle and trailer.

After loading up you stop at a garage to buy fuel.

It's daylight and the weather is dry but windy in open areas.

On the motorway the lanes are very busy. You avoid using the right-hand lane.

Later there's a roundabout. You need to take the second exit going straight on. There are two lanes on approach but no other road markings.

After the roundabout there are signs telling you that roadworks are being carried out further ahead.

1   What important check should you make after buying fuel?

Mark **one** answer

- [ ] Indicator function
- [ ] Tyre pressure
- [ ] Wheel alignment
- [ ] Seat position

`HC` p129 `RES` s15

2   What problem might you face under these weather conditions?

Mark one answer

☐ Being tired and very cold
☐ Being slowed right down
☐ Being overtaken by others
☐ Being blown off course

HC r232–233 **RES** s12

3   Why would you avoid this lane on the motorway?

Mark one answer

☐ Traffic travelling in the right-hand lane moves too fast
☐ You can't see road signs properly from the right-hand lane
☐ Vehicles with a trailer mustn't travel in the right-hand lane
☐ Only cars are allowed to travel along in the right-hand lane

HC r265 **RES** s11

4   How should you approach the roundabout?

Mark one answer

☐ In the right-hand lane while signalling left
☐ In the left-hand lane without giving a signal
☐ In the left-hand lane while signalling right
☐ In the right-hand lane without giving a signal

HC r186 **RES** s9

5   After the roundabout what people might you expect to see?

Mark one answer

☐ Police officers
☐ Traffic wardens
☐ Crossing patrols
☐ Road workers

HC r288 **RES** s8

You're going on holiday.

You'll be carrying a heavy tent. You put your luggage into panniers and a tank bag. The first part of your journey is along a dual carriageway. The national speed limit applies.

Later you visit a garage where you check your oil level. You leave your motorcycle to buy a snack at the shop.

Near your destination you follow a tractor along a country road.

1   Where should you put the tent?

Mark **one** answer

☐   In a back pack

☐   In the tank bag

☐   In a pannier

☐   In the top box

RES s14

2   What's the speed limit on the first part of your journey?

Mark **one** answer

☐   50 mph

☐   60 mph

☐   70 mph

☐   80 mph

HC r124, p40 RES s7

3   Why might your check at the garage not be accurate?

Mark **one** answer

☐ Because the engine is warm

☐ Because your fuel is low

☐ Because your hands are cold

☐ Because your motorcycle is fully loaded

RES s15

4   What should you do when you go and buy a snack?

Mark **one** answer

☐ Leave your helmet and gloves on the seat

☐ Lock your motorcycle and remove the key

☐ Make sure you remove your helmet first

☐ Chain your motorcycle to a fuel pump

HC p131 **RES** s8

5   What should you do on the country road?

Mark **one** answer

☐ Ride closely behind the tractor so that the driver can see you

☐ Sound your horn to allow the tractor driver to hear you

☐ Flash your lights to allow the tractor driver to see you

☐ Drop back slightly so that the tractor driver can see you

HC r164

On a summer day you plan to make an early start on a trip.

Before you leave you're given some very upsetting news over the phone.

It's a sunny day and you think about what you should wear on your journey.

At the beginning of your trip you're cut up by a driver at a roundabout.

Riding through town you stop at a red traffic light alongside a cyclist.

Later you witness a crash between a car and another motorcycle.

1 What should you do after your phone call?

Mark **one** answer

☐ Make as early a start as you can

☐ Calm yourself down before you set off

☐ Start your journey but ride slowly

☐ Set off quickly to make up lost time

RES s1

2 What should you wear on a day like today?

Mark **one** answer

☐ A brightly coloured helmet

☐ A dark full-face helmet

☐ Summer clothing and a helmet

☐ A dark one-piece suit and helmet

HC r86 **RES** s4

3 What should you do at the roundabout?

Mark **one** answer

☐ Catch up with the driver and complain

☐ Sound your horn twice at the driver

☐ Flash your headlight at the driver

☐ Ignore the driver and continue riding

RES s9

4 What should you do when the traffic light turns green?

Mark **one** answer

☐ Ride off quickly ahead of the cyclist

☐ Allow the cyclist plenty of room

☐ Follow closely behind the cyclist

☐ Ride around the cyclist to get in front

HC r212 **RES** s10

5 What should you do at the crash scene?

Mark **one** answer

☐ Warn other road users of the danger

☐ Move the driver out of their vehicle

☐ Remove the motorcyclist's helmet

☐ Give the people involved a drink

HC r283 **RES** s16

You're shopping for new clothing to wear while riding your motorcycle.

You're about to go on a camping holiday for two weeks.

The day before you leave you realise that your tax disc will expire while you're away.

On the day you leave it's raining heavily.

You ride along a busy 'A' road, using the throttle rapidly and braking heavily.

You reach the scene of a crash between a cyclist and a car. The cyclist is unconscious but breathing and lying in the road.

1 What should you buy when out shopping?

Mark **one** answer

☐ Clothing that's the right colour
☐ Clothing that's tight fitting
☐ Clothing that's loose and light
☐ Clothing that keeps you warm and dry

 RES s4

2 What should you do before your holiday?

Mark **one** answer

☐ Make a note to renew your tax disc after the holiday

☐ Renew your tax disc immediately

☐ Borrow a friend's tax disc for now

☐ Tell DVLA your motorcycle is off the road

HC p122 **RES** s2

3 What should you be careful of on the day you leave?

Mark **one** answer

☐ Slippery roads

☐ Sticky tarmac

☐ Large potholes

☐ Loose gravel

RES s12

4 What will be the effect of riding in this way on the 'A' road?

Mark **one** answer

☐ Increased journey time

☐ Economical use of fuel

☐ Uneconomical fuel use

☐ Decreased journey time

RES s17

5 What should you do for the cyclist?

Mark **one** answer

☐ Drag her to the side of the road

☐ Try to remove her cycle helmet

☐ Place her in the recovery position

☐ Administer chest compressions

RES s16

Section sixteen
Answers

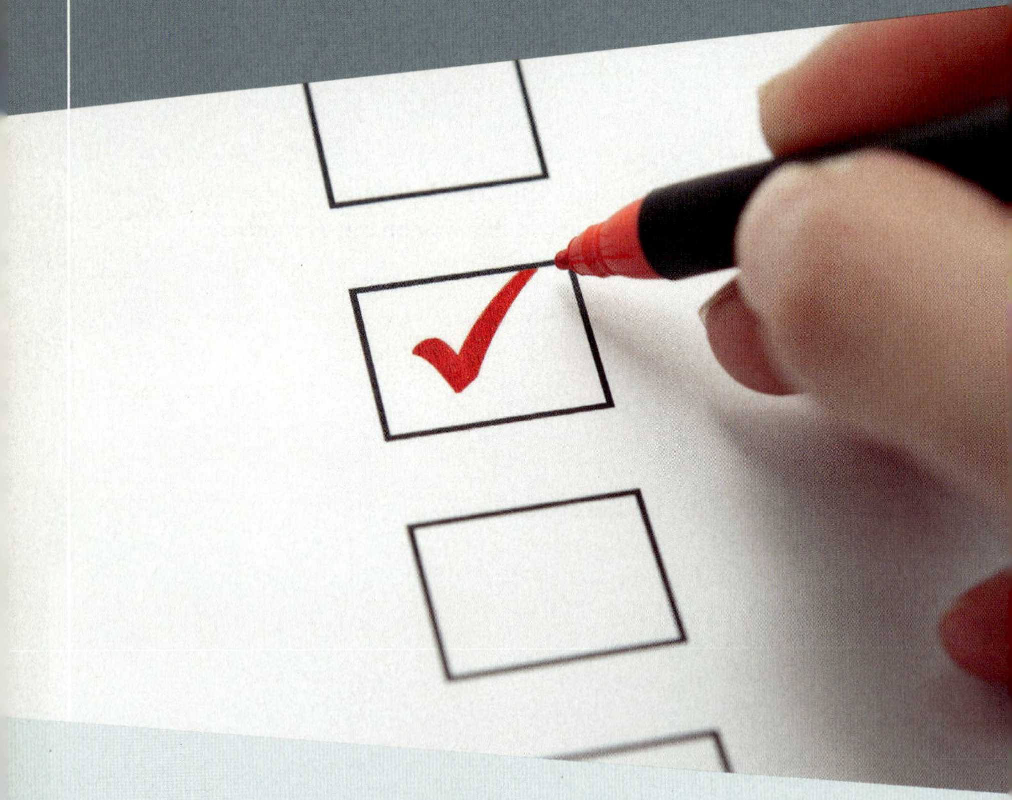

> 1. Alertness

(Section sixteen Answers)

1.1	Take a 'lifesaver' glance over your shoulder	1.17	Check that the central reservation is wide enough
1.2	A final, rearward glance before changing direction	1.18	be sure you know where all controls and switches are
1.3	Slow down before the bend	1.19	take a 'lifesaver' glance over your left shoulder
1.4	extend the mirror arms	1.20	Take a 'lifesaver' glance over your left shoulder
1.5	have parked in a safe place	1.21	Before moving into the left lane
1.6	As soon as the other vehicle passes you	1.22	concentrate on what is happening ahead
1.7	look over your shoulder for a final check	1.23	look over your shoulder for a final check
1.8	lose concentration	1.24	slow down / consider using your horn / beware of pedestrians
1.9	Slow down and stop	1.25	Approaching a dip in the road
1.10	moving off	1.26	overtaking drivers to move back to the left
1.11	changing lanes	1.27	pull up in a suitable place
1.12	To give you the best view of the road behind	1.28	To make you aware of your speed
1.13	Never, you should always look for yourself	1.29	be ready to stop
1.14	Use your mirrors	1.30	Use the mirrors
1.15	Mirrors may not cover blind spots / Drivers behind you would be warned	1.31	allows the driver to see you in the mirrors
1.16	Make a 'lifesaver' check		

1.32	☐ To assess how your actions will affect following traffic
1.33	☐ Stop and then move forward slowly and carefully for a proper view

> 2. Attitude

2.1	☐ showing off and being competitive	2.12	☐ four seconds
		2.13	☐ Slow down
2.2	☐ slow down and prepare to stop	2.14	☐ Bomb disposal
			☐ Blood transfusion
2.3	☐ well back so that you can see past the vehicle		☐ Police patrol
2.4	☐ slow down and be ready to stop	2.15	☐ pull over as soon as safely possible to let it pass
2.5	☐ the pedestrians have reached a safe position	2.16	☐ Doctor's car
		2.17	☐ tram drivers
2.6	☐ pull in safely when you can, to let vehicles behind you overtake	2.18	☐ Cycles
		2.19	☐ To alert others to your presence
2.7	☐ the driver ahead to see you in their mirrors	2.20	☐ in the right-hand lane
	☐ you to be seen by traffic that is emerging from junctions ahead	2.21	☐ To help other road users know what you intend to do
2.8	☐ give way to pedestrians already on the crossing	2.22	☐ Toucan
2.9	☐ there may be another vehicle coming	2.23	☐ allow the vehicle to overtake
2.10	☐ following another vehicle too closely	2.24	☐ to let them know that you are there
2.11	☐ your view ahead is reduced	2.25	☐ Slow down and look both ways

2.26	☐ give way to pedestrians who are crossing
2.27	☐ to keep a safe gap from the vehicle in front
2.28	☐ Steady amber
2.29	☐ Slow down, gradually increasing the gap between you and the vehicle in front
2.30	☐ slow down and give way if it is safe to do so

CASE STUDY PRACTICE – ANSWERS

Section 2 – Attitude

2.1   60 mph
2.2   Carefully, while increasing the distance from the vehicle in front
2.3   Slowly, leaving plenty of room
2.4   To allow the driver to see him in the mirrors
2.5   Doctor attending emergency call

> 3. Safety and your motorcycle

3.1	☐ the rear wheel to lock
3.2	☐ To keep the machine roadworthy
3.3	☐ Carefully, until the shiny surface is worn off
3.4	☐ be seen more easily by other motorists
3.5	☐ continue to wear protective clothing
3.6	☐ It helps other road users to see you
3.7	☐ To be seen better at night
3.8	☐ Touring
3.9	☐ replace it
3.10	☐ 1 mm
3.11	☐ Using a dipped headlight ☐ Wearing a fluorescent jacket ☐ Wearing a white helmet

3.12	☐ stop as quickly as possible and try to find the cause
3.13	☐ be correctly inflated ☐ have sufficient tread depth
3.14	☐ cause much more engine wear
3.15	☐ Slow gently to a stop
3.16	☐ have lower exhaust emissions
3.17	☐ Soapy water
3.18	☐ Stop as soon as possible and wipe it
3.19	☐ Boots
3.20	☐ Velcro tab
3.21	☐ Reflective clothing ☐ A white helmet
3.22	☐ exhaust emissions
3.23	☐ Your wheel alignment

3.24	☐ Between 1 and 2 times
3.25	☐ The rear wheel alignment
3.26	☐ Worn steering head bearings
3.27	☐ Dripping oil could reduce the grip of your tyre
3.28	☐ Your brakes could be affected by dripping oil
3.29	☐ Incorrect rear wheel alignment
3.30	☐ Replace the tyre before riding the motorcycle
3.31	☐ By checking the vehicle owner's manual
3.32	☐ oiled
3.33	☐ increased tyre wear
3.34	☐ Because it gives best protection from the weather
3.35	☐ use the steering lock
3.36	☐ give extra security
3.37	☐ Leave it in a low gear
3.38	☐ stop the engine in an emergency
3.39	☐ Maintain a reduced speed throughout
3.40	☐ Before a long journey
3.41	☐ Take it to a local authority site
3.42	☐ Check out any strong smell of petrol
3.43	☐ Wearing a black helmet

3.44	☐ the helmet is not fastened correctly
3.45	☐ When carrying a passenger ☐ When carrying a load ☐ When riding at high speeds
3.46	☐ Number plate ☐ Headlight
3.47	☐ stop the engine in an emergency
3.48	☐ rear wheel alignment
3.49	☐ It may be damaged
3.50	☐ Tread less than 1 mm deep ☐ A large bulge in the wall ☐ A recut tread ☐ Exposed ply or cord
3.51	☐ by regular adjustment when necessary ☐ by oiling cables and pivots regularly
3.52	☐ better fuel economy ☐ cleaner exhaust emissions
3.53	☐ lock the rear wheel
3.54	☐ In poor visibility
3.55	☐ carrying a pillion passenger
3.56	☐ Oil leaks
3.57	☐ Not on any occasion
3.58	☐ Use the engine cut-out switch
3.59	☐ ride with your headlight on ☐ wear reflective clothing

3.60	☐ Braking
	☐ Steering
3.61	☐ between 11.30 pm and 7 am in a built-up area
3.62	☐ reduces noise pollution
	☐ uses electricity
	☐ reduces town traffic
3.63	☐ they use electric power
3.64	☐ help the traffic flow
3.65	☐ traffic calming measures
3.66	☐ When tyres are cold
3.67	☐ under-inflated
3.68	☐ Take it to a local authority site
	☐ Take it to a garage
3.69	☐ Harsh braking and accelerating
3.70	☐ Distilled water
3.71	☐ Where the speed limit exceeds 30 mph
3.72	☐ air pollution
	☐ damage to buildings
	☐ using up of natural resources
3.73	☐ The braking system
	☐ Wheel alignment
	☐ The suspension

3.74	☐ Just above the cell plates
3.75	☐ left with parking lights on
3.76	☐ Use a route planner on the internet
3.77	☐ Print or write down the route
3.78	☐ You will have an easier journey
3.79	☐ you are less likely to be delayed
3.80	☐ Your original route may be blocked
3.81	☐ allow plenty of time for your journey
3.82	☐ increased fuel consumption
3.83	☐ Brake fluid level

CASE STUDY PRACTICE – ANSWERS

Section 3 – Safety and your motorcycle

3.1 Continue using protective gear

3.2 White with a full-face visor

3.3 With visibility and safety

3.4 So that her view is completely unobstructed

3.5 At least 1 mm over three-quarters of the tread breadth and all around

> 4. Safety margins

4.1	☐ with a passenger
4.2	☐ Use both brakes
4.3	☐ ease off the throttle
4.4	☐ think if you need to ride at all
4.5	☐ It helps other road users to see you
4.6	☐ visibility is 100 metres (328 feet) or less
4.7	☐ at night when street lighting is poor ☐ on motorways during darkness ☐ at times of poor visibility
4.8	☐ make it hard to see unlit objects
4.9	☐ brakes
4.10	☐ slowly in a low gear
4.11	☐ use tinted glasses, lenses or visors
4.12	☐ Use your dipped headlight ☐ Keep your visor or goggles clear
4.13	☐ The painted lines may be slippery
4.14	☐ wear reflective clothing
4.15	☐ Wear suitable clothing
4.16	☐ ride with your headlight on dipped beam ☐ wear reflective clothing
4.17	☐ in the rain

4.18	☐ Potholes ☐ Drain covers ☐ Oil patches ☐ Loose gravel
4.19	☐ Traffic could be emerging and may not see you
4.20	☐ Heavy braking
4.21	☐ Ease off the throttle smoothly
4.22	☐ Ride slowly, braking lightly
4.23	☐ switch on your dipped headlights ☐ be aware of others not using their headlights
4.24	☐ the separation distance when riding in good conditions
4.25	☐ the painted area
4.26	☐ overtaking a large vehicle ☐ riding in exposed places
4.27	☐ A bus may have left patches of oil
4.28	☐ 38 metres (125 feet)
4.29	☐ ten times the normal distance
4.30	☐ ten times
4.31	☐ passing pedal cyclists
4.32	☐ To improve your view of the road
4.33	☐ go slowly while gently applying the brakes

4.34	☐ The grip of the tyres ☐ The braking
4.35	☐ On an open stretch of road
4.36	☐ 96 metres (315 feet)
4.37	☐ 73 metres (240 feet)
4.38	☐ Drop back to regain a safe distance
4.39	☐ 53 metres (175 feet)
4.40	☐ 36 metres (118 feet)
4.41	☐ Allow extra room
4.42	☐ 38 metres (125 feet)
4.43	☐ Increase your distance from the vehicle in front

4.44	☐ Reduce your speed and increase the gap in front
4.45	☐ reduce speed in good time ☐ choose an appropriate lane in good time ☐ keep the correct separation distance

CASE STUDY PRACTICE – ANSWERS

Section 4 – Safety margins

4.1 Tyre pressures and headlight angle
4.2 Blow them off course
4.3 Swerve to avoid cracks and holes
4.4 With more care
4.5 Check over his right shoulder for overtaking vehicles

❯ 5. Hazard awareness

5.1	☐ You may lose concentration ☐ Your reaction times may be slower
5.2	☐ By signalling with your right arm
5.3	☐ find a way of getting home without riding
5.4	☐ Reduced coordination ☐ Increased confidence ☐ Poor judgement
5.5	☐ At all times when riding

5.6	☐ slow down your reactions to hazards ☐ worsen your judgement of speed ☐ give a false sense of confidence
5.7	☐ Tinted
5.8	☐ When riding on a motorway to warn traffic behind of a hazard ahead
5.9	☐ To help to prevent ear damage
5.10	☐ Stick to non-alcoholic drinks
5.11	☐ Your insurance may become invalid

5.12	☐ To check for overtaking vehicles	**5.29**	☐ react very quickly
		5.30	☐ A school crossing patrol
5.13	☐ Ask your doctor ☐ Check the medicine label	**5.31**	☐ Yes, regular stops help concentration
5.14	☐ When your motorcycle has broken down and is causing an obstruction	**5.32**	☐ Stop before the barrier
		5.33	☐ Be prepared to stop for any traffic.
5.15	☐ A soft road surface	**5.34**	☐ Wait for the pedestrian in the road to cross
5.16	☐ Traffic emerging		
5.17	☐ On a large goods vehicle ☐ On a builder's skip placed on the road	**5.35**	☐ Stay behind until you are past the junction
		5.36	☐ Be prepared to give way to large vehicles in the middle of the road
5.18	☐ The cyclist crossing the road		
5.19	☐ The parked car (arrowed A)	**5.37**	☐ They give a wider field of vision
5.20	☐ Slow down and get ready to stop	**5.38**	☐ approach with care and keep to the left of the lorry
5.21	☐ Pedestrians stepping out between cars ☐ Doors opening on parked cars ☐ Cars leaving parking spaces	**5.39**	☐ stay behind and not overtake
		5.40	☐ The bus may move out into the road
		5.41	☐ a school bus
5.22	☐ bend sharply to the left	**5.42**	☐ Car doors opening suddenly ☐ Children running out from between vehicles
5.23	☐ slow down and allow the cyclist to turn		
5.24	☐ There is reduced visibility	**5.43**	☐ The cyclist may swerve out into the road
5.25	☐ buses		
5.26	☐ Lorry	**5.44**	☐ stop and take a break
5.27	☐ behind the line, then edge forward to see clearly	**5.45**	☐ travel at a reduced speed
		5.46	☐ Because of the bend ☐ Because of the level crossing
5.28	☐ ignore the error and stay calm		

5.47	☐ To enable you to change lanes early
5.48	☐ Traffic in both directions can use the middle lane to overtake
5.49	☐ A disabled person's vehicle
5.50	☐ Stop
5.51	☐ It may suddenly move off ☐ People may cross the road in front of it
5.52	☐ If you are turning left shortly afterwards ☐ When you are approaching a junction ☐ When your view ahead is blocked

5.53	☐ Less control ☐ A false sense of confidence ☐ Poor judgement of speed

CASE STUDY PRACTICE – ANSWERS

Section 5 – Hazard awareness

5.1	Convex
5.2	Stick to soft drinks the whole time
5.3	By making you less visible to others
5.4	Red and yellow
5.5	Four seconds

> 6. Vulnerable road users

6.1	☐ it will reduce your view ahead
6.2	☐ slow down ☐ stop if necessary ☐ give plenty of room
6.3	☐ be ready to slow down and stop
6.4	☐ keep calm and be patient
6.5	☐ slow down gradually to increase the gap in front of you
6.6	☐ be prepared to stop
6.7	☐ The rider may be blown across in front of you

6.8	☐ allow the person to cross ☐ be patient
6.9	☐ At junctions
6.10	☐ To check for any overtaking traffic
6.11	☐ Sounding your horn ☐ Revving your engine
6.12	☐ Lack of experience and judgement
6.13	☐ They are often over-confident of their own ability
6.14	☐ You should not wait or park your motorcycle here

6.15	☐
6.16	☐ wait and allow them to cross
6.17	☐ overtaking on your right
6.18	☐ cyclists can use it
6.19	☐ By displaying a stop sign
6.20	☐
6.21	☐ A route for pedestrians and cyclists
6.22	☐ deaf and blind
6.23	☐ Be patient and allow them to cross in their own time
6.24	☐ be careful, they may misjudge your speed
6.25	☐ Give the cyclist plenty of room
6.26	☐ Motorcycles ☐ Bicycles
6.27	☐ They are harder to see
6.28	☐ Motorcycles are small and hard to see
6.29	☐ So that the rider can be seen more easily
6.30	☐ drivers often do not see them
6.31	☐ stay behind
6.32	☐ they need to check for traffic in their blind area

6.33	☐ Cyclists ☐ Motorcyclists ☐ Pedestrians
6.34	☐ when approaching junctions
6.35	☐ be prepared to stop ☐ give them plenty of room
6.36	☐ wait because they will take longer to cross
6.37	☐ Reduce speed until you are clear of the area
6.38	☐ On a school bus
6.39	☐ Any direction
6.40	☐ stay behind until the moped has passed the junction
6.41	☐ stay well back
6.42	☐ Be patient and prepare for them to react more slowly
6.43	☐ be patient as you expect them to make mistakes
6.44	☐ Pedestrians
6.45	☐ be aware that the driver's reactions may not be as fast as yours
6.46	☐ hold back until the cyclist has passed the junction
6.47	☐ go in any direction
6.48	☐ They will have a flashing amber light.
6.49	☐ just before you turn left
6.50	☐ slow moving
6.51	☐ With-flow pedal cycle lane

6.52	☐ Slow down and be ready to stop
6.53	☐ children's view of the crossing area
6.54	☐ Watch out for pedestrians walking in the road
6.55	☐ allow extra room in case they swerve to avoid potholes
6.56	☐ Cycle route ahead
6.57	☐ The cyclist is slower and more vulnerable
6.58	☐ prepare to slow down and stop
6.59	☐ deaf
6.60	☐ pedestrians and cyclists may cross
6.61	☐ To allow cyclists to position in front of other traffic

6.62	☐ The cyclist might swerve
6.63	☐ Allow plenty of room ☐ Go very slowly ☐ Be ready to stop
6.64	☐ You are approaching an organised walk
6.65	☐ By taking further training

CASE STUDY PRACTICE – ANSWERS

Section 6 – Vulnerable road users

6.1 Turn the engine off and wait until the animals have crossed

6.2 Stop and wait patiently until they've crossed

6.3 Wait until the pedestrians have crossed safely

6.4 A vehicle which is slow-moving

6.5 By waiting until the road is clear of oncoming traffic

> 7. Other types of vehicle

7.1	☐ keep well back
7.2	☐ They cannot steer to avoid you ☐ They move quickly and quietly
7.3	☐

7.4	☐ The large vehicle can easily hide an overtaking vehicle
7.5	☐ stay well back and give it room
7.6	☐ Wait behind the long vehicle
7.7	☐ keep well back
7.8	☐ To get the best view of the road ahead

7.9	☐ Watch carefully for pedestrians ☐ Be ready to give way to the bus
7.10	☐ drop back until you can see better
7.11	☐ drop back further
7.12	☐ Do not overtake, stay well back and be prepared to stop
7.13	☐ allow it to pull away, if it is safe to do so
7.14	☐ keep well back until you can see that it is clear
7.15	☐ Cars

7.16	☐ Slow down and be prepared to wait
7.17	☐ Do not overtake when at or approaching a junction
7.18	☐ 8 mph
7.19	☐ It takes longer to pass one

CASE STUDY PRACTICE – ANSWERS

Section 7 – Other types of vehicle

7.1 By using dipped headlights
7.2 Allow it to pull out if it's safe to do so
7.3 The lines could be very slippery in wet weather
7.4 Diamond
7.5 Pull a little over to the right

> 8. Road conditions and motorcycle handling

8.1	☐ push the motorcycle forward to check the rear wheel turns freely ☐ glance at the neutral light on your instrument panel
8.2	☐ prepare to slow down ☐ sound your horn
8.3	☐ Anticipate the actions of others
8.4	☐ Leaning too far over when cornering ☐ Braking too hard ☐ Changing direction suddenly
8.5	☐ ride slower in as high a gear as possible ☐ slow down as there may be black ice

8.6	☐ at all times
8.7	☐ Check that your lights are working ☐ Make sure that your visor is clean
8.8	☐ on firm, level ground
8.9	☐ keep your speed down
8.10	☐ about central in your lane
8.11	☐ left and apply the front brake
8.12	☐ practise off-road with an approved training body
8.13	☐ reduces your control of the motorcycle
8.14	☐ Slow down

8.15	☐ heavy and sharp braking ☐ excessive acceleration ☐ leaning too far when cornering
8.16	☐ the front brake just before the rear
8.17	☐ Slowing down
8.18	☐ upset your balance
8.19	☐ when the motorcycle is upright and moving in a straight line
8.20	☐ How fast you are going ☐ The tyres on your motorcycle ☐ The weather
8.21	☐ your motorcycle is broken down on the hard shoulder
8.22	☐ leave parking lights on
8.23	☐ Close the throttle and roll to a stop
8.24	☐ By a rainbow pattern on the surface
8.25	☐ more difficult to control
8.26	☐ White lines ☐ Tar banding ☐ Yellow grid lines ☐ Loose chippings
8.27	☐ apply the front brake just before the rear
8.28	☐ braking
8.29	☐ The steel rails can be slippery
8.30	☐ release the brakes and reapply

8.31	☐ Fuel spilt on the road
8.32	☐ Wheelspin when accelerating
8.33	☐ Release both brakes together
8.34	☐ Apply both brakes smoothly
8.35	☐ place both feet on the ground
8.36	☐ slippery
8.37	☐ cornering
8.38	☐ cause you to crash
8.39	☐ When you are in a one-way street ☐ When the vehicle in front is signalling to turn right ☐ In slow-moving traffic queues when traffic in the right-hand lane is moving more slowly
8.40	☐ doubled
8.41	☐ be careful because you can see less ☐ beware of bends in the road ahead
8.42	☐ When oncoming traffic prevents you turning right
8.43	☐ **Humps for ½ mile**
8.44	☐ slow traffic down
8.45	☐ Red
8.46	☐ alert you to a hazard ☐ encourage you to reduce speed

8.47	☐ leave plenty of time for your journey
8.48	☐ you do not dazzle other road users
8.49	☐ slow down and stay behind
8.50	☐ To make you aware of your speed
8.51	☐ white line markings ☐ a different coloured surface ☐ a different surface texture
8.52	☐ stop at a passing place
8.53	☐ To prevent the motorcycle sliding on the metal drain covers

8.54	☐ Your brakes will be soaking wet
8.55	☐ It is more difficult to see events ahead

> 9. Motorway riding

9.1	☐ in an emergency
9.2	☐ in the left-hand lane
9.3	☐ adjust your speed to the speed of the traffic on the motorway
9.4	☐ 50 cc or more
9.5	☐ Left-hand lane
9.6	☐ 70 mph
9.7	☐ Continuous high speeds may increase the risk of your motorcycle breaking down
9.8	☐ give way to traffic already on the motorway
9.9	☐ 70 mph

9.10	☐ any vehicle
9.11	☐ A vehicle towing a trailer
9.12	☐ It allows easy location by the emergency services
9.13	☐ gain speed on the hard shoulder before moving out onto the carriageway
9.14	☐ on a steep gradient
9.15	☐ They are countdown markers to the next exit
9.16	☐ the central reservation and the carriageway
9.17	☐ White
9.18	☐ Green

9.19	☐ in the direction shown on the marker posts
9.20	☐ To build up a speed similar to traffic on the motorway
9.21	☐ Face the oncoming traffic
9.22	☐ Red
9.23	☐ Left
9.24	☐ keep a good distance from the vehicle ahead
9.25	☐ In the left-hand lane
9.26	☐ Obey all speed limits
9.27	☐ Learner car drivers ☐ Farm tractors ☐ Learner motorcyclists ☐ Cyclists
9.28	☐ keep in the left-hand lane
9.29	☐ Overtaking
9.30	☐ Stopping in an emergency
9.31	☐ move to the left and reduce your speed to 50 mph
9.32	☐ are told to do so by flashing red lights
9.33	☐ move to another lane
9.34	☐ keep to the left-hand lane unless overtaking
9.35	☐ there is a queue of slow-moving traffic to your right that is moving more slowly than you are

9.36	☐ To use in cases of emergency or breakdown
9.37	☐ are able to stop and direct anyone on a motorway
9.38	☐ You should not travel in this lane
9.39	☐ The hard shoulder can be used as a running lane
9.40	☐ reduce congestion
9.41	☐ all speed limit signals are set
9.42	☐ Your overall journey time will normally improve
9.43	☐ When signs direct you to
9.44	☐ For overtaking other vehicles
9.45	☐ Variable speed limits
9.46	☐ If red lights show above every lane ☐ When told to by the police ☐ When signalled by a Highways Agency Traffic Officer
9.47	☐ In an emergency or breakdown
9.48	☐ 70 mph
9.49	☐ an Highways Agency control centre
9.50	☐ stop and wait

9.51	☐ the hard shoulder is for emergency or breakdown use only
9.52	☐ all the lanes including the hard shoulder
9.53	☐ pull in at the nearest service area

CASE STUDY PRACTICE – ANSWERS
....

Section 9 – Motorway riding

9.1   Steering and braking

9.2   All traffic should do so unless they're overtaking other vehicles

9.3   Slower than normal

9.4   Temporary maximum speed advised

9.5   300 yards

> 10. Rules of the road

10.1	☐ check for cyclists
10.2	☐ Cycle lane ☐ Tram lane
10.3	☐ Parking for solo motorcycles
10.4	☐ use mirrors and shoulder checks
10.5	☐ not park there unless permitted
10.6	☐ Pull into a passing place on your left
10.7	☐ see approaching traffic
10.8	☐ watch for hidden vehicles emerging from side roads ☐ look for vehicles changing course suddenly ☐ look for pedestrians walking between vehicles
10.9	☐ Wait for the green light
10.10	☐ Headlight deflectors
10.11	☐ 125 cc
10.12	☐ 60 mph

10.13	☐ When involved in a collision ☐ At a red traffic light ☐ When signalled to do so by a police officer
10.14	☐ National speed limit applies
10.15	☐ 70 mph
10.16	☐ By street lighting
10.17	☐ 30 mph
10.18	☐ End of minimum speed
10.19	☐ not overtake if you are in doubt
10.20	☐ Horse riders ☐ Long vehicles ☐ Cyclists
10.21	☐ at any time
10.22	☐ Waiting restrictions
10.23	☐ in a one-way street
10.24	☐ overtaking or turning right
10.25	☐ continue in that lane

10.26	☐ Either on the right or the left
10.27	☐ indicate left before leaving the roundabout
10.28	☐ Long vehicle
10.29	☐ your exit road is clear
10.30	☐ oncoming traffic is preventing you from turning right
10.31	☐ A police officer ☐ A school crossing patrol ☐ A red traffic light
10.32	☐ stop, let them cross, wait patiently
10.33	☐ cyclists riding across
10.34	☐ Cyclists ☐ Pedestrians
10.35	☐ wait for pedestrians on the crossing to clear
10.36	☐ To pick up or set down passengers
10.37	☐ keep the other vehicle to your RIGHT and turn behind it (offside to offside)
10.38	☐ Vehicles may be pulling out ☐ Drivers' doors may open ☐ Children may run out from between the vehicles
10.39	☐ give way to oncoming traffic
10.40	☐ Turning right ☐ Overtaking slower traffic
10.41	☐ No one has priority

10.42	☐ 10 metres (32 feet)
10.43	☐ Near the brow of a hill ☐ At or near a bus stop ☐ Within 10 metres (32 feet) of a junction
10.44	☐ carry on waiting
10.45	☐ Neither of the vehicles
10.46	☐ No waiting zone ends
10.47	☐ not exceed the speed limit
10.48	☐ Near a school entrance ☐ At a bus stop
10.49	☐ be easily seen by others
10.50	☐ Wait until the road is clear in both directions
10.51	☐ 60 mph
10.52	☐ with parking lights on
10.53	☐ a concealed level crossing
10.54	☐ A Highways Agency Traffic Officer
10.55	☐ Signal left just after you pass the exit before the one you will take

CASE STUDY PRACTICE – ANSWERS

Section 10 – Rules of the road

10.1 Blue and white
10.2 Stop and wait until the light turns green
10.3 Take a final look over his right shoulder
10.4 To help slow traffic down
10.5 Circular

11.1	☐
11.2	☐ Because you will have less steering control
11.3	☐ side winds
11.4	☐
11.5	☐
11.6	☐ that they are warning you of their presence
11.7	☐ To avoid misleading other road users
11.8	☐ also give an arm signal
11.9	☐ Pass on the left
11.10	☐ red circles
11.11	☐
11.12	☐
11.13	☐ Maximum speed limit with traffic calming

11.14	☐
11.15	☐
11.16	☐ End of 20 mph zone
11.17	☐ No motor vehicles
11.18	☐ No entry
11.19	☐ No right turn
11.20	☐
11.21	☐ Route for trams only
11.22	☐ High vehicles
11.23	☐
11.24	☐ No overtaking
11.25	☐ Do not overtake
11.26	☐
11.27	☐ Waiting restrictions apply

11.28	☐ End of restricted parking area
11.29	☐
11.30	☐ no stopping
11.31	☐ Distance to parking place ahead
11.32	☐ Vehicles may park fully on the verge or footway
11.33	☐ Give priority to oncoming traffic
11.34	☐ You have priority over vehicles from the opposite direction
11.35	☐
11.36	☐ Stop
11.37	☐ Minimum speed 30 mph
11.38	☐ Pass either side to get to the same destination
11.39	☐ Route for trams
11.40	☐ Give an instruction
11.41	☐ On a one-way street
11.42	☐ Contraflow bus lane
11.43	☐ Tourist directions
11.44	☐ tourist attraction
11.45	☐ To give warnings
11.46	☐ T-junction

11.47	☐ Risk of ice
11.48	☐ Crossroads
11.49	☐ Roundabout
11.50	☐ Road narrows ☐ Low bridge ☐ Children crossing ☐ T-junction
11.51	☐ Cycle route ahead
11.52	☐
11.53	☐
11.54	☐ Give way to trams
11.55	☐
11.56	☐ End of dual carriageway
11.57	☐ Danger ahead
11.58	☐ hold back until you can see clearly ahead
11.59	☐ Level crossing with gate or barrier
11.60	☐ Trams crossing ahead
11.61	☐ Steep hill downwards
11.62	☐ Water across the road
11.63	☐ No through road on the left
11.64	☐ No through road

11.65	☐
11.66	☐
11.67	☐ The right-hand lane is closed
11.68	☐ Contraflow system
11.69	☐ Lane for heavy and slow vehicles
11.70	☐ you must stop and wait behind the stop line
11.71	☐ stop at the stop line
11.72	☐ When your exit from the junction is blocked
11.73	☐
11.74	☐ Traffic lights out of order
11.75	☐ Nobody
11.76	☐ Lifting bridges ☐ Level crossings ☐ Fire stations
11.77	☐ No parking at any time
11.78	☐ To pass a road maintenance vehicle travelling at 10 mph or less
11.79	☐ You are approaching a hazard
11.80	☐ On road humps

11.81	☐
11.82	☐ Visibility along the major road is restricted
11.83	☐ Give way to traffic from the right
11.84	☐ Flash the headlights, indicate left and point to the left
11.85	☐ stop at the stop line
11.86	☐ The driver intends to turn left
11.87	☐ On a motorway slip road
11.88	☐ Temporary maximum speed 50 mph
11.89	☐ Right-hand lane closed ahead
11.90	☐ move to the lane on your left
11.91	☐ The number of the next junction
11.92	☐ an overtaking lane
11.93	☐ On the right-hand edge of the road
11.94	☐ At slip road entrances and exits
11.95	☐ leave the motorway at the next exit
11.96	☐ End of motorway
11.97	☐
11.98	☐ 60 mph

11.99	☐ End of restriction
11.100	☐ follow the route diversion
11.101	☐ To warn of road works ahead
11.102	☐ a compulsory maximum speed limit
11.103	☐ Give an arm signal
11.104	☐ No motorcycles
11.105	☐ pass the lorry on the left
11.106	☐ Move into another lane in good time
11.107	☐ Turn to the left
11.108	☐ To warn others of your presence
11.109	☐ unless a moving vehicle may cause you danger
11.110	☐ No parking on the days and times shown
11.111	☐ Quayside or river bank
11.112	☐
11.113	☐ hazard warning
11.114	☐ To prevent queuing traffic from blocking the junction on the left
11.115	☐ It is to separate traffic flowing in opposite directions
11.116	☐ To warn you of their presence
11.117	☐ 20 mph

11.118	☐ trams must stop
11.119	☐ At a junction
11.120	☐ Pull up on the left
11.121	☐ Red alone
11.122	☐ there is a hazard ahead of you
11.123	☐ Leave the motorway at the next exit
11.124	☐ To prevent the junction becoming blocked
11.125	☐ Stop, even if the road is clear
11.126	☐
11.127	☐ Mini-roundabout
11.128	☐ Two-way traffic crosses a one-way road
11.129	☐ Two-way traffic straight ahead
11.130	☐ Hump bridge
11.131	☐
11.132	☐ Direction to park-and-ride car park
11.133	☐ wait for the green light before you cross the stop line
11.134	☐ 'give way' sign
11.135	☐ Wait

11.136	☐ Direction to emergency pedestrian exit
11.137	☐
11.138	☐ With-flow bus and cycle lane
11.139	☐
11.140	☐ Zebra crossing
11.141	☐
11.142	☐

11.143	☐
11.144	☐
11.145	☐ all traffic is going one way
11.146	☐ Red and amber
11.147	☐ Tunnel ahead

CASE STUDY PRACTICE – ANSWERS

Section 11 – Road and traffic signs

11.1 Regulatory

11.2 The joining side roads are slightly offset from each other

11.3 Blue with white arrow

11.4 Green

11.5 The lane is in operation at all times for buses

> 12. Essential documents

12.1	☐ Make and model ☐ Engine size and number ☐ Year of first registration
12.2	☐ any DSA (Driving Standards Agency) approved training body
12.3	☐ the motorcycle is insured for your use
12.4	☐ display it clearly on your motorcycle
12.5	☐ three years old

12.6	☐ Registered keeper ☐ Make of the motorcycle ☐ Engine size
12.7	☐ you change your motorcycle ☐ you change your name ☐ your permanent address changes
12.8	☐ damage to other vehicles ☐ injury to others
12.9	☐ Third party only

12.10	☐ the year of first registration
12.11	☐ To make sure your motorcycle is roadworthy
12.12	☐ a CBT (Compulsory Basic Training) certificate
12.13	☐ your health affects your riding ☐ your eyesight does not meet a set standard ☐ you change your motorcycle
12.14	☐ retake your theory and practical tests ☐ reapply for your provisional licence
12.15	☐ ride on a motorway ☐ carry a pillion passenger ☐ ride without L plates displayed
12.16	☐ 125 cc
12.17	☐ require L plates while learning with a qualified instructor
12.18	☐ the rider holds a full licence for the category of motorcycle ☐ the motorcycle is fitted with rear footrests ☐ there is a proper passenger seat fitted
12.19	☐ two years
12.20	☐ A valid certificate of insurance

12.21	☐ you must have passed your test for a full motorcycle licence
12.22	☐ You must have passed your test for a full motorcycle licence
12.23	☐ You will have to pay the first £100 of any claim
12.24	☐ one year after the date it was issued
12.25	☐ insurance certificate
12.26	☐ Retake your theory and practical tests ☐ Reapply for your provisional licence
12.27	☐ 12 months
12.28	☐ A notification to tell DVLA that a vehicle is not being used on the road
12.29	☐ to tell DVLA that your vehicle is not being used on the road
12.30	☐ £5,000
12.31	☐ The registered vehicle keeper
12.32	☐ When a police officer asks you for it
12.33	☐ obtain a tax disc
12.34	☐ renew your road tax disc

12.35	☐ A valid driving licence
	☐ A valid tax disc clearly displayed
	☐ Proper insurance cover
12.36	☐ valid insurance
12.37	☐ 7 days
12.38	☐ Valid insurance
12.39	☐ When you move house

Section 12 – Essential documents

12.1 Twelve months

12.2 It's allowed in order to get the machine to a repairer

12.3 Vehicle Excise Duty

12.4 It's a legal réquirement

12.5 Third party

> 13. Incidents, accidents and emergencies

13.1	☐ By following an arrow on a marker post
13.2	☐ stop the engine in an emergency
13.3	☐ there is a danger ahead
13.4	☐ for the number on the telephone that you are using
	☐ for details of yourself and your motorcycle
	☐ whether you belong to a motoring organisation
13.5	☐ When you slow down quickly because of danger ahead
13.6	☐ Switch on hazard warning lights
13.7	☐ Stop at the next emergency telephone and report the hazard

13.8	☐ Whether the driver owns the other vehicle involved
	☐ The other driver's name, address and telephone number
	☐ The make and registration number of the other vehicle
	☐ The details of the other driver's vehicle insurance
13.9	☐ a disabled person
13.10	☐ When stopped and temporarily obstructing traffic
13.11	☐ Keep a safe distance from the vehicle in front
13.12	☐ when an emergency arises
13.13	☐ Apply pressure over the wound and raise the arm
13.14	☐ 10 seconds
13.15	☐ 10 minutes

13.16	☐ 10 minutes
13.17	☐ 100 per minute
13.18	☐ Pale grey skin
13.19	☐ Check the airway is clear
13.20	☐ seek medical assistance
13.21	☐ go to the next emergency telephone and report the hazard
13.22	☐ Variable message signs
13.23	☐ 4 to 5 centimetres
13.24	☐ Make sure engines are switched off ☐ Call the emergency services promptly
13.25	☐ not put yourself at risk
13.26	☐ Switch on your own hazard warning lights ☐ Make sure that someone telephones for an ambulance ☐ Get people who are not injured clear of the scene
13.27	☐ Only when it is essential
13.28	☐ try to stop the bleeding ☐ check their breathing ☐ check their airways
13.29	☐ breathing
13.30	☐ Circulation ☐ Airway ☐ Breathing

13.31	☐ Clear the airway and keep it open ☐ Check that they are breathing ☐ Stop any heavy bleeding
13.32	☐ Keep injured people warm and comfortable ☐ Keep injured people calm by talking to them reassuringly ☐ Make sure that injured people are not left alone
13.33	☐ Stop any severe bleeding ☐ Check they are breathing ☐ Clear their airway and keep it open
13.34	☐ Offer someone a cigarette to calm them down
13.35	☐ Reassure them ☐ Not leave them alone
13.36	☐ reassure them constantly
13.37	☐ warn other traffic
13.38	☐ gently
13.39	☐ remove anything sticking to the burn
13.40	☐ douse the burns with clean cool non-toxic liquid
13.41	☐ Apply firm pressure to the wound ☐ Raise the leg to lessen bleeding
13.42	☐ there is further danger
13.43	☐ not move them
13.44	☐ keep them in the vehicle

13.45	☐ 2YE 1089		**13.52**	☐ reassure them constantly	
13.46	☐ Driving licence ☐ Insurance certificate ☐ MOT test certificate			☐ keep them warm ☐ avoid moving them if possible ☐ avoid leaving them alone	
13.47	☐ As soon as possible		**13.53**	☐ This could result in more serious injury	
13.48	☐ It will help to reduce the blood flow				
13.49	☐ Variable message signs				
13.50	☐ Warn other traffic				
13.51	☐ remove anything that is blocking the mouth ☐ tilt the head back gently to clear the airway				

CASE STUDY PRACTICE – ANSWERS

Section 13 – Incidents, accidents and emergencies

13.1 Shock symptoms
13.2 Because removing it could cause further injuries
13.3 To warn following traffic of the incident hazard
13.4 Keep them warm
13.5 He witnessed the incident

⟩ 14. Motorcycle loading

14.1	☐ ease off the throttle and reduce your speed		**14.9**	☐ stopping distance may increase	
14.2	☐ keep your speed down ☐ approach corners more carefully		**14.10**	☐ cause low-speed wobble	
			14.11	☐ The rider of the motorcycle	
14.3	☐ headlight ☐ suspension ☐ tyres		**14.12**	☐ check that the motorcycle is suitable	
			14.13	☐ They could make your motorcycle unstable	
14.4	☐ solo with minimum power of 35 kW (46.6 bhp)		**14.14**	☐ Your ability to steer	
14.5	☐ securely fastened when riding		**14.15**	☐ hold a full motorcycle licence	
14.6	☐ always wear a helmet		**14.16**	☐ tyre pressures	
14.7	☐ lean with you on bends		**14.17**	☐ Keep further back than you normally would	
14.8	☐ Headlight				

14.18	☐ they can reach the handholds and footrests
14.19	☐ is correctly aligned
14.20	☐ may increase your stopping distance
14.21	☐ Preload on the rear shock absorber(s)
14.22	☐ 1 metre (3 feet 3 inches)
14.23	☐ The trailer should NOT be more than 1 metre (3 feet 3 inches) wide
14.24	☐ Increase stopping distance
14.25	☐ Ride a motorcycle with an engine capacity greater than 125 cc ☐ Pull a trailer ☐ Carry a pillion passenger
14.26	☐ have a full motorcycle licence ☐ ensure that your engine is more than 125 cc

14.27	☐ rear footrests ☐ a proper pillion seat
14.28	☐ reduce stability ☐ cause high-speed weave ☐ cause low-speed wobble
14.29	☐ Not at any time
14.30	☐ handling
14.31	☐ not exceed 60 mph ☐ use only the left and centre lanes

CASE STUDY PRACTICE – ANSWERS

Section 14 – Motorcycle loading

14.1 To ensure it's correctly connected up

14.2 Uneven load distribution can affect balance

14.3 60 mph

14.4 Stopping distance is increased on a fully loaded vehicle

14.5 That lane mustn't be used by vehicles with trailers

> 15. Case study practice

Case study on pages 461–463

1 Look over your shoulder for a final check
2 Slow down
   Consider using the horn
   Beware of pedestrians
3 Find a suitable place to stop
4 Go slowly past
   Give plenty of room
5 There may be another vehicle coming

Case study practice A

1 Leather clothing, hi-vis waistcoat and white helmet
2 Wait as another train may be coming
3 Slow down to go round the potholes and cracks
4 The blue sign will show a motorcycle
5 Take a look over your right shoulder

Case study practice B

1 Tyre pressure
2 Being blown off course
3 Vehicles with a trailer mustn't travel in the right-hand lane
4 In the left-hand lane without giving a signal
5 Road workers

Case study practice C

1 In the tank bag
2 70 mph
3 Because the engine is warm
4 Lock your motorcycle and remove the key
5 Drop back slightly so that the tractor driver can see you

Case study practice D

1 Calm yourself down before you set off
2 A brightly coloured helmet
3 Ignore the driver and continue riding
4 Allow the cyclist plenty of room
5 Warn other road users of the danger

Case study practice E

1 Clothing that keeps you warm and dry
2 Renew your tax disc immediately
3 Slippery roads
4 Uneconomical fuel use
5 Place her in the recovery position

Other official DSA publications

Driving Standards Agency

From the Driving Standards Agency –
the official route to Safe Riding for Life™

Theory test learning materials

Every theory test question is taken from the information in these books – make sure you have a copy for complete test preparation.

The Official DSA Guide to Riding – the essential skills

Packed with advice for all motorcyclists.
Book
ISBN 9780115526442 £12.99

Downloadable PDF*
ISBN 9780115530616 £12.99

The Official Highway Code

Essential reading for all road users.
Book
ISBN 9780115528149 £2.50

Interactive CD-ROM
ISBN 9780115528460 £9.99

British Sign Language pack
ISBN 9780115529849 £9.99

eBook
Also available as an eBook from your device's eBook store.

Know Your Traffic Signs
Book
ISBN 9780115528552 £4.99

The Official DSA Theory Test for Motorcyclists Interactive Download

Check how much you have already learnt to see if you're ready to pass the multiple choice part, with mock tests and much more.
Interactive download*
ISBN 9780115531989 £9.99

Hazard perception

Develop your hazard perception skills and learn more about this part of the theory test.

The Official DSA Guide to Hazard Perception
DVD
ISBN 9780115528651 £15.99

Practical test

For help with practical skills for your test and beyond.

The Official DSA Guide to Learning to Ride
Book
ISBN 9780115530562 £7.99

Downloadable PDF*
ISBN 9780115530630 £7.99

Better Biking – the official DSA training aid
DVD
ISBN 9780115529559 £10.99

*for instant access from tsoshop.co.uk

learningtodrive

@DSA_Publishers

Official Highway Code iPhone app
All the rules of the road at your fingertips. Available on the iPhone app store.

For the full range of official DSA titles and to place your order visit **tsoshop.co.uk/dsa**
or call **0870 850 6553** quoting **CQD** when ordering
Also available from all good high street book stores.

TSO (The Stationery Office) is proud to be DSA's official publishing partner. Prices, savings and images are correct at time of going to press but may be subject to change without notice.

The **OFFICIAL DSA**
THEORY TEST
for Motorcyclists

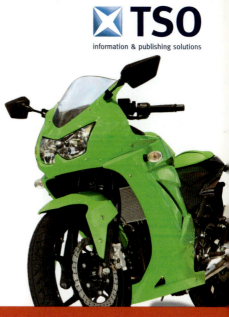

2013 WIN
BIKE GEAR
COMPETITION

TSO, DSA's official publishing partner, is offering you the chance to win new clothing or accessories.*

To enter, simply answer the questions and tell us in 25 words or less how learning to ride will make a difference to your life. The winner will be the entrant who answers the first three questions correctly and writes the most apt and original 25-word essay, as decided by the judges. Closing date: 31 December 2013.

Please send the entry form to:
Win Bike Gear Competition 2013, TSO, Freepost, ANG 4748, Norwich, NR3 1YX (no stamp required).

1.   What is the minimum motorcycle engine size allowed on a motorway?

....

2.   What is the legal minimum depth of tread for motorcycle tyres in millimetres?

....

3.   You hold a provisional motorcycle licence. When are you allowed to carry a pillion passenger?

....

Tie Breaker: Learning to ride will change my life.... (complete in 25 words or less)

....

....

....

* Terms and conditions apply

Name of shop or website that you bought this product from?

....

Why did you choose this particular product?

....

....

How would you improve this, or any other DSA product?

....

....

....

Name ....

Address ....

.... Date of birth ....

Daytime telephone number ....

Mobile telephone number ....

Email ....

TSO would like to continue to keep you informed of products and services that may be of interest to you. If you do not wish to receive these updates in future please let us know.

☐ I do not want to receive these updates from TSO in future

I have read, accept and agree to be bound by the Competition Rules

Signature .... Date ....

If you would like us to send you email updates on your specific area(s) of interest register at tsoshop.co.uk/signup.

Competition Rules

The following rules apply to this competition. By entering this competition, entrants will be deemed to have accepted these rules and to agree to be bound by them.

1. Only one entry will be accepted per purchase of The Official DSA Theory Test for Motorcyclists.
2. All entries must be on original official entry forms. No photocopies will be accepted.
3. Entries must be received by the Promoter by no later than 5.00pm on Tuesday, 31 December 2013 (**Closing Date**). Entries must be submitted by ordinary post to the Promoter's free mailing address at: TSO, Freepost, ANG 4748, Norwich, NR3 1YX.
4. The competition will run from 10 September 2012 to 31 December 2013 and one prize shall be awarded to a winner chosen from valid entries received by the Promoter by the Closing Date. No responsibility can be taken by the Promoter for lost, late, misdirected or stolen entries.
5. The prize awarded to the winner will be a range of bike clothing to a value of approximately £1000 (at the time of these rules going to press (Prize)). The Promoter may in its absolute discretion substitute this Prize with a similar prize of approximate equivalent value. There will be one Prize only and accordingly only one winner. Prizes cannot be transferred or exchanged and there is no cash alternative.
6. Only entrants over the age of 16 and resident in the United Kingdom are eligible to enter the competition. The Promoter reserves the right to request evidence of proof of age and residence from the winner before any prize will be awarded.
7. The winning entry will be decided by the judges in their absolute discretion from correct entries submitted by eligible entrants received by the Closing Date. A "correct" entry means a fully completed entry, with the first three questions answered correctly, the most apt and original essay and otherwise in compliance with these rules.
8. The winner will be notified by 22 January 2014. Only the winner will be contacted personally via the email address or telephone number they provide.
9. If the winner cannot be contacted by the means provided, the Promoter reserves the right to have the judges decide on an alternative winner from other correct entries received by the Closing Date, using the same criteria as for the original "winner" and subject to these rules.
10. The winner's name will be published on the Promoter's website at tso.co.uk on or about 1 February 2014 for a period of approximately 60 days.
11. The prize will be made available within six weeks of the Closing Date by arrangement between the Promoter and the winner, provided that the Promoter shall not be responsible for any delivery costs.
12. By entering this competition, an entrant agrees they will be deemed to consent to the use for promotional and other purposes (without further payment and except as prohibited by law) of their name, city/town/county of residence and competition entry, including any opinions or comments provided; an entrant, if they accept any Prize further agree they will be deemed to consent to:
    (a)   the use for promotional and other purposes (without further payment and except as prohibited by law) of their likeness;
    (b)   participate in the Promoter's reasonable marketing and promotional activities.
    The entrant agrees that all rights including copyright in all works created by the entrant as part of the competition entry shall be owned by the Promoter absolutely without the need for any payment to the entrant. They further agree to waive unconditionally and irrevocably all moral rights pursuant to the Copyright, Designs and Patents Act of 1988 and under any similar law in force from time to time anywhere in the world in respect of all such works.
13. No entries will be returned to entrants by the Promoter. Therefore, entrants may wish to retain a copy.
14. The Promoter reserves the right to cancel this competition or amend these rules at any stage without prior notice, if deemed necessary in its opinion, especially if circumstances arise outside of its control. Any such cancellation or changes to the rules will be notified on the Promoter's website.
15. This competition is not open to employees or contractors of the Promoter or the Driving Standards Agency or any person directly involved in the organisation or running of the competition, or their direct family members. Any such entries will be invalid.
16. By entering this competition, entrants warrant that all information submitted by them is true and correct and that they are eligible and have legal capacity to enter this competition. The Promoter reserves the right to disqualify any entrant if it has reasonable grounds to believe that the entrant has breached these rules.
17. Any personal data provided in any entry will be dealt with by the Promoter in accordance with the requirements of the Data Protection Act 1998, provided that the winner expressly consents to the information set out in rule 12(a) being used in the manner specified therein.
18. The judges' and the Promoter's decisions in relation to any aspect of this competition are final and no correspondence will be entered into. Neither the judges nor the Promoter will have any liability to any person in relation to their decisions or any damage, loss, injury or disappointment suffered arising from the competition (except to the extent that such liability cannot be limited or excluded by law).
19. The competition and these rules shall be governed by English law.
20. The "Promoter" means The Stationery Office Limited, St Crispins, Duke Street, Norwich, NR3 1PD (the publishers of The Official DSA Learner Range). The competition judging panel will be made up of a combination of the Promoter's employees and independent judge(s).

Learning to ride?

Don't forget to prepare for your theory and practical tests using the official materials for expert information from the people who set the tests. For the full range of DSA titles go to **tsoshop.co.uk/dsa**

Did you know you can:

- book your theory test
- book your practical test

and much more by visiting: **direct.gov.uk/drivingtest**

or call customer services on 0300 200 1122

 Join the conversation
Questions about learning to ride? Follow **@Liz_DSA @John_DSA @Linda_DSA**
Keep up-to-date with the latest rules of the road **@HighwayCodeGB**

You Tube Find out what to expect when you take your theory and practical motorcycle tests: **youtube.com/dsagov**

f **start2ride**
Scan to become a fan for hints, tips and news for learners
(you'll need a phone with a QR code reader app to read the code)

HighwayCodeGB
Find out about all the latest rules of the road